Hidden

Cathy Glass

Hidden

Betrayed, exploited and forgotten

How one boy overcame the odds

HarperElement
An Imprint of HarperCollins*Publishers*
77–85 Fulham Palace Road,
Hammersmith, London W6 8JB

The website address is:
www.thorsonselement.com

and *HarperElement* are trademarks
of HarperCollins*Publishers* Ltd

First published by HarperElement 2007

1 3 5 7 9 10 8 6 4 2

A catalogue record of this book is
available from the British Library

HB ISBN-13 978-0-00-726096-6
HB ISBN-10 0-00-726096-2
PB ISBN-13 978-0-00-726097-3
PB ISBN-10 0-00-726097-0

Printed and bound in Great Britain by
Clays Ltd, St Ives plc

To my parents – with love

Acknowledgements

My sincere thanks to my agent Andrew Lownie; Carole Tonkinson and all the team at HarperCollins; and Kirsty Fowkes, my editor.

Prologue

There are 11.8 million children known to be living in the UK. But it is thought there could be as many as one million other children living here who are unregistered and therefore unknown. Some have been trafficked into the country to work in the sex industry, or as cheap labour in our sweatshops. Others have been smuggled in, or sent from Third World countries by desperate parents to be privately fostered in the hope of saving them from the abject poverty at home.

Some will have come in on forged passports, or under visitors' visas that have since expired. Others may have been born here to parents who are not themselves registered. No one really knows the true picture, but these children live isolated and perilous lives. They are outside our society, unprotected and vulnerable. They only come to our attention when something goes dreadfully wrong.

This is the story of one such child who came into my care. Certain details, including names, places and dates have been changed to protect that child.

Chapter One

A New Year

The call came at eleven o'clock on the morning of Friday 2nd January.

My daughter Lucy was expecting her boyfriend to ring her, so she rushed into the hall to answer the telephone. Then, with disappointment in her voice, she called through to the lounge. 'Mum, it's for you! It's Jill.'

I was surprised. This was really the first working day since Christmas Eve, as many people had tagged another day's leave on to the winter break, giving them a full week off between Christmas and New Year. I hadn't expected a call from Jill, my contact at the fostering agency, quite so soon. I picked up the extension in the lounge.

'Hi Jill. Did you have a good Christmas?'

'Lovely, thanks. And you?'

'Quiet. Unnaturally so, if I'm honest,' I said. 'It's taking a bit of getting used to. I'm almost missing all the chaos.'

Jill laughed. My previous foster placement of twin seven-year-old girls had ended on 14th December when they had returned to live with their mother, and for the first time since

I couldn't remember when, we hadn't had a foster child with us for Christmas. I wasn't sure whether I'd liked the quiet or not.

'Thank everyone for the present and card,' I added. Every year, the agency gave all their foster carers a large tin of chocolate biscuits and a Christmas card signed by the staff.

'I will, when they're back,' Jill said. 'There's only me in today. I think I drew the short straw.' She paused – it was the pause I'd come to recognize as heralding a possible new foster placement. I wasn't wrong. 'Cathy, I've just had a phone call from the council's duty social worker – the placement team's still away. It concerns a twelve-year-old boy.' She stopped.

'Yes?' I prompted.

'That's it.'

It was my turn to laugh. 'What? That's all?'

'He's twelve,' she repeated, 'and they're going to court for an ICO' – I knew that was shorthand for an Interim Care Order – 'on Monday morning. They'll need to show the judge they have somewhere to take him.'

'Yes, they will,' I said. 'So you must be looking for a home for him. Has this young man got a name?'

'The duty officer doesn't know it.'

'So where is the child now?'

'I don't know.'

I raised my eyebrows. I was used to things often being rushed and confused in the world of fostering but even I was surprised by the lack of information. Jill went on.

'Sorry, Cathy, I think the duty officer is just responding to a note left by a social worker from the Children and Families team between Christmas and the New Year. I'll speak to the team leader first thing on Monday morning for more details.'

My twenty or so years of fostering had taught me that stopping to think didn't gain me anything. I had to be prepared to take anyone who needed a home. 'Yes, OK, Jill, put my name forward. Possibly it won't come to anything, especially if it's a minor family crisis that's flared up over Christmas.'

'That's my feeling too. The chances are it will all be forgotten. Thanks Cathy. And Happy New Year.'

'And you, Jill.'

I returned to my book, *Italian Cooking At Its Best*, a Christmas present from my other daughter, Paula. We had spent a week in Italy the previous October and we had all loved the local cooking, feasting on delicious pasta, grilled meat, seafood and fantastic vegetables. The children had been badgering me ever since our return to have a go at making some of the dishes they'd enjoyed so much, but my Italian repertoire comprised lasagne, spag bol and not much else. Now there was no excuse. Paula had obviously bought me this cookery book to give me some inspiration and a bit of a prod to try my hand at something a bit more exciting, and no doubt Lucy and Adrian were hoping that they'd reap the benefits as well.

I turned the pages of colourful pictures showing fresh pasta in all shapes and sizes glistening with homemade sauces, risottos studded with peas or chicken and covered in shavings of Parmesan cheese, salads of wonderful fresh vegetables in lashings of olive oil. It all looked beautiful and mouth-wateringly delicious. But where would I find the ingredients for these lovely recipes? Would I be able to find artichoke hearts, truffle oil and yellow pimentos in Sainsbury's in the middle of winter?

My thoughts were interrupted by Lucy poking her head around the lounge door. 'What did Jill want? To wish us a happy New Year?'

I winked. 'She did actually, and a possible referral. A twelve-year-old boy. But I've got a feeling that it won't come to anything.'

She shrugged. All my children were remarkably sanguine about the little strangers who turned up on our doorstep. Some stayed for a short time, and some for months or even years. In Lucy's case, she'd become a permanent member of the family when I'd eventually adopted her. I was proud of the way all my children were happy to open their home to others who needed a port in a storm, and they'd certainly been tested by some of the more difficult and challenging of my foster placements, but they'd always come through. Lucy said casually, 'Is it all right if I go out later?'

'Yes, of course, love. Anywhere nice?'

'Cinema, maybe, with Helen.'

'Not David?'

She shook her head. 'If he can't be bothered to phone when he said, he'll find I've gone out.'

I smiled. Lucy's no-nonsense approach to life was obviously going apply to what was her first proper relationship. Poor David. I felt a bit sorry for him. Although he was seventeen, the same age as Lucy, he seemed much younger than she was, and I guessed his first foray into dating was going to prove quite a sharp learning curve. 'OK, but don't be too hard on him,' I said. 'Many boys his age sleep until lunchtime. I mean, have you seen Adrian yet this morning?'

'No.'

'Exactly, and he's nineteen. Actually, Lucy, if you're going back upstairs, could you knock on his door and wake him? He wants to go shopping for some things he needs for uni.'

'OK, Mum. And if David phones, tell him I'm in the bath.'

I turned the page of my Italian cookbook, found a recipe that looked reasonably straightforward and jotted down the ingredients on a scrap of paper. I was thrilled that the family still had fond memories of our week in Italy. We had taken the twins, and although I'd worried about how they would fare with a foreign holiday, especially one without a beach, they'd enjoyed themselves as much as we had. By then they were six months into the placement, well settled, and Paula and Lucy were still enamoured enough of the novelty of twins to keep the little girls amused. That meant I could have a real break and had also given me a chance to spend some time catching up with Adrian after his first few weeks away at uni. Fortuitously he'd had a week's study leave which had coincided with half term, so he had been able to come away with us. I had been reassured to learn from him that he *did* know how to open a can and work a washing machine, although judging from the amount of drinking that appeared to have gone on, I think the cans he opened were mainly cans of lager.

Remembering the holiday, I wondered what sort of Christmas the twins and their mother, Sashi, had enjoyed. Sashi had given birth to the twins when she was just sixteen. She had been dabbling in drugs at the time and by the age of twenty-three she was a crack-cocaine addict. The drug was so cheaply available that it could be bought for as little as ten pounds a rock, and Sashi was able to fund her habit on Income Support and still manage to take reasonable care of her daughters. The twins hadn't been badly neglected or abused, and a drug habit alone wasn't grounds for taking a child into care, rather the standard of care-giving when the parent is under the influence. Sashi had actually requested that her children be brought into care. With no family support network and after struggling alone for seven years, she'd reached the point where she'd felt she could no longer cope so she'd asked her social worker if the twins could be looked after so she could sort out her life and get off the cocaine. The girls had been placed under what is known as a Voluntary Care Order, and Sashi had brought them to my house with her social worker, spending the rest of the day with us and helping them settle in. The media image of heavy-handed social workers snatching children from their beds in the middle of the night is, I'm glad to say, usually a far cry from the truth. Whenever cooperation with the parents is an option, it's always the method chosen as it's clearly in the best interests of the child for them to see everyone working together in harmony for their benefit.

The aim of this placement had been respite for Sashi and the eventual return of the twins. I was wary at first, because I'd known plenty of cases where the mother fully intended to turn her life around but in the end, she wasn't able to and couldn't have her family back. This time, however, it worked like a dream. It was a shining example of good textbook social work practice (and – dare I say it – good fostering practice). The twins suffered as little disruption as possible; they were able to attend the same school, and their mum visited them at our house three times a week. Because there had been no concerns surrounding her treatment of the twins, Sashi was allowed to take them out on her own. When she returned them to us she often stayed for dinner, and sometimes helped put them to bed, and we got to feel that she was part of the family too. During this period she received counselling and began a programme to wean her off the crack-cocaine.

I had wanted her to come with us to Italy, for she needed a holiday as much as anyone, but she'd said she was petrified of flying. She was happy for the twins to go though as she didn't want them to miss out on such a wonderful opportunity. We'd phoned every night from Italy and the twins had loved chatting excitedly about what they had done that day.

On our return we had begun the process of rehabilitating the twins back to live with their mum: as well as continuing to visit during the week, Sashi had them to stay on Saturday nights for four weeks, then the entire weekend for another three. All of this culminated in my packing up all the twins' belongings and moving them back home on 14th December. With hugs, kisses and promises to keep in contact we'd said our goodbyes – but the onus was now on Sashi as to whether she wanted to stay in touch. Some parents do, but, in my experience, the majority do not. They want to forget the episode of having their children in care, and concentrate on the future. I had great hopes for Sashi: she was nearly off the crack-cocaine, and with the package of support the Social Services had put together for her, I thought she could make it, and I hoped she would phone occasionally to tell me. She loved the twins more than she loved herself, which was a sad reflection on her own upbringing.

* * *

'How about this then?' I said proudly, as I presented the home-made Toscana with ciabatta bread. I'd spent a happy hour that afternoon messing around with ingredients and I had to say that the result didn't look too bad at all.

There was a round of applause as I started dishing it up.

'That looks excellent, Mum. It really makes me think of Italy,' said Paula nostalgically, sniffing the air. 'Remember all those gorgeous meals?'

'I wonder how the twins are,' said Lucy. We couldn't help thinking of them whenever we recalled our holiday.

I raised my glass of water. 'Here's to Sashi and the twins.'

'To the twins,' repeated Adrian, Lucy and Paula.

Then they tucked in. And judging from the speed at which my offering disappeared, Paula's investment in a cookbook had already proven its worth.

Chapter Two

Lost and Found

True to her word, Jill phoned at ten o'clock on Monday. 'He's called Tayo,' she said.

'Right,' I said, jotting down the name on the pad I keep by the hall phone. 'Is that T-A-Y-O?'

'I think so, Tayo Mezer, M-E-Z-E-R. And he's not twelve but ten.'

'OK.' My pen hovered above the paper, ready to write down the other essential details that would follow: a brief general background and the reasons for his being brought into care, the name of his school and any special needs or dietary requirements. Anything, in fact, that would help me welcome him into our home and make sure he was properly looked after. I waited. 'Yes?'

Jill sighed. 'That's all I've been given, I'm afraid. The team manager has taken the file with her into court, and no one else in the office knows anything about the case. I've left a message for someone to phone you as soon they know what's happening. I'm in a meeting in Kent soon so I'll get in touch again when I'm finished.'

'So Social Services are definitely going for the Interim Care Order?' I asked.

'Yes, but whether it's granted or not is a different matter. With so little information, I've no idea why they want to take this boy into care or what the causes of concern are. I don't think the family can be known to Social Services or somebody would have something to tell me – some details would be available. I've honestly never experienced a case where there's so little known about the child. So I can't give you any more news, but if I were you, I'd be prepared anyway.'

'OK, thanks, Jill.' I put the phone down, and stared at the receiver thoughtfully.

Be prepared. It could be the foster carer's motto. Well, I was as prepared as I could be at this stage, knowing what I knew of my possible charge. I'd stripped the beds and given the bedroom a thorough cleaning the day after the twins had left – I found it cathartic as well as practical. Now the room was a blank canvas for the next child, but I wasn't about to do anymore. With so few details, the boy's age already changing, and the questionable outcome at court, I knew that I could very well find the child or children that eventually arrived were completely different to the original referral. I had once prepared the bedroom for the arrival of a thirteen-year-old girl, only to have a two-year-old toddler arrive. Situations change in fostering as quickly and dramatically as family situations, and in the space of three hours, the thirteen-year-old had gone to live with an aunt – it's always preferable if a child can be looked after within the extended family – and the toddler had been brought into care on an emergency order after his mother had left him alone in her flat all night. Foster carers have to be very flexible but I wasn't going to pin up posters of Daleks and warlocks, if a cot and big cuddly teddy was required. And I couldn't leave the house either, just in case something happened, and quickly.

What should I do while I waited for the news to come? I supposed I could always give the house a clean – if the child was very demanding, it might be a while before I got another chance – but Lucy and Adrian were still in bed, so I couldn't really start Hoovering now. Paula had left that morning in a rush; it was her first day back at school after the Christmas break and she was feeling stressed and envious of the other two – Lucy's college didn't start again for another week, and Adrian's university for another two.

I decided to tackle the basket of ironing that was waiting for me in the kitchen. While some women (and men) find ironing therapeutic, the only satisfaction I've ever got from it was when it was finished. With resolve, I went through to the kitchen, made a mug of coffee and set up the ironing board.

An hour later I carried the neatly pressed pile of laundry upstairs where I laid it on my bed, ready for distribution. I knocked on Adrian and Lucy's bedroom doors.

'It's eleven-thirty!' I called, then, hoping to prod their consciences. I added, 'Paula's gone to school. Can one of you get up? I need someone to do some shopping and I can't go out. Social Services might call.'

And as if on cue, the phone rang. I went to my bedroom and picked up the extension. 'Hello?'

'Is that Mrs Glass?'

'Speaking.'

'It's Binta Melthew, social worker from Children and Families, about Tayo Mezer?'

'Yes.' I could tell that Binta was on a mobile from the rush of passing traffic in the background.

'I've just come out of court. We've got the ICO. Someone from the team is going to collect Tayo from school. They should be with you by early afternoon.'

'OK. Do you know which school?' I asked, hoping the school run I would eventually be doing wasn't too long.

'No, I don't.'

'And Tayo is ten?'

'Yes, I think so. I'm going down the tube now. Someone will be in touch later.'

'OK.'

She was gone. I replaced the receiver and went back along the landing, knocking again on the bedroom doors, this time slightly more insistent. 'Come on, people. Time to get up! A ten-year-old boy is on his way, and I need some shopping.'

I continued along the landing and into the spare bedroom. A ten-year-old boy was very different to seven-year-old girls, and although political correctness said I shouldn't gender stereotype, experience had taught me that the things that appealed to little girls – the fluffy toys, Barbie play-scene, jewellery-making set, and Cinderella duvet covers – would not appeal to a little boy. So I packed them away and in their place I laid out a set of model dragons, a Star Wars castle with dubious inhabitants, and a Simpsons duvet cover showing a big picture of Homer saying 'D'oh'. These were always a safe bet with boys.

I still had no details about Tayo but I would learn more when the promised 'someone' from the team phoned. I only hoped I'd get the call before the child arrived. This wasn't the best way to start a placement and I felt uneasy about the lack of preparation. What if the little boy arrived and I discovered he had dietary or health requirements and no time to address them?

I was also worried about the fact that Social Services were taking Tayo from school. In ideal circumstances, the child would visit a few days before the move to get a sense of the new environment and have time to adjust emotionally. Even if this couldn't be arranged, most foster children had time to pack their favourite toys and some clothes. Not so in this case. Tayo had gone to school this morning, presumably expecting to finish his day and go home to his mother as usual. Instead, his life would change abruptly and he would be sent on an entirely different course, ending up at my house. With no warning of what was to come, he would probably arrive angry, upset and very confused, with just what he stood up in. I was sure I would have some clean pyjamas and underwear that would fit him until we had time to get his belongings – I had most sizes tucked away in my cupboards.

With all of this playing on my mind, I went downstairs to get some lunch. I heard bedroom doors open and footsteps along the landing as Lucy and Adrian emerged from their bedrooms and stumbled to the bathroom and shower. Just as I was sitting down for a quick sandwich, the phone rang. I hurried over to answer it. 'Hello?'

'Mrs Glass?'

'Speaking.'

'It's Brian Williams, social worker from Children and Families. Binta asked me to phone you. About Tayo Mezer?' He was on his mobile too.

'Yes.' I reached for the pen and paper; I always kept a set beside all of the four phones in the house.

'I'm on my way to the school,' Brian continued, 'but we're not sure if Tayo's there. I've already alerted the police and they're going to meet me there.'

'Which school?' I got in quickly.

'Meadway.'

I jotted it down. 'But you don't know if he's there?'

'Mum said in court that he was at home, but the Head said he was at morning registration. When I phoned the school half an hour ago, they couldn't find him. Once we've searched the building, the police will put out an alert. It's possible Mum's snatched him from the playground but not likely, as she was pretty drunk in court.'

'I see,' I said, concerned. This did not sound at all good. If the boy had been snatched by his mother, then they were now on the run. But if she hadn't taken him then it appeared that he'd vanished of his own accord. My heart went out to him. Poor little boy. Somehow he must have found out what was happening, and had probably run for his life, petrified by what he thought must be waiting for him. Now he was going to be picked up by the police, which would only increase his distress, even though they were excellent at dealing with runaways. This placement was quickly going from bad to worse.

'I'll keep you posted,' Brian said.

'Before you go, do you have any more details about the child?' I asked. 'Other than his name and age, I have nothing.'

14

'Neither have we. Didn't Binta tell you?'

'No? What?'

'There's no record of the child or his mother anywhere in the UK. They're still searching computer data but it looks like they could be here illegally, although the boy's English is perfect, which is odd.'

'Which country are they from?'

'Don't know. His mother, Minty, didn't produce any documentation in court.' He paused. 'I'm at the school now, I'll phone as soon as I have anything.'

'All right, Brian. Thank you.'

I put the phone down and looked at my notes. All I had written was the name of the boy's school. This was a first for me. I'd never dealt with any placement with so little to go on but if Tayo and his mother were here illegally it would explain the lack of information.

I went back to the table and sat down. I'd just taken a bite of my sandwich when the phone rang again. I dashed over and picked it up.

'Hi, Cathy. It's Jill.'

I made a muffled noise of acknowledgement.

'Sorry, have I caught you in the middle of lunch? I've just come out of my meeting. I phoned the team and they said Brian had been in touch. Any news?'

I swallowed and gave her a quick précis of the situation. 'If Brian and the police can't find Tayo at school then the police will put out an alert,' I finished.

'Oh dear.' I could hear the concern in Jill's voice. 'The poor kid's going to be in a right state by the time they get him to you. Do they have any idea where the family's come from?'

'No.'

'OK, take him as an emergency placement. I'll be back in the office in an hour. I'll phone from there.'

'Talk to you later then.'

I returned to my now forlorn-looking lunch and managed to finish it just before the phone rang again.

'Cathy Glass speaking.'

'Cathy, it's Brian Williams. There's no sign of him at the school, so the police are beginning a search. Hopefully we'll find him before the end of the day, but he could be anywhere. I'll phone when I have news.'

'Thanks, Brian.'

Foster carers are used to feeling in the dark about the great goings-on in courts and council offices, and all the machinations that bring some little soul to our door. Often we feel that social workers don't update us as much as they should, that there's barely time in their busy days to tell us what's going on. Not so in this case. I'd never had so many phone calls keeping me updated but in effect telling me nothing. And if I was starting to feel jittery with all this non-productive activity, how much worse must the child be feeling?

Lucy appeared, washed and dressed. 'What's going on with the phone, Mum? It's been non-stop all morning. You're blocking the line.'

I smiled at this role reversal. I was usually the one reprimanding Lucy for hogging the phone. 'I know, it's about the ten-year-old boy, Tayo. They can't find him.'

She raised her eyebrows. 'Is he on the run? I'm sure he'll turn up. Look, I'll get the shopping. I've got to go into town anyway to get some more hair gel. Can I borrow five pounds until Saturday?'

I nodded. 'Take it from my purse, and another twenty for the shopping. The list is on the side in the kitchen. Thanks, love, I really appreciate it.'

She disappeared.

There was a fifteen-minute phone respite while I made a mug of tea and tidied up the lunch things, before the phone rang again.

'Cathy?'

'Yes, hello, Brian.'

'The police have found him.'

'That was quick.' I couldn't help imagining a scared little schoolboy running for his life, puffing with exertion, before the police caught him.

'He was in the library at school all along. He was reading a book.'

'Really?' I said, relieved. 'Thanks, Brian. I'll see you both later.'

Now all I had to do was wait.

Chapter Three

Manners Maketh Man

It must be distressing for any child to be taken into care, whatever their home circumstances but, as I waited for Tayo, I considered how much worse it must be for him. Here he was in a foreign country and his mother was obviously considered unable to look after him. She must have drowned her sorrows before arriving at court and by turning up drunk, she would have lost any chance of persuading the judge to let her take Tayo back home. No doubt Tayo had seen himself off to school that morning – it was probably the one place he felt safe. And then the police and a social worker had arrived without any warning while he sat in the library and whisked him away from everything that was comfortable and familiar. I felt for him, I really did.

The last telephone call from Brian had come just before one-thirty. The school was a twenty-minute drive away, so I guessed they'd be with me soon after two.

While I prepared myself to meet my mysterious new charge, Lucy left to go into town and Adrian came down, grabbed a bite to eat and wandered out to meet some friends.

The phone rang again, but this time it was an old friend calling to wish me a happy New Year, and by the time we'd finished, it was three o'clock. There was still no sign of Tayo.

Jill phoned fifteen minutes later. 'Is he with you?'

'No. He was due here at two. I can't think what the delay is. They're only coming from Meadway.'

'I'll try and find out what's going on.'

But as soon as we'd hung up, the phone rang again.

'Hi, Cathy. It's Brian. We've stopped by the office for the paperwork. We'll be with you in half an hour.'

'OK, Brian.' I didn't really mind but it was a little irritating. If Brian had told me he was coming via the office, I could have put the time to good use instead of waiting anxiously for the doorbell to ring.

Lucy got back from the shops and we both agreed we were feeling jittery. Despite over twenty years of fostering, I still found that the build-up to the arrival of a new child was nerve wracking. Lucy went up to her bedroom to listen to music. Paula returned from school and quickly disappeared up to her room, while I tried to pass the time plumping cushions and tidying everything within an inch of its life.

At just after four o'clock, the doorbell finally rang and I shot down the hall, my heart pounding.

'Hello – Cathy?' said the man I took to be Brian.

'Yes, hello.'

'This is Tayo.'

I was already looking at the boy standing confidently beside him. With pleasant open features, large dark smiling eyes, light brown skin and short black hair, he really was a very handsome little chap. Except he wasn't little – at just under five feet, he was nearly as tall as me. He gave me a broad smile and offered his hand for shaking. I shook it and smiled back.

'Hello Tayo. It's lovely to meet you. Come in, both of you.'

'Thank you, ma'am,' Tayo said.

Did I hear him right? I thought, astonished. In all my years of fostering, I'd never been addressed as ma'am. I don't think most of my foster children would ever have heard the word. I exchanged a glance with Brian, who stood aside to let the boy come in first. Tayo stepped in and walked past me, confident and assured, but not brash.

'Straight down the hall,' I called to Tayo, who was already heading that way. 'The lounge is directly in front.' As Brian and I followed, I said quietly, 'Is everything all right?'

He nodded. I wondered if Brian was new at the offices, as I hadn't met him before. He looked like he'd been through the wringer today.

'Would you like tea, or a coffee?' I asked him as we entered the lounge.

'Coffee please, milk and no sugar. Thanks.'

'And what about you, Tayo? Would you like a drink?'

'Yes, please, ma'am. Black tea with no sugar.'

I was slightly taken aback, not only with the continued use of ma'am but with the request of black tea, not a drink I was used to children asking for. I smiled. 'OK, but please call me Cathy.'

He nodded. I went through to the kitchen, wondering where on earth the boy had acquired such impeccable, if slightly old fashioned, good manners. And his English was faultless with no trace of an accent. It didn't add up.

I made the drinks, arranged the biscuits on a plate, and carried the tray back through to the lounge.

Tayo stood as I entered, and Brian and I exchanged another pointed glance.

'Good boy,' I said to Tayo, and passed him his drink and offered him the plate of biscuits.

'Thank you,' Tayo said, and was about to say ma'am again but stopped himself in time. I watched him as he sat upright on the sofa and sipped his tea, then, setting the mug on the coaster (which not even Brian had managed to do), he began eating his biscuit, cupping his free hand under it to avoid dropping the crumbs. Perhaps I should have used the best china cups and saucers, I thought. I noticed that Tayo's shoulders and chest were quite broad and muscular under his fleece, and his neck thick and firm.

'Do you like sport, Tayo?' I asked curiously. He seemed to have an athletic physique.

'Very much so ...' He hesitated, reluctant to use my name.

'What do you play?'

'Everything from table tennis to rugby, when I get the chance. Recently I've been doing more skate-boarding and roller-skating.'

His English was indeed perfect, and his accent was almost a public school one. With his confidence and good manners, he was nothing like the child I'd been expecting, nor like any child I'd ever fostered or known to have come into care.

I assumed Brian would now throw some light on Tayo's background with the documents he'd collected from the office. He had finished his coffee and was delving into his briefcase. I smiled at Tayo. 'This is the boring bit, I'm afraid, Tayo. There's always lots of paperwork when someone comes to stay with me. But we'll try not to take too long and once we've finished, I'll show you your room.'

He smiled. 'Thank you for having me. You're very kind. Is all your family white?'

I glanced at Brian, surprised by the directness of Tayo's question. 'Yes. Well, my adopted daughter Lucy is part Thai. I've looked after children from many different ethnic backgrounds, though,' I said quickly, to reassure him. 'Why do you ask, Tayo?'

'Mum was worried I'd be placed with black carers. But I'm not black – I'm white.'

I didn't know what to say. Tayo was quite clearly mixed race, or of dual heritage as we're now supposed to say – one of his parents or grandparents was obviously Afro-Caribbean. It was very concerning that he saw himself as white, and that it was an issue he had raised almost at once. A child's cultural identity is of paramount importance if a positive self-image is to be cultivated. Why was he so vehemently opposed to the black part of him? What circumstances had made him that way? It sounded as though his mother might have had something to do with it, but now was not the time to question him.

'Here we go – the dreaded paperwork. Placement Agreement and Essential Information Part One,' Brian said, passing me two wads of stapled papers.

I reached over and took them just as his mobile went off. He answered: 'Speaking. I'm here now.' He listened, then looked at me. 'It's Jill, your support worker. She's been called to an emergency and wants to know if you're OK to continue alone?'

I nodded. Normally Jill, variously referred to as a link worker, support or supervising social worker, would be with me when a child was placed, but it was only really essential for new carers. By now I knew which forms to sign and what questions to ask.

'She'll phone you this evening,' Brian said, closing his phone and returning it to his pocket.

'Fine.' I smiled again at Tayo. He had finished his drink and biscuit, and was now sitting patiently, his back upright, and hands folded in his lap. 'Help yourself to another biscuit,' I said.

'Thank you, ma'am,' he said, before he could stop himself. 'Whoops, sorry, I mean, Cathy.'

'It's OK. Whatever you feel comfortable with.'

I began flicking through the ten pages of the Placement Agreement, which was in a different format to the one I'd had for the twins the previous year. The administration department did have a habit of changing them, usually for the worse. I noticed the boxes for the information, which were normally hand-written by the social worker at the time of placement, were now already computer printed, and not very successfully.

'We've just gone over to the new computer system,' Brain explained, seeing my expression.

'Another one?' There always seemed to be some new system being implemented.

''Fraid so. It's not without its teething problems, as you can see.'

'No,' I agreed. The first page contained the child's full name, sex, and date of birth, which was shown as 12–12–1996 – or would have if it hadn't collided with the heading.

'So you've had a birthday recently?' I asked Tayo, and he nodded. 'Did you get anything nice?'

'This jumper.' He pulled at the bobbled and stained nylon sweatshirt he was wearing that appeared to be a cheap imitation of Nike and looked as though it had been worn every day since his birthday on 12th December.

'Do you wear it for school?' I asked. It didn't look to me like a Meadway uniform.

He nodded, and suddenly looked downcast.

'Oh, yes. I meant to say. He'll need a full school uniform,' Brian put in. 'I'll authorize the allowance, of course.'

'Fine.' Carers are given an extra payment towards the cost if a child needs a whole new uniform. 'Is Tayo going to school tomorrow?'

'Yes,' Brian said.

I looked at Tayo. 'We'll go in early and I'll introduce myself to the Head, then we'll get you sorted out with some uniform.'

His expression lifted. 'I've been wearing these trainers for school. I'm not supposed to.'

I looked at the badly worn grey plastic trainers. They were in a dreadful state. 'If you can make do for one more day, we'll go to the town after school tomorrow and buy school shoes. I'll need you with me if I'm going to buy shoes so you'll have to wear those until we can go shopping. Don't worry, another day won't hurt and I'll explain to the Head why you're still in them. Do you have any clothes at home?'

'I did,' he said, 'but they got lost in the last move.'

'OK, no problem,' I said. *Last move.* That suggested there may have been others. 'We'll get you what you need tomorrow.'

I returned to the Placement Agreement and checked that my name and contact details were entered correctly, which they were, albeit at an odd angle, then looked down the page. *Child's legal status: Interim care order,* I read. That was normal. I turned over the page to the set questions and their answers.

Is the child on the Child Protection Register? Yes. Have the carers been given a copy of the Care Plan? Yes – it was part of the form I held. *Other significant information* was blank. *Mother's name: Minty.* The surname was blank, so too were her contact details, apart from a mobile phone number. *Child's health concerns: Mild asthma?* Below that, *Behavioural difficulties* was answered with a blank space. Then the boxes containing the social worker's contact details were filled in, except that the computer had missed the box and overprinted the line above.

'Can I write down your extension number, Brian?' I said. 'It's not come out on the form.'

'Of course, but I don't know how much use it will be to you. I'm only placing Tayo. Another team member will be taking over the case tomorrow.'

'Do you know who?' I asked, aware this was normal procedure.

'Not yet. I'll make a note on the file for them to call you first thing in the morning.'

I nodded and looked down again. The penultimate page was the actual contract of the placement, which the social worker and I would have to sign and date. The social worker would be signing to say all the information was correct to the best of his knowledge, and that he agreed to carry out duties specified in Section 11 of Foster Placement Requirements 1991. I would be signing to agree to look after the child under the same 1991 schedule, and also 'to cooperate with all arrangements made by the local authority', or in other words, the social workers. As if I wouldn't!

I signed and passed it to Brian. 'Is that my copy or yours?' I asked helpfully, as he put his signature in the appropriate box.

He tutted. 'Oh dear. I only brought one copy. That's annoying – I'll have to get it photocopied and put it in the post first thing tomorrow.'

'Don't worry, that's fine,' I said. 'But I'd be grateful if you could make sure you do – you know that without it I don't have any legal right to look after Tayo. And I've just noticed that the medical consent form isn't signed either.'

This form gave me permission to seek any medical treatment that might be necessary and it was supposed to be signed by the parents, but in practice it rarely was when the child had been removed on an Interim Care Order. The parents were often angry and uncooperative and not in the mood for agreeing to anything. Without it, though, I couldn't give Tayo so much as a spoonful of Calpol, the mild analgesic designed for young children. 'Obviously I'll need that too, so could you also ask whoever is taking over the case to send the medical consent form, please?'

'Will do.' Brian made a note.

I glanced at Tayo who was still sitting patiently, then down at the information form. 'It says here you have mild asthma. Do you have an inhaler?'

'No. I don't need one now, only when I have a cold. Last year I borrowed a friend's.'

Struth, I thought, shocked. A child borrowing medication! No one should use anything prescribed for someone else and certainly not a child, especially when an inhaler would be free. 'Have you been to see the doctor about it?'

Tayo looked at me cautiously and seemed to be choosing his words very carefully. 'Not since I've been in this country, no.'

'And how long is that?'

He looked down and shrugged. 'I don't know, four or five years, maybe.'

I hid my shock at this and turned to Brian, saying quietly, 'Is that right? Tayo's been here for five years and has never seen a doctor?'

'We don't know. I'll have a word with you later.' He gave me a meaningful look, which clearly meant we'd discuss it out of Tayo's earshot. 'But could you take him for a check-up at the doctors as soon as possible please?'

'Yes, of course.' I smiled at Tayo. 'It's important to have your own medicine if you need it, not to borrow a friend's. Everyone's needs are different, and if you have asthma it should be monitored. OK?'

He smiled back but didn't look wholly convinced.

I returned to the second set of forms: Essential Information Part 1. This was supposed to tell the carer everything they needed to know about the foster child. To quote from the guidance notes at the top of the form: 'All questions must be answered before any child/young person can be left in a placement.' Well, that's the theory!

The form started well, with the correct name, date of birth, and Tayo's gender. Below that were several blank boxes for dates and contact details, then the address and telephone number of the Social Services offices, which I was already very familiar with.

There was no home address but the principal carer was given as Minty, his mother. Ethnic origin was given as British/African, followed by a question mark, while the boxes for the ethnic origin of the birth mother and the father were blank. *What culture does the child/young person identify with?* was answered with *White UK?* From then on, box after box was blank. According to the form, he had no religion, spoke English, suffered from mild asthma and went to Meadway School. Minty's mobile phone number was also included. There was nothing about Tayo's father, or any siblings, or any extended family he might need to keep in touch with.

So, at the end of ten pages of official forms, all I had was what I knew to start with, and for once I didn't think it was entirely the fault of Social Services.

I glanced up at Brian, resisting the temptation to quip something about it being a bit sparse.

'Can we go somewhere to talk?' he asked, his face sombre.

I glanced at Tayo. I didn't want to leave him alone, all too aware we were discussing him. With a child of his obvious intelligence and understanding, it seemed downright rude and marginalizing.

'Tayo,' I said, 'you've been great, sitting there through all of this. How about if I introduce you to my daughter, Lucy, and the two of you can have a game of cards or something, while Brian and I finish off?'

Although Paula was closer to Tayo's age, I volunteered Lucy, not just because she'd been relaxing while Paula had been at school all day, but also because she had a gift for bonding with children I fostered, always being the first to connect with the new arrival. Perhaps it was because she had been fostered herself once, and knew what it felt like.

'Lucy is with her sister, Paula, upstairs listening to music,' I said, standing up. 'I'll just get her.'

I went upstairs, knocked on Lucy's door and went in. She was sitting on her bed listening to her MP3 player but when she saw me, she took her earphones out. 'Hi, Mum. What's up?'

'Tayo's here. Could you do me a favour and keep him occupied while I have a chat to the social worker?'

'Sure.' She switched off the music and jumped off the bed. She was used to lending a hand when a child first arrived. 'Is he hyperactive then?'

'No. Not at all, he's fine. It's just that the social worker wants a word in private.'

She followed me back downstairs. As we went in, Tayo stood up politely and offered his hand for Lucy to shake.

'Lucy, this is Tayo,' I said, as a surprised Lucy shook the proffered hand.

'Hi, Tayo,' she said brightly. 'Do you fancy a game of Uno?'

'Very nice to meet you, Lucy. And yes, please, I would like to play Uno. I know that game.'

'Great, I'll get the cards.'

Brian and I left the two of them dealing a hand in the lounge and went through to the front room.

'So I take it you're still very much in the dark about Tayo's past,' I said, as I closed the door.

Brian nodded. 'We still haven't come up with anything. Other than what you have on the forms, there's nothing. No doctors' records, no benefit records, no immigration records —

not on the names they've given us, anyway. There's just Tayo and his mother. No family, no history, nothing.'

'I see,' I said, thoughtfully. It certainly made a change from the usual thick case files of my foster children. 'And what about the school? They must know something. How long has he been there?'

Brian sat down. 'One term. Tayo appeared at the end of September. The school was one of the parties that raised concerns. The Head contacted us in December.'

'One? There were others?'

'Yes. There was also a taxi driver, who picked up Tayo's mum a few times from home and thought there might be a child left alone, and an anonymous caller. We tried to see Tayo at school before Christmas but he vanished, then reappeared today. It's their first day back.'

'So you don't know where he was over Christmas?'

'No. He says he stayed with friends. And I gather he didn't see Mum from when school broke up last year until yesterday.'

'What? He wasn't with her over Christmas?'

'It seems not.'

'Didn't that make him anxious? Frightened?'

Brian shrugged. 'Apparently not.'

This little boy was becoming more of a mystery. It was hard to imagine a child who didn't seem to mind being apart from his mother over Christmas. I frowned. 'And he's been in the country for possibly five years?' I asked.

'That was the first I'd heard of it just now,' Brian said. 'Mum's not saying anything. Perhaps Tayo will open up to you.'

'Well, let's hope so but it won't happen overnight. He's got to trust me first, and that takes time. How was Tayo when you collected him from school? He seems very relaxed now.'

'It all went very smoothly, actually. He was playing chess with a friend in the library, and when we told him what was happening, he just put down his chess piece and said, "We'll have to continue this tomorrow" and happily came with us.'

'I see.' I'd never heard of such a calm and collected response to being taken into care.

'Whoever takes over the case will arrange the placement meeting,' continued Brian. 'They'll invite Mum, but I'm not hopeful of her coming, even if we can contact her. There's only her mobile and that's not often switched on.'

'And does she know our address?'

'We're not giving it yet. There are too many unknowns. Further down the line maybe, if you haven't any objections.'

'None that I can think of.'

'Good.' Brian smiled. 'Well, that's everything for now, Cathy. I'll just say goodbye to Tayo.'

We went back to the lounge where Tayo and Lucy were finishing a second game of Uno and Tayo was about to win again, much to his obvious delight.

'I'm going now,' Brian said to Tayo as he picked up his brief-case.

Tayo stood to shake Brian's hand. 'Thank you, sir, for every-thing.'

Lucy raised her eyebrows and shot me a glance. I motioned for her not to say anything, although I doubted she would. We were well used to different, unusual, even bizarre behaviour in the children we fostered, although extreme politeness wasn't something we usually had to contend with. If that's as bad as it gets, I thought, we can certainly count our blessings.

After Brian left, I offered to show Tayo round the house before dinner. He was immediately on his feet, more relaxed now the social worker had left. I gave him my usual guided tour of the downstairs first, then upstairs to his bedroom.

'Hopefully, we'll be able to get some of your bits and pieces from Mum,' I said. 'It'll make you feel more at home.'

'This is fine, Cathy,' he said, at last managing to use my name comfortably. 'I don't know where my things are.' He abruptly stopped, and I knew he was saying nothing further.

I marvelled again at his self-possession. It was completely outside my experience. How long, I wondered, would it take a child like this to open up, and begin to reveal the truth about himself and his past?

Chapter Four

Settling In

Our first night seemed to go extremely smoothly.

Tayo asked me if it was all right if he stayed in his bedroom to watch the portable television until dinner was ready.

'Of course,' I said. 'That's your room – you can come and go as you please. You won't be disturbed there. And by the same token, Tayo, you must respect other people's privacy when they're in their rooms. We don't go into each other's bedrooms without being asked. OK?'

Tayo nodded and said, 'Yes, Cathy', before disappearing upstairs.

I wouldn't normally have left a child unattended in their room for an hour on the first night but Tayo was different. It was obvious he had a maturity well beyond his age and, with no sign of any behavioural difficulties, there was no reason why he shouldn't relax in his bedroom, as the girls were doing in theirs.

Adrian returned just after six o'clock and I served dinner at six-thirty. I showed Tayo his place at the table and as Paula and Adrian arrived, he stood and shook their hands. I saw Tayo instantly warm to Adrian, another male in the house, and I thought it was a pity for Tayo that Adrian would be going back to university in two weeks.

As I could have predicted, Tayo's manners were impeccable at the meal table. He shook out his paper napkin and laid it across his lap, sat upright, used his knife and fork properly, and never once spoke with his mouth full, which was a glowing example to everyone. His gratitude at what for us was a routine and rather mundane meal of roast chicken, boiled potatoes and peas, knew no bounds. When I produced the dessert of a shop-bought apple crumble and instant custard, I thought he was going to hug me. He was the perfect guest, polite and grateful.

'Tayo,' I said, as a thought struck me, 'have you often had meals at other people's houses?'

He nodded. 'Mum had some good friends and they were very kind to me.'

'And you spent Christmas with some of her friends?'

'Yes. I …' He stopped and returned to his pudding, and I knew that was as far as any talk about Mum and home was going at this point.

At the end of the meal, Tayo helped clear the table without being asked, and then hovered, and asked if I needed help with the washing up, which again was a fine example to the others, although unfortunately there was no one around to witness it. The girls had gone to watch television and Adrian was getting ready to go out.

'That's very kind of you, but don't worry,' I said. 'I have a dishwasher, I'll load it.'

He still hovered, almost as if he liked the domestic feel of being in the kitchen and watching me go about my chores.

'Have you lived in the house a long time, Cathy?' he said after a while.

'Yes, over twenty-two years.'

'That's nice. So your children have never had to move?'

'No, darling, they haven't.'

He was looking thoughtful and slightly sombre and I thought this was another opportunity to find out a little more.

'Have you had lots of moves, Tayo? It can be very unsettling if you never get to stay anywhere for long.'

His eyes met mine. 'Yes. I don't like it. I lose my things and some of the people are nice but not all.' He thought and then said, 'Will I have to move from here?'

'Not until everything is sorted out. Did Brian explain to you about the court process?'

'Yes, he said he thought it would take nearly a year.'

'That's right. I know it sounds a long time but it goes very quickly. The judge will want to make sure your next move is the last one and that you're looked after properly until you are an adult. He'll also ask what you want to do so that he can bear it in mind when he makes his decision. Did Brian mention the Guardian Ad Litum?'

Tayo nodded. 'He said that was the person appointed by the court to watch out especially for me.'

'Yes. Well, that person will talk to you and then tell the judge your wishes. At your age you won't have to go to court. It all takes time and during that time you'll stay with us, go to school, and try not to worry. If you like sport, we could enrol you in some clubs.' I was mindful that a child of Tayo's age and intelligence could well spend a year of his life fretting. Younger

children and those with learning difficulties were in some ways
protected by their limited understanding.

'Thank you, Cathy,' he said. 'But I know what I want right
now.'

'Do you?' I asked, and I expected him to say, 'Yes, I want to
stay with my mother.'

He nodded. 'I want to live in Nigeria.'

I stopped what I was doing and looked at him. 'I see,' I said
slowly. 'Is that where you used to live?'

He gave a small nod, then his gaze slid away and I knew that
he would say no more at present. 'I'll watch the television now,
if that's all right?' he said.

'Yes, of course, love. See you later.'

He smiled as he turned, and with a little hop, jogged off
down the hall and upstairs, with the ease of someone who had
been with us for years rather than a couple of hours.

Nigeria? Nigeria had not been mentioned before or Brian
would have said. This must be a new piece of information, and
could be the first bit of the jigsaw of Tayo's past that would,
I hoped, slowly be pieced together over the months ahead.

When I'd finished clearing away, I went through to the
front room to start a file on Tayo. It was something I had to
do for all the children I fostered. Once the child had left me
and the file was complete, I had to lock it away in a filing cabinet in my room; these files are highly confidential and have to
be kept for twenty years. They could be wanted by a judge in
a court case in years to come, and are available for scrutiny by
the Social Services or the child at any time now or in the
future. The five-drawer metal filing cabinet was already
pretty full.

I hole-punched the forms Brian had given to me and hooked them into the folder, then took a fresh record sheet from my desk drawer and headed it with today's date and the time Tayo arrived. I noted how Tayo was on arrival, and included what he'd said about where he'd been at Christmas, and his comments about Nigeria. We used to keep the daily record in a large diary but, like many things, this had changed and we were now required to use the pre-printed forms. Details of his first night, I would add in the morning. I placed it in the folder, closed the file and locked it in my desk.

It was after eight o'clock already, and with Tayo going to school the next day, I needed to start a bedtime routine. I went upstairs, found a pair of pyjamas and toothbrush from my emergency hoard, then took a towel from the airing cupboard and knocked on Tayo's door.

'Come in,' he called.

I pushed the door open. He was sprawled on the bed, holding the remote, and leisurely flicking through the channels. As I entered, he immediately switched off the television and jumped off the bed, almost standing to attention.

'You can have your shower now,' I smiled. 'These pyjamas will do for tonight, they should fit. We'll buy some more tomorrow.'

He thanked me, then followed, as I led the way along the landing and to the bathroom. I showed him where the shower gel was, how to work the shower, and placed his toothbrush in the mug with ours and left him to it. Fifteen minutes later I heard the bathroom door open, and his footsteps along the landing. I went up to say goodnight and to make sure the television was off.

He'd left his bedroom door slightly open, but I knocked all the same before I went in. He was comfortably settled under the duvet, and the television was off. I noticed his towel was neatly folded at the foot of his bed with his toothbrush on top. To the right was a pile of his dirty clothes, also folded with incredible precision. It reminded me of a young army cadet's bed, ready for inspection.

'Are the pyjamas OK?' I asked.

He grinned. 'Yes, thank you.'

'I'll wash and dry your clothes so you can have them for the morning.' I went to the end of the bed and removed the pile of clothes. 'Shall I put your towel and toothbrush with ours in the bathroom?'

His face registered concern. 'Can I keep them here?'

'Yes, if you prefer.' I guessed that Tayo had lost his things many times as he moved about and, as a result, felt anxious about letting things out of his sight. Many children I'd fostered had been through similar experiences and felt safer keeping their possessions close to them. I'd once looked after an eight-year-old girl who'd slept with the new shoes I'd bought her under her pillow every night for a month. In the past, anything of hers that was half-decent had been taken by her older siblings, and she wasn't going to risk having her first pair of new shoes disappear.

I drew Tayo's bedroom curtains. 'I'll wake you at seven-fifteen tomorrow. That should give us plenty of time to get ready and be at school for eight forty-five.'

'School starts at eight-fifty,' he emphasized. 'I mustn't be late again.'

'No. You won't be,' I reassured him. 'No one is ever late with me.'

I watched him relax. I was used to this too – children who have had to devise and oversee their own routines often find it a great relief to know they can relinquish some of the responsibility.

'Goodnight then, love,' I said. 'It's bound to be a bit strange sleeping in a different bed for the first night. You know where I am if you need me.' He looked quite relaxed and comfortable, though, snuggled under the duvet with only his head showing. 'Shall I close your door so you're not disturbed when Adrian and Lucy come up later?'

'Yes. And Cathy?'

'Yes, love?'

'Can I have a goodnight kiss?'

'Of course.' I bent down and kissed his forehead. He smiled, and suddenly all the maturity that had seen him through goodness knows what, vanished, and he was a little boy again, vulnerable and in need of a mother's goodnight kiss. 'Night, love. Sleep tight.'

'And don't let the bed bugs bite,' he added.

'Is that what your mother used to say?'

'No, my gran. When I was little in Nigeria.' He closed his eyes and I gave his forehead a little stroke, then I came out and closed the door behind me.

I never sleep well on the first night of having a new child or children in the house. I listen for any sound that might suggest they are unsettled, upset, or even out of bed. Often I'm up and down like a yo yo, particularly with very young children who don't understand what's happening. In fact, I have been known to abandon my bed altogether and doze in a chair on the landing, resettling the new arrival as soon as they cry, shout or come out of their bedroom. My insomnia on this occasion, however, was none of Tayo's doing; there wasn't a sound from his room all night.

Nevertheless I tossed and turned into the early hours, trying to fathom out what had brought him here. It was both puzzling and perplexing. Most children fit a type, a kind of mould formed by what has happened in their lives; abuse and neglect can make them angry, withdrawn, obsessive, anxious, or just plain naughty. But not so with Tayo. He may have been neglected but he was one of the most well adjusted children I had ever met, in or out of care. And while it was obviously early days yet and things could change, I failed to see how his self-possession could all be an act.

No – at some point in this boy's past, someone had done some good parenting, which was a hopeful sign. It meant that his mother might well be able to have him back. If Tayo's mother was prepared to work with the Social Services and willing to rectify whatever had gone wrong, then it was quite possible that Tayo would eventually be able to return to live with her, either here or in Nigeria.

With this optimism, I managed two hours' sleep before the alarm rang.

Chapter Five

A Promising Start

The following morning I was up, showered and dressed by six-thirty, as usual, then I woke Paula at seven, and Tayo at seven-fifteen.

When I went into his bedroom and presented him with his pile of washed and ironed clothes, he looked at me with such admiration that you would have thought I had performed a miracle. It was just a pity no one else in the house viewed my domestic achievements in the same celestial light.

He got up straight away, washed and dressed, then made his bed (without being asked), before coming down to breakfast. He chose cereal from the selection in the cupboard, then followed it with two slices of toast and marmalade, and black tea with one sugar.

'Are you sure you wouldn't prefer fruit juice?' I asked.

'No, this is fine, thank you. And it's so nice not to have to eat in my room.'

Paula, who had just joined him at the table, felt duty bound to set Tayo straight on this point. 'You can't eat in your bedroom here, not unless you've been away to uni. Then when you come back you can do anything.'

She shot me a look but I said nothing, while Tayo lowered his eyes diplomatically and concentrated on his toast. Adrian had brought some student habits back with him, snacking in his room being one. Paula knew that age brought certain privileges but that didn't stop her moaning occasionally when she felt things were unfair.

'Come on, Tayo,' I said. 'Let's get going.'

Tayo hadn't brought any school things with him so there was nothing to remember other than himself. He told me he had been having school dinners, so I didn't make him a packed lunch. As I unlocked the car he asked if he could sit in the front passenger seat but I explained it was safer in the back, and that was where all children under twelve had to sit, which he accepted. It also had the hidden advantage of the child security lock, which meant that the door couldn't be opened from the inside.

I watched him in the rear-view mirror as we started the twenty-minute journey to school. He was quiet but seemed to be taking everything in, with more than a passing interest in the scenery outside. His head flicked back and forth as though he was noting the route and the road signs we passed. It crossed my mind that he might be planning an escape – he wouldn't be the first child to try and find his way back to his mum.

'Do you know this part of town?' I asked after a while.

'Yes. I used to live down there.'

I glanced back at the road we had just driven past and made a mental note of Gresham Gardens. 'With your mum?'

'No, with friends.'

A couple of minutes later as we slowed for traffic lights, Tayo was craning his neck back again. 'Do you know Salisbury Road?' I asked casually.

'Yes, I lived there.'

'What? Recently?'

'A few months ago, I think.'

'With Mum?'

'No, with friends.'

Another hundred yards and it happened again, and then again. During the remaining ten minutes of the journey, Tayo pointed out another six roads where he had lived or stayed 'with friends' in the last few months. I began to doubt it. Time and location can be very confusing to children, particularly when they have been moved, and I thought he had more than likely visited the houses, perhaps to play or possibly stay for a meal, rather than actually living there. Even so, he appeared to know the area very well, and it was something else I should mention to the social worker who took over the case when they phoned later.

It was eight-forty as I parked in a side street a short way from Meadway School.

'Can I go straight into the playground with my mates?' Tayo asked.

'I'd like you to come with me into reception first to sort out your uniform. Then, while I see the Head, if there's time, I'm sure you can go in the playground.' For the first time, I saw something like dissension cross Tayo's face, and I thought I heard the quietest of groans. 'Don't worry, I won't embarrass you,' I added. 'As soon as we've got your uniform, you're free to go.'

He smiled and I knew I had hit the right note. It can be very embarrassing for a child to appear in the playground with a new carer – it sparks curiosity and questions from friends and also their parents. Sometimes I arrange to meet foster children, particularly the older ones, just outside the school gates so I'm not so visible.

As I climbed out of the car and then opened Tayo's door, a boy of about the same age, in Meadway uniform and laden down with a schoolbag, walked by the car.

'Hi, Sam!' Tayo called unselfconsciously as he climbed out.

The boy stopped, smiled at Tayo, and then predictably looked at me.

'This is Cathy, my carer,' Tayo said, with only a small dismissive shrug. So having a carer wasn't a problem for Tayo, it was more just having an adult with him.

I smiled. 'Hello, Sam. Nice to meet you.'

Tayo walked on ahead beside his friend while I followed a few steps behind. As we approached the main entrance, Sam went off to the left to go into the playground and Tayo returned to my side. 'He seemed very nice,' I said.

'Yes,' Tayo said casually. 'I lived with him once.'

I pressed the security buzzer, gave my name and added that I was Tayo Mezer's carer. The door was unlocked and Tayo pushed it open, then stood aside to let me in first.

'Thank you,' I said. 'Now, you lead on and show me the way. We'll go to the secretary's office.'

Pleased to be given this authority, Tayo proudly went ahead. We made a right turn and saw a woman approaching us along the corridor.

'Hello, Mrs de la Haye,' Tayo said.

'Hello, there, Tayo.' She smiled at him, then at me. 'Roberta de la Haye, I'm the deputy head,' she said. 'I'm also the designated person for looked-after children.' We shook hands. 'Shall we go into my office? It's more private.'

Tayo and I followed her a little way down the corridor and into an office on the left.

'Do sit down,' she said, closing the door.

The three of us sat in a small semi-circle. Roberta de la Haye had a comfortable but businesslike manner. She addressed Tayo first. 'So, how are you, young man? It was quite a day yesterday.'

'Good,' he grinned. 'I've got my own room with a television, and it's a nice house. I've had dinner and breakfast, and I won't have to move again.'

Roberta de la Haye nodded. 'Excellent.' She looked at me. 'Tayo's been rather unsettled in school recently and has fallen behind with his work. I'm sure it will all change now.'

'Yes,' I agreed. 'I'm sure he'll soon catch up. Do you have my contact details?'

'No. Not even your name.'

'It's Cathy Glass. I'll give you the other details later.' I threw a glance in Tayo's direction, hoping she understood that he shouldn't be party to the information in case he passed it to his mother, though given his level of understanding it was likely he would soon know his address if he didn't already.

Roberta nodded

'I need to buy Tayo a school uniform,' I added. 'He's only got what he's wearing.'

'We can do that now. I'll take you to the office and Mrs Saunders, our welfare lady, will sort you out. Then I think it would be helpful if we had a chat.' It was her turn to glance in Tayo's direction and I knew she meant out of earshot.

'Yes, of course.'

'Come on then, Tayo,' she said, standing. 'A whole new uniform. That sounds good.'

We followed her back along the corridor and into the school secretary's office. She introduced me to Mrs Saunders, explained what we wanted, then left us, saying she'd be back in ten minutes.

'I'm sorry, I don't know Tayo's size yet,' I said, as Mrs Saunders opened a very tall cupboard with shelves full of school uniform.

'No problem. I've had a lot of experience in fitting out children.' She looked Tayo up and down, then started taking down polythene bags containing blue sweatshirts and jumpers emblazoned with the school's logo, grey trousers and PE kit.

'I'd like three of everything,' I said.

Tayo's eyes grew wide with excitement at the growing pile of new clothes. This was evidently a novel experience for him. 'And can I have the school bag for the PE kit?' he asked, spying it in the cupboard.

'Yes, of course.' I opened the packets of PE kit containing shorts and sweatshirt, again bearing the school's emblem, and held it up against him. 'It looks a perfect fit.'

'I need to hang the bag on my peg,' he said.

'OK.' I placed the PE kit in the bag and closed the draw-string. 'Is there somewhere he can go to change into the uniform?' I asked Mrs Saunders.

'Go in the stockroom, Tayo. Over there.'

While he went off to change I wrote a cheque for £137, seventy of which I would recover from the additional payment Brian had mentioned.

Mrs Saunders placed the other sets of uniform in a carrier bag and we waited for Tayo to reappear. 'He's such a nice kid,' she said. 'God knows what's been going on.'

'No,' I agreed, but I wasn't about to enter into a discussion. The deputy head would inform the staff of what they needed to know, and the rest was confidential. Then something else occurred to me. 'Tayo's having school dinners. Has the bill been paid for this term?'

'No,' Mrs Saunders said. 'Nor for last.'

'I'll pay for this term but I'm not responsible for last. Tayo wasn't in my care then. I'm afraid you'll have to try and recover it from Social Services. How much is it for this term?'

'It's £1.75 a day or £122.50 for the whole term.'

I wrote out another cheque as Tayo reappeared, his old clothes stuffed in a ball under his arm.

'You look smart!' Mrs Saunders and I chimed together.

'Thanks, Cathy.' Grinning proudly, Tayo came over, gave me his old clothes, then shook my hand in gratitude.

'You're welcome,' I said with a smile. His happiness was infectious. 'I'll put your name in your things tonight, so be careful you don't lose them today.'

'I won't,' he said fervently, and I knew for certain he wouldn't; they were obviously his first new clothes since goodness knew when.

Roberta de la Haye came into the office, echoing our praise for Tayo's smart new things. I explained that Tayo would have to wear his trainers until we bought school shoes in the evening. 'That's fine,' she said, then told him to join his class-mates, who were lining up ready to come in for registration.

'Where shall I meet you after school?' I asked Tayo.

'In the playground, over by the gates, please,' he said, eager to be off. I guessed this was his way of saying, 'I want you there, but not too obvious.'

'Have a good day, and see you later,' I said.

He turned and, with a massive smile, loped off.

'One satisfied client,' I said to Roberta.

'Yes.' She nodded. 'He really is a nice kid. Shall we go back to my office?'

I followed her again down the corridor and into her office. I liked Roberta de la Haye already, and guessed that her kind but efficient manner would make my future deal-ings with the school run smoothly. Having a designated person in school specifically to monitor looked-after chil-dren is a fairly recent development, and not all schools have a well-trained and responsible staff member to take the role on. I often have a lot of explaining to do about social work and court procedure but not this time. Roberta was obvi-ously on the ball.

'I suggested an Interim Care Order well before Christmas,' she said as we entered her office. 'We raised concerns at the beginning of November. Heaven only knows what took Social Services so long – unless it was that they couldn't find his mother.'

'It might have been,' I replied. 'The social worker yesterday said she was difficult to contact.'

Roberta de la Haye sat behind her desk and lifted a pen. 'Let me write down your address and phone numbers first.'

I told her, adding that it was confidential at present, and Tayo's mother wasn't to be told.

'Good,' she said, and I guessed her dealings with his mum hadn't been too positive.

'I don't have any background information at all,' I said. 'Can you tell me what you know, and why you raised the concerns?'

'Certainly, although Tayo only started here in September and we don't know where he was before that. Mum said she couldn't remember the name of the school. She couldn't remember their previous address, GP, or even her own telephone number. There doesn't appear to be a father on the scene.'

'No, but he did mention a gran in Nigeria to me.'

Roberta raised her eyebrows. 'I haven't heard that before. Mum brought him here on the first day and as far as we know hasn't done so since. She's been in the playground to collect him a few times at three-fifteen, but more often he goes home, wherever that is, alone, or with someone else. His mother seems to search out and latch on to good families and then she leaves Tayo with them, sometimes for one night, other times for days on end. Tayo has no way of contacting her, and says he doesn't know where she is. When she can't find another family to take him, they go to Bed and Breakfast – but she can't pay, so the two of them have to do a runner in the early hours. We learnt this from the families he's stayed with. He told their children. My hunch is that now he's in care, she'll disappear completely.'

'Really?' I asked, surprised. In my experience, even mothers who appear very neglectful don't give up their children without a fight.

She nodded. 'He seems to be just a burden to her.'

'While I was driving here Tayo pointed out a number of places where he'd stayed. I thought it was too many to be true but it makes sense now from what you've said.'

'The poor boy has been all over the place. People are kind and feel sorry for him. One family had him for nearly a week in November with no word from his mother. Then one morning she turned up drunk on their doorstep at two a.m. She was very aggressive and demanded Tayo back. He went with her, but reluctantly. They told us, and we alerted the Social Services again. It's a clear case of neglect, I'm afraid. Tayo has been in the same clothes since he started school. The families he's stayed with have washed them but when he's in Bed and Breakfast we often find him in the toilets here trying to sponge the stains off his sweatshirt. To be honest, I think it was a relief for him yesterday when the social worker arrived – although we did have a job finding Tayo.'

'Yes, what was all that about?'

'I'm not sure. We searched high and low and couldn't find him. We *had* looked in the library, but he wasn't there to begin with. Tayo said he was in the toilets.' She shrugged. 'It's a mystery. But it doesn't really matter now.'

'I suppose not.' I paused. 'If I'm frank, Tayo is a bit of a puzzle. He's not like the children who usually come into care. At some point he must have had some good parenting from someone. And his English is unusually good, isn't it? Some of the children born and brought up in this country can't speak as well as he does.'

'I know, but it wasn't from his mum. We haven't seen that much of her, but we've seen enough to know she's got a big drink problem, and possibly a drug one too. She calls herself a dancer, but I suspect that's a euphemism for something else. She's not on benefit but she's getting money from somewhere and I don't think it's cleaning. That's all the information we have, really. I take it you don't know any more?'

'Only that Tayo said he thought he'd been in this country for five years but he isn't saying any more at present. Despite everything, he's likely to be quite protective of Mum. Children often are when they're taken into care.'

Roberta nodded. 'I know. All that loyalty and love, after everything they go through. It's heartbreaking.'

As I drove home, I wondered if Roberta de la Haye had been right when she'd said Tayo's mother would disappear. I hoped not. If she vanished, there would be no hope of Tayo going back to live with her, or even of any kind of contact, and I knew that a complete rejection would be very hard for him to come to terms with. In my experience, some contact with a natural parent is usually better than none.

When I got home, Adrian was up and about.

'A social worker phoned, about Tayo,' he mumbled, still half asleep. 'Here's the extension number.'

I took the piece of paper he held out to me. The social worker's early call was a promising sign of efficiency; after all, it wasn't ten o'clock yet. 'No name?'

'Didn't say.'

'Male or female?'

'Female.'

'Thanks.'

'Can you leave the answer phone on next time?' Lucy added as she came down the stairs rubbing her eyes. 'The phone woke me up.'

'You'll have to get back into the morning routine before long,' I called as they both disappeared back upstairs to bed.

I left the bags of Tayo's old clothes in the hall and went to the lounge to call the number Adrian had written down. The extension was a direct line and I was surprised when it rang and rang. Eventually a male voice answered.

'Social Services.'

'It's Cathy Glass. I'm Tayo Mezer's carer. Someone phoned a few minutes ago to speak to me. I'm returning the call.'

There was an ominous silence, then: 'I don't know anything about it. Do you know who's dealing with it?'

'No. Brian Williams placed Tayo yesterday, and he said someone else would be taking over today. She phoned a few minutes ago and gave this extension.'

Another ominous silence. I was fairly used to ominous silences followed by someone denying all knowledge of anything to do with my case. 'I'll try and find out. Can I have your telephone number?'

I gave my landline number, more in hope than expectation. I don't know how many times I'd given out my details and waited in vain for a call to be returned, only to learn in the end that the message had disappeared into the void.

'And what did you say your name was?'

'Cathy Glass.'

'And who's it about?'

'Tayo Mezer.'

There was a pause while he wrote. 'Is Tayo your child?'

'No. I'm his foster carer. He was placed with me yesterday.' My patience was being tested.

There was another silence, when I assumed he was writing some more, then: 'And what was the query about?'

I spoke slowly, enunciating every word. 'A social worker is taking over Tayo's case and that person phoned me. I am returning the call.' I gave him enough time to write, then added, 'So will you tell that person I'm at home now, on this number.'

'Yes. I'll have to speak to someone.'

'Thank you.' Another frustrating, repetitious call, but there was nothing for it but to wait for whoever it was to ring me back.

I put the laundry on, then made a cup of coffee. I was just sitting down with it when the phone went and I answered it immediately.

'Is that Cathy Glass?' It was a female voice.

'Speaking.'

'It's Sandra Braxley. I'm taking over Tayo Mezer's case.'

'Ah good.' I was relieved. Contact established, thank goodness. 'Hello – did you get my message?'

'No. Why, is there a problem?'

'No, it was just to say I was returning your call.' But, I thought, no surprises to learn that the last conversation had been a total waste of time.

'Sorry. I was away from my desk, on another line. How was Tayo last night?'

'Fine,' I said, and gave her a brief résumé of his first night and what had happened that morning.

'Thank you so much, that's very helpful. I'll need to see Tayo this week. Can I come tomorrow after school?'

'Yes, certainly. We should be back by four at the latest.'

'I'll make it four-thirty, then. I expect he'll want a drink and a snack when he first gets in.'

I was warming to Sandra Braxley already. First a quick follow up on her initial call, and now some consideration for Tayo. I'd lost count of the number of social workers who visited at four on their way home from the office, and then wondered why the child, having just come in from school, was cranky and more interested in a drink and a biscuit than in what the social worker had to say.

'We've found his mum,' Sandra continued, 'but I want to discuss with you whether we should tell Tayo or not.'

'Yes?'

'The police have been in touch. Minty is in Holloway prison.'

'Oh dear. Can I ask what for?'

'She was arrested yesterday for being drunk and disorderly, and she hit one of the arresting officers so it's assault as well, which is why she's still there. I'm hoping they'll keep her for a few more days as I need to speak to her and once she'd released we won't know where she is. She's virtually impossible to contact.'

'Will Tayo be seeing her in prison?'

'My instinct is no. She won't be in for long and it's not the nicest of places for a child to visit.'

Sensible woman, I thought. I had once had to take a child to visit a parent in prison every month for a year, and it was upsetting for everyone involved. The child had only just recovered from one emotional parting when it was time for the next.

'I agree,' I said firmly. 'And from what the deputy head said, it's not as though Tayo's used to seeing his mother every day.'

'Do you think we should tell him where she is?' she asked.

'If we don't have to, then I wouldn't. Has she been in prison before?'

'Yes, but under different names. The police have turned up other charges of drunk and disorderly, and also of soliciting.'

So Roberta had been right about his mum's work, I thought.

Sandra continued. 'She gave her name as Minty Mezer this time but her fingerprints matched up with others under different names. She's broken bail before on two other occasions. She probably won't get it this time. Minty is in court tomorrow so let's wait and see what happens then.'

'Yes.'

'We've also found out that Tayo attended a school in Kent for two terms, when he was six. I spoke to the headmistress this morning, but she was very guarded when I told her Tayo had been taken into care. It's the same head as when he was there, but she said they'd had very few dealings with Minty. Apparently they had no concerns about Tayo, though when I asked for the address he'd had then, their records showed five different addresses. I checked, and they are all B&Bs.'

No wonder the head was guarded, I thought. That in itself should have raised concerns.

'As you probably know,' Sandra continued, 'Kent is struggling with the high number of children coming in through immigration, so I guess Tayo wasn't a priority. Apart from that, we haven't turned up anything else. The rest of his life is a blank. It's interesting though, what Tayo told you about Nigeria. When we've finished I'll give the Home Office a ring, and also the Nigerian Embassy. Mum insists both she and Tayo have British passports but hasn't produced them yet.'

'You presumably know about the different addresses in recent months?' I asked. 'Tayo pointed out some on the way to school.'

'Yes, but if you can keep a note of any he mentions, it would be helpful. The taxi driver who contacted us last year gave us a list. He kept picking Minty up from different addresses late at night, and thought there was a child left alone.'

'These were the B&Bs?'

'Some were, others were bedsits. He saw Tayo looking out of the window as he drove Mum away.'

'Tayo told me he had stayed with friends.'

'Sometimes he did, but other times he was alone. The taxi driver had been picking up Minty since June last year so it's been going on for quite a while.'

'Where did he take her?' I asked, curious.

'No specific address. Just various streets around Leicester Square.'

'I see.'

'I'll see you tomorrow then. And say hello to Tayo for me. Would you tell him I'm looking forward to meeting him?'

'Will do.'

I put the phone down, feeling that things were looking up: Roberta de la Haye and now Sandra Braxley – both efficient and aware of what was going on.

Adrian came bounding down the stairs three at a time. 'Dad phoned my mobile,' he said as he got to the bottom. 'He's seeing us on Sunday.'

'OK. Are you and Paula both going?'

'She's not sure yet.'

'I'll have a word with her. I think she should. She missed last time.'

Although my husband had run off with someone half his age eight years previously, leaving me with two young children, he had, to his credit, maintained contact with Adrian and Paula. They both now had commitments of their own and friends to meet, but I still encouraged them to see their father whenever possible. Lucy, adopted by me after a long foster placement, saw her natural mother twice a year. It had been difficult when the children were young, explaining why there was this difference, and that they couldn't all go on one of the 'treat' outings together, but now they were older they obviously understood and it also gave them another bond; they often discussed their estranged parents in quite a therapeutic manner.

It wasn't long before the phone rang again. It was the secretary from the agency I fostered for.

'Morning, Cathy,' she said. 'I'm afraid Jill has been called away with a personal family crisis and will be off work for a while. She asked me to let you know.'

'Oh dear,' I said. 'Tell her not to worry. Everything's ticking along here. And send her my regards.'

'Will do. And if you need anything, Joan is covering.'

'OK. Thank you.'

Jill had been my link worker for over six years, and I'd got to know her quite well so I was well aware that her own family wasn't without its problems. One of her two sons was a heroin addict, and the family had endured repeated failed attempts at weaning him off it. I thanked my lucky stars that my children had so far steered clear of drugs, even cigarettes, but I had never become complacent. After all, drugs were such a huge problem for parents bringing up teenagers and even those children from good families, like Jill's, weren't exempt from their evil claws.

While I wished Jill luck, I wasn't too worried about not having her support and input for a while. After so many years of fostering and dealing with Social Services, I was confident that I could manage. The only thing troubling me was the niggling mystery of Tayo himself. How on earth had his mother managed to produce this bright, well-mannered, articulate child, and then neglect him so badly that he'd had to be taken into care?

Chapter Six

Heritage

Adrian had taken down the Christmas decorations and the house looked strangely bare as I set off to collect Tayo from school.

I arrived in plenty of time and waited, as arranged, just inside the school gates. The bell sounded inside at three-fifteen and the children began streaming out, but there was no sign of Tayo. I waited a little longer, then checked with one of the last parents still waiting in the playground that there was no other exit. At three-thirty I went in. A member of staff immediately approached me and asked if I needed help.

'I'm Cathy Glass, Tayo Mezer's carer. I was supposed to meet him at the gates but he hasn't shown up,' I explained.

'I'll take you to his classroom,' she said. It was empty. We checked the boys' toilets but they were empty too. The corridors were now more or less devoid of children, except for the ones taking part in a gym club in the hall; we looked in but Tayo wasn't there.

We went to Roberta de la Haye's office where she was busy at her desk. I explained that we couldn't find Tayo, and she joined in the search. I was beginning to get worried. Where on earth could he be? He was too intelligent to have misunderstood our arrangement and I couldn't believe he would have forgotten either.

'Was he dismissed with the rest of his class?' I asked.

'Let's go to the staff room and ask his class teacher,' Roberta said. 'You haven't met Mrs Gillings yet.'

In the staff room I was introduced to Sonya Gillings who confirmed Tayo had been in class until the bell rang, and he'd left with the others, saying he was meeting me in the playground. 'I'm sorry,' she said, looking worried. 'I wouldn't have let him go if I'd have known there was going to be a problem.'

'It's not your fault,' Roberta reassured her.

The four of us continued searching the empty classrooms, the dining hall, and library. As time went on, it seemed more and more likely that Tayo had left the building. By the time we'd been searching for half an hour, I was getting nervous.

'If we don't find him soon, I'll have to alert Social Services and the police,' I said.

'Where on earth can he be?' muttered Roberta de la Haye grimly, as we retraced our steps back to her office to use her phone.

I glanced into Tayo's classroom as we passed, and gasped. There he was, sitting calmly at a table with an open book before him. We hurried in.

'Tayo, where have you been?' I asked, both annoyed by the anxiety he'd caused, and also relieved. 'We've been looking for you everywhere!'

He looked up at me, his eyes widening in innocence. 'You weren't in the playground so I came back in here,' he said. His expression was similar to the one I'd seen the previous night, that of a vulnerable little boy – only whereas then it was genuine, this time it had an artful and almost practised edge to it.

'Tayo,' I said firmly, 'I've been waiting by the school gates since just after three. You certainly didn't come out.'

'I did,' he said, his voice rising in protest and still looking me straight in the eyes. 'Then when you weren't there, I did what they tell us to do and came back in here to wait.'

And so adamant and convincing was he that for a few seconds I could feel the others begin to doubt my version of events. Then Roberta de la Haye said, 'You weren't here fifteen minutes ago, Tayo. We looked.'

His gaze left mine and went to her. 'I went to the toilet first, Miss, then I came here.' And I could tell by his look that he knew there was no way we could disprove it and he wasn't going to back down. Roberta saw it too.

'That's twice in two days you've vanished, young man,' she said. 'A third time and I will become highly suspicious.'

He lowered his gaze, and I saw the briefest flicker of a smile cross his lips as though he knew he was safe and had won a victory.

I turned to his class teacher. 'Mrs Gillings, perhaps for the next few weeks, until Tayo is more settled, he could wait with you in the classroom, and I'll come in here to collect him. Then there's no possibility of my missing him, or him me.'

'Yes, that's fine with me,' she said knowingly.

I returned my gaze to Tayo whose face had now set in a disgruntled acknowledgement of his defeat. Yes, my friend, I thought. You'll have to get up earlier if you're going to play games with me. 'Thank you so much for all your help,' I said to the teachers. 'I'm very sorry you've had your time wasted. I'm sure you had better things to do.' Then I said to Tayo, 'Come on, as quick as you can, please. We're supposed to be going shopping. I don't think you want to spend another night in those Winnie the Pooh pyjamas, do you?'

He heaved himself from the desk and sauntered over to me with what I could only describe as attitude. I caught the eyes of the teachers. We all knew for sure then that Tayo had been giving us the run around, as he probably had yesterday lunchtime when the social worker and police had tried to find him.

My perfectly mannered little visitor was going to prove somewhat of a challenge after all.

Tayo was very quiet in the car as I drove into town. I didn't mention what had happened again: it had been dealt with, and I never dwelt on negatives or bore grudges.

Tayo knew as well as I did that this particular escapade wouldn't happen again, so it was perhaps his defeat that kept him sulky and silent in the back of the car. I had seen another side to Tayo but it didn't worry or surprise me. He was an intelligent child with a troubled past, and he'd used his intelligence to try and put one over on me and place me in the wrong, probably having a bit of fun in the process. He was, after all, only ten. It was perfectly normal for a child to test boundaries and discover what he could get away with.

'I think you're going to be very happy staying with us,' I said, as I entered the multistorey car park and reached out of my window for the ticket. 'The nice thing about being in care and being looked after is that you don't have adult worries and responsibilities. A lot of children I've looked after have spent so much time worrying about grown-up things – like where they were going to live, or how they were going to pay the bills – that they didn't have time to play like children should. So I think we should consider some clubs we could enrol you in. You like sport, so how about Saturday morning football?'

'Oh yes!' he cried, at last forgetting his pique. 'Could I?'

'Of course. I'll get permission from your social worker tomorrow, then you can start on Saturday.'

'Thanks, Cathy. That's great!' A big grin covered his face. I was back in favour.

I smiled at him in the rear-view mirror. 'You're a good boy, Tayo, and I know things haven't been easy for you, but that's going to change now. OK?'

He nodded.

I reversed into the parking bay and we got out. As we walked down the stairs to the shopping centre, I told Tayo about his new social worker Sandra and how nice she'd sounded on the phone, and that she was looking forward to meeting him tomorrow. He asked why he had to have a social worker and I briefly explained her role and how, like me, she was here to help him.

'Does my mum have a social worker?' he asked.

'Not exactly, but Sandra will be meeting her and making sure she's all right.'

63

'Good,' he said. 'My mum needs help more than me.'

I glanced at him sadly, thinking how true that was. Like so many other children I'd known, Tayo had probably struggled for years in an adult role, having to make decisions in a world he was ill equipped for and had little control over.

With only an hour to closing time, we rushed in and out of the shops buying from the list I had drawn up that afternoon. Fortunately, Tayo was an easy shopper, happy just to have new clothes. We bought his school shoes first, black lace-ups, and also a pair of trainers and slippers. At only ten years old, he was already a shoe size 4 which meant that undoubtedly he was going to be a big lad.

'I bet you'll be as tall as Adrian,' I said, as I paid.

He said, 'Good. My dad was big—' and then stopped abruptly.

'Have you seen your dad recently?' I asked casually, as we left the cash desk. But he shrugged and said nothing, so I dropped the subject; it would only raise his defences further if I tried to pursue it.

In the boys' department we bought two complete outfits of casual clothes, then pants, socks, two sets of pyjamas with Action Man pictures on the front (his choice), and a winter coat. I wrote a cheque for £297.35. Part of the foster carer's weekly allowance was designated for clothes, the scale rising according to the child's age. At ten years, it was about £16 a week, which in my experience just about kept them in T-shirts so I paid for the rest myself and got my recompense from the pleasure of seeing the delight on a child's face.

As we left the store, Tayo said he was thirsty so I popped next door into Marks and bought a bottle of juice and a muffin just as they were closing. Then we made our way back to the car carrying our bags of shopping.

'Have you got enough money for the car park?' Tayo asked anxiously as we entered the multistorey and began the climb up.

'Of course.' I smiled to reassure him. 'It's my job as an adult to make sure of these things. It's not for you to worry about.'

Five minutes later, as I approached the exit barrier, he said nervously, 'You need the correct change.'

I lowered my window. 'It's all right, Tayo. I always keep change for car parks here.'

He watched as I retrieved £1.50 from the small well in front of the gear stick, and fed it into the machine. Not until the barrier had lifted and I drove out was he convinced I had the means or wherewithal to get us out.

'Do you keep change for the gas and electricity meters at home?' he asked a few minutes later.

'No. I don't need to. I have a quarterly bill.'

'Do the lights go off when you don't pay it?'

'No, never. I always pay the bill. I expect that when you were with your mum in bedsits, the electricity stopped and the lights went off when she didn't have the money to put in the meter. Is that right?'

'Yes. It was frightening. I don't like the dark when I'm alone.'

'No one does, love. But I promise you, it won't happen when you live with me, and you won't be left on your own, either. You're ten, Tayo, and that's far too young to be left. Occasionally I go out in the evening, but someone will always be with you – Adrian or Lucy, or my sitter. You will never be at home alone, day or night. Do you understand?'

'Yes,' he said quietly. 'Thank you. And thank you for my clothes.'

'You're welcome.'

When we arrived home it was after six and the smell of cooking greeted us in the hall.

'Dinner's ready!' Lucy called from the kitchen.

We left our shopping in the hall and went to kitchen where Adrian and Lucy were about to dish up homemade chicken curry, rice and Naan bread.

'Oh, my angels,' I said. 'What a lovely surprise!' And it was. I sometimes grumbled that they could all do more in the way of domestic chores now they were older, but this was a timely reminder that when necessary everyone could pull together to make the house run smoothly.

'Where's Paula?' I asked.

'Upstairs, doing her homework.'

Another pleasant surprise. Perhaps I should stay away more often, I mused, because certainly it had a very positive effect.

I called Paula down for dinner and we sat around the table while Adrian and Lucy served the meal. As we ate, I told them of the successful shopping trip Tayo and I had had.

'We did very well, didn't we, Tayo?' I said, trying to draw him into the conversation.

Tayo nodded, then he looked over at Paula and said pointedly, 'Your mum spent over four hundred and fifty pounds on me today.' He waited for a response.

I was taken aback, first that Tayo had even known what the total was – he must have been watching over my shoulder as I wrote the cheques in the shops, and then added it to the cost of the school uniform, which was displayed on a board in the school's reception – and secondly by the manner in which he had said it. It was designed to provoke. But if Tayo thought it was going to elicit jealousy in Paula, he was very much mistaken.

'You're lucky, aren't you?' she said, more interested in eating than in the edge to his remark. Fortunately the family were well aware that when a child arrived with nothing, there was always a huge initial outlay.

I didn't like the way Tayo had aimed his comment at Paula. At fifteen, she was suffering from teenage lack of confidence and low self-esteem, and was therefore the most vulnerable. Tayo had spotted this and homed in on it.

'Have you got much homework, love?' I said to Paula, changing the subject.

'Loads. And it's maths!' She pulled a face.

I looked at Adrian.

'OK,' he said, knowing what my request was going to be before I asked. 'I'll have a look, but straight after dinner. I'm going out later.'

'Thanks, Adrian,' I said. It was just as well there was one person in the house whose strong point was maths, because it certainly wasn't mine. 'Have you got any homework, Tayo?'

'No.'

'But presumably you get some from time to time in Year Six?'

He shrugged. 'Not often.'

I decided to check that with his class teacher, as Roberta de la Haye had told me that Tayo was behind with his work, and in my experience Year 6 children were usually set a fair bit in preparation for going up to secondary school in September. 'Would you like me to set you some?' I teased.

'No, thanks.' He laughed openly and naturally, his face relaxing into a truly charming, genuine little boy grin.

We all cleared away, and Tayo asked if he could take his bags of new clothes up to his room.

'Certainly, love,' I said. 'If you could hang them up in the wardrobe, that would be a great help. You'll find your other set of school uniform already there. I've put your name in it.'

'Then can I watch television?' he asked.

'Yes, if you like. Or there are games and activities in that cupboard I showed you in the conservatory.'

He disappeared down the hall and I heard him make two trips up and down the stairs with the bags. Adrian went up with Paula to her room to help her with the maths, while Lucy slipped off to watch *Coronation Street*. They were let off loading the dishwasher tonight in view of their splendid work in the kitchen earlier, and homework. I cleared up, wrote my log notes, then it was nearly eight o'clock. I went up to Tayo's room, knocked on the door.

'Enter,' he called.

I went in. 'Shower time.'

He jumped off the bed immediately and switched off the television. 'I've hung up my clothes,' he said. 'Would you like to see?'

'Yes please.'

Opening the wardrobe doors, he proudly stood aside for me to view the contents. He had certainly done a good job. The trousers, creases aligned, were over the hangers, and on the shelves beside were neatly folded piles of his new sweatshirts and T-shirts.

'This is my pants drawer.' He opened the top drawer of three. 'And this is for my socks.' He opened the second. I'd never seen a ten-year-old boy set out his clothes with such neat precision: the arrangement of socks and pants could only be described as meticulous.

'Well done,' I said. 'That's fantastic. You're a very good boy. There aren't many children who'd be so neat and tidy, and so conscientious. Now, get a pair of your new pyjamas and go through for a shower.'

'Cathy?' he said, as I began towards the door.

I stopped and turned. 'Yes, dear?'

'There's just one thing I'm not certain about, well two things really, and I need to ask you.'

'Yes, love, of course. You know you can ask me anything, and I'll try my best to answer.'

He paused. 'Well, you know the trainers you bought me?'

'Yes.' I glanced down at them. They were in a neat line beside his school shoes and slippers, at the end of his bed.

'They're not Nike,' he said. 'And I noticed all the rest of your family have Nike or Adidas trainers. I wondered why I wasn't allowed them.' He was looking at me intently, watching closely for my reaction, and I knew his choice of the word *allowed* had been carefully designed to highlight the apparent injustice.

'It's not that you're not allowed them, Tayo, but designer trainers are very expensive, as I'm sure you know. Paula's were her birthday present, and Lucy and Adrian bought theirs from the money they earned at their Saturday jobs. I have a rule in this house that applies to all children. I buy the clothes and shoes everyone needs but if anyone wants a designer label, that has to be a Christmas or birthday present. Otherwise I'd be bankrupt, wouldn't I?'

He nodded, but for the second time that day his expression was one of reluctant defeat, as it had been earlier in the classroom. It was though he was trying to catch me out and gain imaginary points. Why, I'd no idea.

'You said there were two things you wanted to talk about,' I said. 'What was the other?'

'The meal tonight,' Tayo said, still watching me carefully.

'Yes?'

'I don't eat curry. I'm not Indian.'

'Neither are we, love, but we can enjoy a curry. And as I recall, you had a clean plate.'

'I was hungry, but my mum would be furious if she knew you'd given me curry. They don't eat curry in her country, it's foreign muck.'

I looked at Tayo and he stared back. Why, oh why did issues that needed dealing with always raise themselves at bedtime, when I was looking forward to the chance of sitting down with a coffee and the paper?

'All right, Tayo. I think we need to have a chat. You sit on the bed and I'll take this chair.'

Suddenly he looked frightened. 'Why? I only—'

'Don't worry. You haven't done anything wrong. I just want to talk to you. You'd don't have to say anything unless you want to, OK?'

He nodded, and sat on the edge of the bed as I pulled up the chair. It wasn't going to be a marathon session, but I needed to nip a few things in the bud before they had a chance to grow.

I leaned forward and looked him straight in the eyes. 'Tayo, you really are a nice boy, and you're very polite which counts for a lot.' He smiled. 'You're also intelligent so I know you're going to understand what I say. It won't take long – then you can have your shower.' He nodded again; I had his attention and cooperation. 'Now, Tayo, you said your mother would be furious if she knew what I'd given you to eat—'

'I—' he began.

'No, just listen for a moment, then you can have your say. First of all, I'm sure it wasn't intended as a threat, but it did sound like one. I've been fostering for a long time and trying to use your mother in this way won't work, and doesn't help anyone, OK? I know it's difficult to adjust to being in care but it's not a good idea to start playing people off against each other. Do you know what I mean by that?' He nodded. 'Good. Now, if there are certain things that you and your mother don't eat – we usually call them cultural needs – then all you have to do is tell me, and I'll make sure you're not offered them. According to the papers Brian brought here yesterday, you don't have any special dietary needs so you must tell me if you do. When your new social worker comes tomorrow we can discuss this with her. And she might have had a chance to talk to your mother as well by then.'

'If she can find her,' Tayo put in quickly.

'Yes. But the Social Services are quite successful at finding people so there's a good chance.' I wasn't about to tell him that she had been found and was in prison. I paused. The next part was going to be more difficult and required all my powers of tact and diplomacy; I could guess that this was a particularly sensitive subject for Tayo. 'Now, love, there are lots of different races and cultures on this planet and some of us have different customs and food from each other. However, we never refer to what other people eat as "foreign muck", it's derogatory. Do you understand?' He nodded, albeit a little sullenly. 'Good. We always respect differences, especially in this house. One of Lucy's parents came from Thailand and so Lucy is slightly different in appearance to Adrian, Paula and me. She was brought up in this country and likes all types of food, but she has inherited her beautiful jet-black shiny hair and some of her features from the part of her that is Thai. Just as you have inherited your lovely light brown skin and black curly hair from the part of you that is African. My guess is one of your parents or grandparents is Nigerian. Would I be right?'

He nodded and looked down. Then said vehemently, 'Yes, and I hate it.'

'I had a feeling you did, but why?'

He shrugged. 'My mum, I guess. I'm not allowed to tell anyone. She said I shouldn't look like this.'

'Why not? Does that mean your father is African, and your mother is not?'

'Yes, and she wants me to look like her.'

I hid my reaction to that. The logic of his mother beggared belief – it was obviously hurtful and damaging to start undermining a child and how they felt about themselves – as if they could do anything about their genetic inheritance anyway.

The whole area surrounding race in fostering is a minefield of political correctness (just as it is in society at large) but while

I was going to tread very carefully, I wasn't about to mince my words. It was ridiculous for Tayo to be walking around calling himself white, when part of his heritage was black. 'Tayo, there's no point in telling or not telling – it's perfectly easy to see that you have an African heritage. Why not be proud of the way you look, like Lucy is? What does your mum want you to look like?'

He shrugged again. 'Like her, I guess.'

'Which is what?'

'Malaysian.'

'I see.' I was silent for a moment, for I could see instantly what had happened. As in many children with dual heritage, one set of genes had dominated and, as a result, outwardly at least, Tayo had inherited none of his mother's Malaysian characteristics other than a lighter skin tone. All his other features, including his hair, were African. It appeared that, for some reason, his mother had rejected that part of her son and tried to persuade herself and him that they didn't exist. I guessed that Tayo now suffered from a very negative sense of himself and it could take a long time to undo. But there were lots of things I could do to start building a positive self-image for him, and there was no time like the present to make a start.

'Tayo, we live in what is called a multicultural area, do you know what that is?' He shook his head. 'It means that in this town, indeed in this road, there are people from many different backgrounds. One of my neighbours is Indian; next door to him is a couple where the lady is Japanese and her partner is Egyptian. Further down the road I am friends with a family who came from Sri Lanka, which is a small island off India and used to be called Ceylon. Adrian, Lucy and Paula have lots of friends who have parents from different countries; some of their friends were born abroad. I have also fostered children from many different races and cultures. One boy I had here was a Muslim and his mother showed me how to prepare the halaal meat. He also had a prayer mat and he had to face in a certain direction when he prayed. I always accommodate the needs of the children I foster, and one of the things I would like to show you is how to oil your lovely hair.'

He looked up, shocked and surprised, as though I had just spoken the unspeakable. 'I have to have my head shaved every four weeks. Number two all over.'

'Why is that?' I asked, although I knew the answer even if Tayo didn't – so that the curl of his African hair was cut off before it had a chance to show.

'I don't know. I didn't have it done last time,' he said, 'because Mum didn't have the money. It needs doing now.' It was only about half an inch long but I'd already noticed it was very dry and in poor condition.

'Tayo, you can still have your number two all over, if you want, but in the meantime I've got some special gel in the bathroom that will give your hair a real shine. If you like, you can use some, I'll show you what to do.' He nodded easily. 'Good. Now I've finished talking. Is there anything you'd like to say?'

He grinned, a perfectly natural smile, and looked more relaxed. 'No, not really.'

'OK, it's getting late and you've got school tomorrow. Have your shower and when you've changed I'll show you how to use the gel.'

He went off to the shower, while I put the chair back under the table and drew the curtains. Five minutes later, Tayo was back, clean and in his pyjamas and sitting expectantly in front of his bedroom mirror.

'Have you towel-dried your hair?' I asked. He gave it another rub on the towel. 'This is the gel,' I said, showing him the pot I'd retrieved from the bathroom. It was called simply *Afro*, and had a picture of a black male on the front who was very macho and seemed to appeal to Tayo. Tayo drew back his shoulders and straightened himself to his full height. 'You only need a small amount,' I said, unscrewing the lid, and dipping in the tip of my forefinger. I set down the jar, rubbed the blob of sheen between my palms and began lightly massaging it into his scalp and hair. 'All right?' I asked. He grinned in the mirror as he watched me, and I had the feeling he was enjoying the scalp massage as much as anything. Gradually his dry and wiry hair began to glisten with a deep black lustre.

'Wow!' he said. 'That's magic. What's in it?'

'I'll have a look in a second.' Once his hair and scalp were shining healthily, I wiped my hands, then inspected the pot. 'Avocado is one of the main ingredients. I'll leave it on your shelf tonight in case you get peckish.'

He looked at me for a second, uncertain, then doubled up, clutching his sides, and laughing heartedly. He really did have a sense of humour when he wanted to, and it was nice that I could share a joke with him – so many of the children I had looked after had learning difficulties and would have taken my remark literally.

'It wasn't that funny,' I said with a grin, but he was still chuckling as I pulled back the duvet and he climbed into bed. I tucked him in, then said goodnight and began towards the door.

'Cathy,' he called. 'Haven't you forgotten something?'

I turned. He was pointing to his forehead and grinning. I returned to the bed, and smiling, leaned over and planted a big kiss on his forehead. 'Night, love. Sleep tight.'

'And don't let the bed bugs bite,' we chorused together, which was to become our nightly refrain for all the months he was with me.

Chapter Seven

Manipulation

'Look at my hair!' Tayo said, still excited the following morning, leaping into his chair for breakfast. 'Cool, or what!'

'It's good,' Paula said, glancing up.

'Wait till my mum sees it.'

For a moment I wasn't sure if this was another play-off comment, revealing that this time he intended to annoy his mother, but then I decided it was no more than an innocent remark. He obviously wanted to share his excitement with his mum.

'What would you like for breakfast?' I asked Tayo from the kitchen. The breakfast room was a small area off the kitchen, and I encouraged the children I fostered to stay there rather than actually come into the kitchen while I was cooking and risk an accident with the hot pots, oven and gas rings.

'Can I have eggs and bacon, please?' Tayo asked.

'There isn't really time for a cooked breakfast on a school morning,' I said. 'I'll do you a big fry up at the weekend. Can you have cereal and toast on a school day?'

'Sure,' he called. 'Weetabix, please. Can I have the milk warm?'

'Yes, of course.'

A moment later I set Weetabix with hot milk in front of him, along with the sugar jar. 'Good service in this hotel,' I joked. He laughed while Paula glanced up, unimpressed by my stab at early morning humour. 'How many pieces of toast would sir like?' I asked. 'And what would sir like on them?'

He was grinning from ear to ear. 'Two please, and can I have the marmalade I had yesterday?'

'Of course you can.'

We arrived at school as planned at eight forty-five, and I left Tayo in the playground with a strict reminder that he mustn't leave it once I'd gone. He was too old to have me wait with him until the bell rang; none of the other children his age had parents or carers waiting with them.

'Have a good day and see you later,' I called.

He smiled and with his characteristic hop, which showed he was feeling good, ran off to join a couple of friends. He looked very smart in full school uniform and obviously felt pleased with himself.

I returned home, cleared up the kitchen, put the Hoover round downstairs and checked that the biscuit barrel was full. Sandra was coming later and, in my experience, social workers liked clean carpets and biscuits. I took some pork chops out of the freezer to defrost for the evening meal, then got back in my car and drove into town. I wanted to have a look in the January sales for some new shoes – for me, this time. With a shoe size of only 3, I can sometimes pick up real bargains in the sales, although occasionally I do end up in the children's department, desperately looking for something to fit my little feet. It was my lucky day; I found a pair of shoes, then boots reduced to less than a third of the original price.

Coming out of the shop I bumped into an old friend, Pat, whom I hadn't seen in ages and she suggested we had some lunch together.

Why not? I thought. All the children were accounted for and I had my mobile on if I was wanted.

Pat and I spent a really pleasant couple of hours in a rather nice bistro, catching up, then reminiscing about our student days, laughing ridiculously as only old friends can. It was like a breath of fresh air and quite therapeutic, and as we said goodbye we made a promise to do it again in another couple of months.

I arrived at Meadway to pick up Tayo at ten past three. I parked in the same spot as the day before – I'm a creature of habit – and waited in the playground until the bell went. Then I slipped into the school building past the children hurrying out all around me, and found my way to Tayo's classroom. He was waiting by Mrs Gillings' desk as the others headed out.

'Hello,' a boy said. I looked down. It was the friend of Tayo's I'd met yesterday.

I smiled. 'Hello, Sam.'

Tayo saw me and gave a little wave. Mrs Gillings looked up and motioned for me to go in.

'Have you had a good day?' I asked Tayo, then looked at Sonya Gillings for confirmation.

'Pretty good,' she said. 'He's got a piece of science to finish for homework. I've given him some new exercise books as the other ones went missing last term. Does he have a school bag?'

I looked at Tayo. 'Do you?'

'No. It got left behind where we stayed after Christmas.'

'And can you get it back?'

He shook his head.

'I'll get him a new one tomorrow,' I said to Sonya Gillings. 'I won't have time tonight, his social worker is coming. Is there anything else he needs for school?'

'Only the basic pen, pencil and ruler. And a set of crayons would be useful, though not essential.'

'I'll see to it,' I said, then smiled at Tayo. 'More new things. It's like Christmas all over again.'

He grinned back.

'Well, let's get going. See you tomorrow, Mrs Gillings,' I said, ready to leave.

'Actually, Mrs Glass, do you think I could have a word?' she said.

I experienced that sinking feeling which only those words, spoken by a teacher can elicit. 'Can I have a word?' usually means that the child has been up to something that needs to be discussed out of earshot – and then dealt with by me later.

'Yes, of course,' I said with an inward sigh.

'Tayo, go and read a book in the library please, until we've finished,' Sonya Gillings said.

Tayo didn't look guilty as he hopped off, although most children also know that 'Can I have a word?' spells trouble for them.

As soon as Tayo was out of earshot, Sonya Gillings said, 'I thought I should tell you that Tayo came to me this morning looking very sorry for himself and said you wouldn't let him have breakfast.'

'What?' I exclaimed, horrified.

'No, it's OK. I know Tayo, and I'm sure that if he didn't have breakfast this morning, it must have been for a good reason. That's what I told him.'

I opened and closed my mouth like a goldfish as the words fought to get out. 'He most certainly did have breakfast, a good one!' I said indignantly. 'Why on earth would he tell such a silly lie?' Then I remembered what had happened that morning. 'It's true that he asked me for bacon and eggs, and I said that there wasn't enough time for that on a school day. He seemed perfectly happy, and had cereal and toast instead. I warmed his milk specially!' I couldn't help feeling hurt and angry. 'I don't believe it! How dare he say such a thing!'

Sonya Gillings placed a reassuring hand on my arm. 'Don't worry. Tayo's done this sort of thing before. I'll explain to the Head.'

'He told the Head as well?' I asked, astounded.

She nodded. 'He told anyone who would listen.'

'Little devil,' I said, my usual sanguinity now completely gone. 'He must realize that's a very damaging accusation to make about his carer. He seems to like being with us – why is he so hell bent on trying to get me into trouble?'

'I think it might be more about making people feel sorry for him,' Sonya Gillings suggested.

I looked at her. 'Why do you say that?'

'Well, for the last term Tayo has had a lot of sympathy from staff and classmates. His unkempt appearance, his mother turning up drunk in the playground, all the different addresses … it was obvious things were bad at home. Often he looked pretty depressed. I supposed he enjoyed all the attention and didn't want to lose it.'

'I give him lots of attention,' I said lamely.

'I'm sure you do,' Sonya Gillings said. 'Look, Tayo is a bright child and we all like him here, but there is another side to him. As his class teacher, I've seen it more than the other staff and I know how good he is at manipulating situations for his own ends – surprisingly good for a boy of his age. I suppose he's had to learn how to look out for himself and manipulate his mother as well, though I've no sympathy with her. But he has tried it on with me a few times so I know what he's like. At the end of last term he went to Mrs Saunders, our welfare lady, looking very sorry for himself and complaining that the class had made mince pies the day before when he'd been absent, and that they'd eaten them all. He said he was very disappointed because he'd never tasted a mince pie as his mother never had the money to buy them. Well, dear Mrs Saunders, who can only see good in anyone, went out at lunchtime and with her own money bought half a dozen mince pies which she gave to him, and he ate them after his school dinner. What Tayo hadn't told her was that I'd saved two mince pies for him, which he knew I was going to give him at home time. When I found out, I was very cross with him for taking advantage of Mrs Saunders' good nature, even though he had misled her rather than lied to her. It's not much of an offence, I know, but I do have to have my wits about me when dealing with Tayo, and I think you will too.'

'That's good to know – thank you,' I said thoughtfully, but while I was grateful for her support, I still felt very deflated by what Tayo had said. After all, in this case he'd not just misled, he'd told a deliberate lie. 'But do you realize that if he'd told his social worker I hadn't let him have breakfast, I'd have been investigated? The Social Services always take complaints from a child seriously and act on them. The complaint would be on my record even if it was found to be untrue.'

She looked at me sympathetically. 'I admire you foster carers, you do a very difficult job. Anyway, I thought I'd better let you know, but please don't worry about the breakfast issue. I'll make everyone aware of the truth of the matter first thing tomorrow.'

'Thank you.' I raised a smile. 'I'll have to talk to him about it. I'm sure he has no idea how serious the repercussions could be. And would you let me know if Tayo doesn't hand in homework? I always make sure homework is done before television time, so if it doesn't appear, there's no excuse.'

'Yes, of course. Thank you,' Sonya said. 'We'll have to work quite closely.'

I nodded 'I'd better get going now. We can't be late for his social worker. Thank you for dealing with this.'

I found Tayo by himself in the library, coat on, poring over a book as though butter wouldn't melt in his mouth. 'Ready?' I asked.

He stood immediately, returned the book to its correct place on the shelf, and trotted up to me. 'Can we get my school bag now?' he asked, excitedly.

'No. Tomorrow. We've got your social worker coming.' I turned and led the way out of the building, with Tayo bobbing along beside me. I was quiet, still subdued from the revelation, and wondering what I was going to say to him. For his part, he chatted away, unperturbed, telling me about his day. Yesterday it would have pleased me, but today I saw it as a tactic to distract me from what he must know I had to say.

I let him continue talking until we got in the car. 'Is your seat belt on?' I asked, as I always do before starting the engine.

'Yes, Cathy. Shall I do my homework before or after my social worker visits?'

'After. There won't be time before.' As I pulled away, I said, 'Tayo, why did you tell Mrs Gillings I hadn't given you breakfast?'

'I didn't!' he exclaimed at once.

I met his eyes in the rear-view mirror.

'Is that what she told you?' he continued. 'If she did, it was a lie. I never said that. What I said was I couldn't have a cooked breakfast because there wasn't time on a school day. Which was right, wasn't it, Cathy?' He looked the picture of wronged innocence. Then he added, 'Mrs Gillings doesn't like me.'

I shouldn't have expected more, but somehow I was disappointed. I'd had foster children lie to me before, of course, but somehow when it came from someone of Tayo's obvious intelligence and pleasant disposition, it felt much worse. I stared at the car in front and kept my voice even. 'Tayo, that's not true.

Mrs Gillings does like you, and so do I. I believe what she told me, and I'm not going to make an issue of it, but it will make my relationship with you very difficult if you lie like this.'

'I didn't—!' he began again.

I was trying to treat Tayo as his maturity required and it was hard to have him go on pretending to me. I raised my voice slightly. 'Tayo, I believe Mrs Gillings, and you need to think very carefully before you do anything like that again.' I glanced in the rear-view mirror and saw his face set into a sulk. I really did feel quite hurt that he was doing this when I had gone to so much trouble to welcome him at home. Fortunately Mrs Gillings was no fool, but someone else – such as too-trusting Mrs Saunders – might have been taken in.

'That's enough,' I said sternly. 'Don't make it worse with more lies. Let's leave it.'

When we arrived home, Tayo was still sulking. There was a quarter of an hour before his social worker was due to arrive and as we went in I called a general hello, then asked Tayo if he wanted a drink and a biscuit. He shrugged.

'I'll leave one at your place at the table,' I said, 'then you can have it if you want to.'

He shrugged again, then went up to his room where I heard the television go on. He was still there fifteen minutes later when the doorbell rang. I answered the door and shook hands with Sandra Braxley. She was young, tall, with a pleasant and efficient manner, and black, which was exactly what Tayo needed. My spirits lifted. I showed her through to the lounge and offered her a drink.

'Just a glass of water please, Cathy,' she said. 'And thank you so much for having Tayo.'

'Not at all,' I said. 'I'm glad I was able to help.' I fetched her the glass of water and some biscuits.

'So, how is young Tayo settling in?' she asked, taking an A4 writing pad and a pen from her briefcase.

I told her the positives first – his courtesy, relaxed attitude and good behaviour – then the negatives, including his poor self-image in respect of his race and the lies he had told about breakfast, which still smarted. She made notes as I spoke and when I'd finished she said, 'Yes. I can see we're going to have to keep an eye on him. Where is he now?'

'Upstairs, in his room.'

'OK, leave him there for now. It won't do him any harm, and it will give me a chance to bring you up to date.'

I really did like her professional and direct approach. The standard of care the child receives depends largely on the competence of the social worker assigned to the case, and in nearly twenty-three years of fostering I'd seen everything from excellent to what could only be described as downright negligent. I was delighted that Sandra was obviously going to fall into the first category – experienced foster carers can tell almost immediately. It was a stroke of luck for Tayo that he would probably never know of.

'I've spoken to Tayo's mother, Minty,' Sandra said. 'She's out on bail.'

'Is she?' I asked, surprised. 'Didn't she jump bail before?'

'Yes, I was surprised too, and I thought she'd disappear again, but she phoned me on her mobile. I've set up a placement meeting for tomorrow.'

'OK.' I reached for my diary. 'What time?'

'I've made it at four, so could you bring Tayo straight from school? I think he's mature enough to attend the meeting. It will be at the offices but I'm not sure which room yet. Could you wait in reception and I'll come and find you?'

I nodded again and wrote the details in my diary. 'Who's been invited?'

'You and Tayo will be there, Minty, myself, my manager – Danuta Boyd – and there'll be someone external chairing. I don't know who yet.'

I nodded again. This was what I would have expected for a placement meeting.

'Minty is angry, obviously,' Sandra continued. 'And she wasn't particularly coherent on the phone. But she says she wants to be involved, and is going to fight to get Tayo back. She'll be assessed, and I'll be working with her to see if rehabilitation is a possibility.'

'Has she got a permanent address now?' I asked, mindful of Tayo's many moves.

'She says so, but when I asked, she couldn't remember what it was, so I'm a little dubious about that. Minty's memory has been extremely faulty in the past. I've told her to bring the address with her tomorrow as I need it for the paperwork as much as anything. I've also told her she needs to get a solicitor, and she's eligible for legal aid, but I'm not sure whether she's taken this on board. I'll explain the position again to her tomorrow. I've asked her to come in an hour before the placement meeting so I can speak to her. Now, contact,' she said. 'Contact' is the term used to describe the meetings that are arranged for parents and children to spend time together. 'I'm going to set up supervised face-to-face contact for Tuesday and Friday, starting this Friday at the Headline Family Centre in Pallin Road. Do you know it?'

'Yes, I've had children there before.'

'Good. Will you be able to take Tayo there straight from school? I was thinking of starting contact at four. Will that give you enough time?'

'Yes, it should do. As long as Tayo comes out of school on time.'

She nodded, and ticked a note on her pad. 'I'm going to make both contact sessions an hour and half each to begin with. Shall I arrange for an escort to bring Tayo home, to save you having to wait around?'

'Yes, please. That would be a great help.' I liked the way Sandra thought things through and was considerate of my time.

She made a note. 'One of the staff at Headline will be supervising. I don't know who yet, but they're all good. And his mum's asked for telephone contact as well. I wasn't sure about that. She's often pretty incoherent when she's under the influence. But I've agreed to two calls a week. Are you happy to monitor them?'

'That's no problem at all.' I was used to helping my foster children have phone contact. 'Do you want the phone on loud speaker, or should I just be present in the room?'

'Let's try being present to begin with and see how it goes. Minty won't be given your contact details so will you phone her mobile at a set time, and block your number? We can discuss the days and times of the calls at the placement meeting tomorrow.'

'Yes.' I paused and then asked, 'Is Minty OK about meeting me?'

I was well aware that parents of children who have just been taken into care are often very resentful of the person who has taken over their parenting and this can manifest itself as anger.

'She didn't say she had a problem with it, so we'll assume not.' Sandra threw me a stoical smile. 'As with all of this, Cathy, we'll just have to see how it goes.' She glanced down at her notepad again. 'I thought you'd be interested to know that I've spoken to the Home Office, and the Nigerian Embassy. There are no records of Tayo or his mother entering this country or residing there. The person I spoke to at the Nigerian Embassy was very helpful and said they'd double check. The problem is that they're looking under the names we have, plus the two I had from the police for Minty, which could be different to the ones on their passports.'

'I see. Didn't Minty say they both had British passports?'

'Yes – Minty is adamant that they do but the Home Office has no record of it, so it's very doubtful. Apart from the school in Kent Tayo attended four years ago, and Minty's three arrests, there's absolutely no trace of either of them. Mum says they have been here for over five years but became vague when I asked her where they'd been living – and I could tell it was a surprise when I told her that I knew about the stay in Kent and Tayo going to school there. I only hope that she'll be more forthcoming as time goes on, if I can win her trust.'

I shook my head. 'Isn't it incredible, when you think about the amount of paperwork that follows us around here, that they've managed to live with none of it and survive for five years?'

Sandra nodded in agreement. 'Absolutely. And, of course, because they are not officially here they have not been able to access help, and Tayo has fallen through the net. I'm not sure he's ever seen a doctor or a dentist.'

'What – never?' I was astonished. There might be a lot wrong with this country but everyone should have access to the basics of life: food, shelter and medicine.

'I don't think so. I told Minty we were still trying to find his medical records, and she became vague again, saying he was never ill. Which reminds me, Cathy – can you register him at your GP?'

'Yes, though it will be interesting if he's not on any system. They like a National Health number or a last GP address – or rather, the computer does.'

'If there's a problem, tell them to phone me, and I'll explain. Also Tayo will need a Looked-After-Children medical in due course. I'll send the forms directly to the doctor.'

'Fine.' It was a pleasure to deal with someone so businesslike and efficient. 'I'll register him tomorrow. Shall I book appointments at the opticians and dentist as well?'

'Yes, please.'

I was used to this as it was standard procedure for any child who first came into care. So many of the children had never seen a dentist or optician, or were well overdue for their next check-up.

'I've spoken to the family where Tayo stayed at Christmas,' Sandra said. 'Mr and Mrs Graham. They were helpful, and relieved that Tayo had been taken into care. They have two children and live in a block of flats in Eastbury Road. Minty and Tayo lived in the flat next door for a week at the beginning of December. The Grahams' children are a similar age to Tayo and they began playing with him. Apparently Tayo was often seen hanging around on the landing while Mum was inside the flat, possibly entertaining. They weren't sure and didn't like to pry. They felt sorry for Tayo and asked him into their flat and often gave him a meal. Minty hardly spoke to them, and Tayo and Minty suddenly disappeared after a week. Mrs Graham thought it was because of non-payment of rent because the landlord knocked on their door and asked if they knew where they'd gone. The couple didn't see either of them again until two days before Christmas when Minty turned up with Tayo and asked if he could stay. They assumed it would be for a day or so, but she left him there for the whole of the Christmas week. Mrs Graham rushed around before the shops closed on Christmas Eve and bought him presents. Minty did phone each day and spoke to Tayo on a mobile she'd given him. He always went out of the room to answer it so he couldn't be overheard.'

My heart went out to Tayo as I again thought of him being dumped with strangers over Christmas, albeit kind and generous ones. 'Wasn't he upset?' I asked.

'Apparently not, he just took it in his stride as though it was perfectly normal. To be honest, I think the Grahams were more upset for him. Minty turned up and took Tayo away three days after Christmas with no thanks for all they'd done, and no forwarding address. Mrs Graham was so worried she phoned Social Services. Added to the concerns we already had from his school, the taxi driver and another family who had looked after him, we applied for the ICO.'

'What about the presents they gave him for Christmas?' I asked. 'Where are they?'

'He took them with him.'

'He hasn't got them now. He arrived with nothing.'

'So I understand. When we call him down we'll try and find out what happened to the presents, and I'll see if I can get them back. The couple has an old jumper of his which I can collect if he wants me to.'

'What a sad state of affairs,' I said.

'Yes. And this only accounts for the last few months. What's been happening in the other four or five years?' Sandra sighed then checked her notes. 'I think that brings you up to date, Cathy. Is there anything else you can think of before we bring Tayo down?'

'I don't think so. Shall I call him now?

'Yes please.'

I went to call Tayo from the bottom of the stairs and found him perched halfway down, with his arms looped around his legs, chin on knees and ears flapping.

'Hello,' I said brightly. 'You should have come and joined in rather than sitting there ear-wigging.' I winked and he grinned mischievously then hopped down beside me. Now I had him sussed I knew we were going to get along just fine.

'Tayo, this is Sandra,' I said as we entered the lounge. I saw Tayo do a double take and I wondered if it was because she was black. He quickly recovered and went immediately to shake her hand.

'Sit down,' Sandra said, patting the space next to her on the sofa.

'I'm hungry, Cathy,' he said with those forlorn-looking eyes, glancing at Sandra for sympathy.

'Well, I did offer you a drink and biscuit when we first came in,' I said, as much for Sandra's benefit as a reminder to Tayo.

'I won't keep you long,' Sandra said. 'Then you can have your dinner.'

He sat next to her, upright and hands in lap.

Sandra turned towards him. 'I've spoken to your mother on the phone, Tayo, and she sends her love. I've told her you're being well looked after, and she's looking forward to seeing you tomorrow. I've arranged what's called a placement meeting. Cathy knows all about it and she'll explain later. After tomorrow you'll be seeing your mum every Tuesday and Friday and phoning her twice a week. Do you still have the mobile she gave you to use over Christmas?'

Tayo shook his head and looked slightly taken aback, probably because Sandra knew about the mobile. 'No,' he said. 'Mum borrowed it and had to give it back.' Good, I thought. Mobiles were always a problem as far as I was concerned because it was almost impossible to supervise and monitor their use.

'You remember that you stayed with Mr and Mrs Graham over Christmas?' Sandra continued. 'Well, they have a jumper of yours. Do you want it? I'll collect it if you do.'

There was another flicker of surprise on Tayo's face at the mention of this other detail Sandra was aware of. He shook his head. 'No, thank you. Cathy's bought me loads of new stuff.'

'Lucky boy,' Sandra said. 'And what about all those Christmas presents Mr and Mrs Graham gave you? You and Mum took them with you. If you know where they are, I can try and get them for you. I understand there was an MP3 player among other things. I'm sure you'd like that.'

'The landlady took them,' Tayo said flatly.

'Which landlady?' Sandra asked. 'Do you know the address?'

'No. It was a long way from here. We went there on a train after Christmas, but only for a few days. The landlady wouldn't let us in one day and kept all my things. Mum said she was a thief.'

I could guess why the landlady had kept them, but I left the explanation to Sandra.

'Tayo, I don't think the landlady was a thief. She's probably kept back any valuables because your mother didn't pay the rent. She's allowed to do that. If you do know the address I could speak with her and explain the things were yours and she might let me have them.'

I watched Tayo as he considered this, and I could tell he was weighing up the attraction of having his Christmas presents returned, with having to be disloyal to his mother. 'I can't remember,' he said, at last, loyalty winning.

'That's fine,' Sandra said lightly.

Then he added despondently, 'You wouldn't get them back anyway. I never do. That's why I haven't got any things.'

Sandra didn't look up as she wrote, not wanting Tayo to appreciate the significance of what he'd said, and might yet say. Instead, she said, 'It must be very sad for you to keep losing your things in all the moves.'

He nodded. 'I had a DVD player, and a bike.'

'When was that?' Sandra asked nonchalantly.

'Last year.'

'And another landlady kept them?'

'No. It was a man. Mum said she'd have him locked up because he was a thief and a liar.'

I doubt that, I thought. Minty was obviously very good at persuading Tayo that their troubles were everybody else's fault. I said nothing.

'Do you know the address where this happened, or any of the other addresses where you stayed?' Sandra asked, still low key and not wanting Tayo to put up his guard.

'No,' he said adamantly, obviously feeling he had said enough, and changed the subject. 'What will happen to me?' he asked, his large brown eyes turning towards Sandra.

Sandra looked at him kindly and smiled. 'You'll be staying here with Cathy until everything is sorted out, and I know you'll be well looked after. I expect Cathy has already explained some of the process to you, about the judge and all the reports that are written.'

Tayo nodded and listened carefully as Sandra went over a few points, and explained her role and that of the Guardian Ad Litum. 'Both the Guardian and I will spend a lot of time talking to you and listening to you before we report back to the judge.'

'And when all that's done? What then?' Tayo asked.

'At the final court hearing the judge will decide where you'll be best looked after until you are an adult.'

'And how long will it take?'

Sandra glanced at me. 'It's difficult to say but about nine months to a year. And I know you'll have a great time here while everything is being taken care of.' Tayo nodded. 'Is there anything else you want to ask me now, Tayo?'

He shook his head, then added, 'Can I have my dinner now?'

Sandra and I smiled. 'Very soon,' I said.

'One last thing, Tayo,' Sandra said. 'You told Cathy you wanted to go and live in Nigeria. Do you have relatives there? If so, I'll try and contact them and see if it's a possibility.'

I watched Tayo's face quickly shut down and I knew for certain he wasn't going to risk further disloyalty to his mum or possibly her wrath, by saying any more at present. 'Not sure,' he said and gave one of his characteristic shrugs.

'OK,' Sandra said, closing her notepad. 'I know you're hungry, so how about if Cathy makes you something to eat, while we have a game of cards before I go. I'll show you some tricks.' She took a pack of cards from her briefcase.

This was my cue to leave the two of them together. Social workers are supposed to spend time alone with the child on each visit in case there are issues the child wants to raise concerning their care or carer. It's not the most pleasant of feelings to know that your best endeavours are up for scrutiny and you're not present to be able to answer criticism, particularly with a child like Tayo who was capable of manipulating the truth to his own ends – but, like all foster carers, I just had to accept it.

In the kitchen, I put the chops under the grill and the vegetables to boil. Quarter of an hour later I heard the lounge door open and went out into the hall.

'Is it all right if I watch *The Simpsons* until dinner's ready?' Tayo called, already halfway up the stairs.

'Yes – but it'll only be about ten minutes.'

'He seems happy enough,' Sandra said, as I walked her to the door.

'I think so. Was everything all right?'

'Absolutely. He's very relaxed here. I'll see you tomorrow then for the placement meeting. I'm not expecting trouble from Mum but I'll have security briefed anyway.'

'OK.'

'And by the way,' she added, 'I didn't eat all the biscuits, Tayo did. He said he was going to blame it on me.'

'Hmmm – you know, I wouldn't put it past him.'

Chapter Eight

A Mixed Day

I was feeling very pleased with myself as I collected Tayo from school and then drove to the Social Services offices on the Thursday afternoon. I'd been up in the loft and stowed away the two boxes of Christmas decorations, enrolled Tayo in a Saturday morning football club, made after-school appointments for him at the opticians and dentist for the following week, and bought the pen, pencil and crayons he needed for school, together with an Adidas school bag (the Adidas being a treat).

I'd also successfully registered him with the doctor, which, as I'd predicted, had been no mean feat. I'd had to go to the surgery and spend half an hour trying to write enough details on the form to persuade the computer that Tayo existed and should be registered. Fortunately the practice manager knew me, and that I was a foster carer, and she had been very help-ful in the past when a child's details had been scant. They'd never been as scant as this, though. The biggest problem was with Tayo's immunization history. I had to cross out all the Yes/No boxes and write 'don't know' beside each one: tetanus, whooping cough, diphtheria, MMR, Hepatitis A, Meningitis C and so on. Because 'don't know' was not a recognized option, the computer rejected it time after time until the practice manager found a way of circumnavigating the registration programme, and managed to sneak Tayo in the back door when the computer wasn't looking.

After all that, I felt doubly pleased with myself as I pulled into the Social Services car park at exactly three-fifty and actually found a parking space.

'Perfect timing,' I said to my captive audience seated in the rear. Tayo grinned, but he was subdued and evidently a little anxious at seeing his mother again. He wasn't the only one. I was nervous myself. The first meeting with the parents of the child I was caring for was always delicate. It was a difficult situation for the parents too, as they had to meet the person who had usurped their role, as a result of their failings as a parent. It could often be very upsetting and humiliating for them, and I tended to keep a low profile, although I always answered any questions the parents had, reassured them, and listened to their advice on how to care for their child – sometimes having to bite my tongue as I did so.

Tayo hopped out of the car and stood beside me. I hadn't told him about the Saturday football club or his Adidas school bag yet; I thought I'd leave it until we got home, when he might need cheering up after separating from his mother again. We went across to the Social Services building and signed ourselves in at reception. I was told by the receptionist that Sandra was in a meeting but would be with us shortly, so we found a couple of seats and waited for her. I thought that

Sandra was probably with Minty, remembering that she had told me she'd asked Minty to go in early.

The whole of the reception area had undergone extensive refurbishment in the last year and as a result was far more light and airy. Tayo and I sat side by side, casually watching people come and go. I noticed that security had been tightened recently. I had a photo ID that I'd pinned to my jacket, but I still had to sign in at every visit. Those who didn't have ID passes were issued with a 'Visitor' label, which they handed in at reception when they left. After a while Tayo, who had noticed these labels being issued, asked what they were for. I explained.

'Why haven't I got a visitor badge?' he said, as though it was a coveted prize and he was disappointed not to be given one.

'I think it's because children are exempt.'

'What age do you have to be before you can have one?'

'Good question,' I said. 'I don't know. Sixteen?'

'How do they know when someone has turned sixteen?'

I laughed. 'That's another good question, Tayo. Maybe you should think about being a lawyer when you grow up. We can ask the receptionist when she's not busy, if you like. But Sandra should be down soon to take us to the meeting. Have you ever been here before?'

'No, but Mum has. She came here and asked them for some money when we were broke but they wouldn't give her any. She said the woman was a bitch.'

Charming! I thought, but of course kept quiet. I knew better than to say anything to a child that might sound like a criticism of a parent, particularly in the early days. Nevertheless, the picture I was forming of Minty wasn't a very impressive one.

We continued to wait in reception, then suddenly a woman's voice could be heard screaming obscenities through the double doors some way over to our right. 'Get your fucking hands off me! You fucking bastard! I'll sue you for physical assault!'

'Oh dear, someone's a bit upset,' I said to Tayo, who had obviously heard, as had everyone else in reception. 'Best put your hands over your ears.'

The shouting grew closer, and everyone in reception looked at the double doors.

'Fuck off! You black bastard! I'll have you arrested,' the woman raged.

Then the doors suddenly burst open and a very large security guard of African descent appeared, and spread himself across the door space, blocking the exit of the woman on the other side. We could see her. She was screaming like a banshee, her long black hair swinging maniacally around her face and shoulders. Tayo and I watched bemused, transfixed, and not a little frightened by the ferocity of the woman's attack on the guard. Everyone else in reception, including the receptionist, was watching too. The woman was only about five feet tall but quite heavily built, and she pummelled her fists into the guard's chest, hissing and spitting through gritted teeth. But the guard was much bigger and stronger and well versed in restraint technique, and he soon regained control. With a couple of deft movements he had her facing away from him with her arms behind her back, and they disappeared. The doors swung shut on the corridor.

The group of visitors at reception were raising their eyebrows and exchanging whispered comments. I looked at Tayo. 'Are you OK?' I asked, aware such a display of anger can be quite unsettling for a child, as indeed it was for me.

He nodded. 'She always gets angry when she's had a few drinks.'

I stared at him, and my stomach tightened. 'Tayo,' I said quietly, 'was that your mother?'

He nodded and looked down. I put a reassuring hand on his arm and we sat in silence. Good God! I thought, but there was nothing I could say.

Ten minutes later Sandra came through the same double doors, looking decidedly shaken. She came straight over.

'Are you all right?' she asked Tayo. He nodded. 'Mum has calmed down now,' she assured him. 'She's had a drink of water and she'll be fine. We're going to go ahead with the meeting, do you still want to come in?' He nodded again. 'Good boy, let's go through.'

Sandra led the way through the double doors. Just as well she hadn't asked me if I still wanted to go to the meeting, because I didn't. My initial nerves at meeting Minty had now developed into full-blown anxiety. But there was no time to ponder this because Sandra led us almost immediately into the meeting room.

In the centre of the room four tables had been pushed together, and there were a dozen or so chairs dotted about. Minty was at the far end, sipping water from a plastic cup. Behind her was the security guard, shoulders back, feet apart, and arms folded. Tayo rushed straight over to his mother, gave her a quick hug, then sat in the chair beside her. On the other side of Minty was Danuta Boyd, Sandra's team manger, whom I'd met previously on another case. And next to her was a woman I hadn't seen before, who must be the chairperson Sandra had mentioned.

Still apprehensive, I took a chair on the opposite side of the table, a good way from Minty and close to the door. Sandra hovered for a moment watching Minty who was now talking to Tayo in a whisper, then said to the security guard, 'Could you wait outside please?'

He moved round the tables and went out, closing the door, and positioning himself just the other side. Minty hadn't acknowledged me in any way yet but, given how angry she had been, I wasn't unduly surprised. I took the opportunity to look at her. She had clearly been a strikingly attractive woman once, but her lifestyle had taken its toll on her looks. She could only be in her early thirties, I guessed, but she looked much older. She was bloated, her face coarse and already quite lined, probably from alcohol and drug abuse, and her long black hair was dull and greasy. Tayo had said she was Malaysian and I could see some of the characteristics, but there was also something else, possibly Caucasian. But what hit me more than anything was that Tayo looked absolutely nothing like her. He had undoubtedly inherited all his appearance from his father

'All right, Mrs Mezer?' the chairperson said. Minty ignored her or didn't hear her, and carried on whispering to Tayo. She tried again, looking at Minty and saying more loudly, 'Shall we begin?'

Eventually Tayo pointed at the chairperson, and said, 'Mum, look—'

Minty reluctantly stopped talking but didn't look up. She crossed her arms, sat back, and stared at the table like a petulant child. Tayo looked up and met our gaze. The chairperson smiled at him.

'We'll start by introducing ourselves,' she said. 'I'm Anne King and I shall be chairing this meeting.'

Sandra had sat between Anne and myself, and at the opposite end of the table to Minty and Tayo. 'Sandra Braxley,' she said. 'I'm Tayo's social worker.'

'Cathy Glass,' I said. 'Tayo's foster carer.'

Tayo was next and having watched us introduce ourselves, knew exactly what to say, so in a nice, loud and confident voice he said, 'Tayo Mezer. I'm the foster child.'

Sandra and I smiled.

It was Minty's turn but she remained silent. 'Mum,' he said, giving her a little nudge with his elbow. 'Say your name.' He looked embarrassed that she couldn't even get this right.

She's doing this on purpose, I thought. She's certainly not drunk – the meeting wouldn't have been held if she hadn't been considered compos mentis. Judging from the way her face was set, I could see that her silence was a refusal to acknowledge or participate in the proceedings.

'It's Mrs Mezer,' Tayo said at last.

'And I'm Danuta Boyd,' Sandra's team manager said. 'My role is one of observer. I won't be contributing much.' I guessed that she was probably present as part of Sandra's evaluation for her annual review.

Anne King, the chairperson, was also minute taking, which tended to happen in small meetings. She wrote down who was present, then looked up. 'Thank you for coming,' she said. 'As you know, this is the placement meeting for Tayo Mezer, and Tayo, I'm really pleased you felt you could come. This meeting is about you, and it's important we hear from you. Well done.'

Tayo grinned, and Minty at last glanced up and looked at her son, before returning her gaze to the table.

'This is only a short meeting,' Anne continued, 'and it's really about making sure Tayo has settled in and answering any questions he or his mother, or his carer, may have.'

I liked Anne's approach. Placement meetings did tend to vary slightly but if the child was present and the chairperson was relaxed and friendly, they were low key and aimed at helping the child understand everything and feel able to join in.

'Now, Tayo,' she said. 'This is all about you. I'll start by briefly outlining why you were brought into care, and what's going to happen.'

Tayo looked at her, nodding and taking in every word, a contrast to his mother, who still sat with her arms fiercely crossed and face set, concentrating on the table. For want of a better term, she was sulking.

Anne went on. 'As I'm sure you know, Tayo, we've been very worried about you recently. You've had a lot of moves and may not have had all the care that a boy of ten needs. We also don't know much about where or how you've been living. So Cathy will be looking after you until we've had a chance to learn more.' She briefly explained the court process, which Sandra and I had already outlined to Tayo. He kept eye contact, nodded and took it all in, apparently very relaxed.

'So,' Anne said, 'how do you like living at Cathy's? I know you haven't been there long, but what are your first impressions?'

'It's good,' he said. 'I've got my own room, and there's lots to eat.' He looked over at me and I smiled back.

'That's terrific,' Anne said. 'And is there anything you need that we should tell Cathy about?'

I waited for his response, wondering if he'd say a cooked breakfast every morning, but that had run its course. He shook his head.

'Your social worker, Sandra, will be visiting you, and you'll have a chance to speak to her then.'

'She already has,' Tayo said.

Anne glanced at Sandra, clearly impressed.

'Yesterday,' Sandra said. 'Tayo appeared to be fine and I've given him my telephone number.'

It was standard practice for a child of Tayo's age to be able to contact his social worker personally. He had to feel that there was someone outside the fostering family he could turn to if he needed them. Although Tayo was living with me for now, it was actually the local authority that had legal parental responsibility for him.

'Good,' Anne said, then turned to me. 'Cathy, could you tell us how Tayo has settled in so far?'

'He's doing very well,' I said. 'We've been shopping and he now has a full school uniform, and casual clothes. He's eating well, sleeping well and integrating into family life. I've made myself known at his school, registered him at our doctors and arranged a check-up. I've also made appointments at the optician and dentist for next week.'

'Thank you,' Anne said. 'So there are no concerns at present?'

'No,' I said, and smiled again at Tayo. There was no point mentioning the minor problems we'd had, especially with Tayo present. Like Sandra, I purposefully kept my report brief and positive. Minty wasn't looking up but I was sure she was listening – she must be, it was her son I was talking about after all.

'Anything else?' Anne asked.

'No. He's a good boy and I'm sure he'll do very well,' I said.

'And is Tayo able to stay with you until the final court hearing?'

'Yes.'

'Good. Thank you, Cathy.' Anne finished writing and looked down the table to Minty. 'Mrs Mezer, is there anything you'd like to say or comment on? I appreciate you are not happy with Tayo being taken into care, but is there anything that we should know that might be useful in looking after him?'

Minty said her first words without looking up. 'She needs to give him a deodorant, he smells. I took him to the doctors. There's something wrong with his blood, that's why he smells.'

Tayo visibly squirmed.

Is that all you can think of to say? I thought disbelievingly, and felt sorry for Tayo that his mother could only think of something like that to say about him. 'I can assure you that Tayo has a shower every day, and I've bought him a deodorant,' I said, unsure of what else to say. Tayo didn't smell, I knew that, and he was a very clean and neat little boy. I'd seen some personal hygiene disasters in my time, and Tayo was certainly not one of them. Anne came to my aid.

'If a doctor has raised concerns about Tayo's blood, can you give me the details please?' she asked Minty. 'The doctor's name? It's important we know of any medical conditions Tayo has.'

Tayo glanced sideways at his mother and I thought I detected a slight look of triumph, as though he felt she'd been caught out.

Minty shrugged. 'I don't know. I can't remember. It was some time ago. Tayo, you tell them.'

We looked at Tayo, who quite clearly hadn't the least idea what she was talking about. He shrugged in an exact imitation of his mother. So that's where he got that little habit.

'All right,' Anne said. 'If you do happen to recall anything, Mrs Mezer, please let Sandra know.' She turned to Sandra. 'Are there any medical concerns?'

'Not as far as we know, but we haven't been able to trace Tayo's medical records.'

Anne wrote. 'Have you been to a doctor recently?' she asked Tayo.

'No. I went to the hospital once.'

Sandra and I exchanged a glance. This was the first we'd heard of it.

'And what was that for?' Anne asked.

'I fell off my bike and banged my head.'

'Who took you?' Anne asked kindly.

'The friends I was staying with.'

'Do you know which hospital? Or where the friends lived?'

'Birmingham, I think.'

Anne glanced at Sandra who shook her head. It was clearly the first time Sandra had heard Birmingham mentioned and she made a note – it might be another clue to unravelling Tayo's past.

'OK. That's fine.' Anne said, smiling at Tayo. 'Mrs Mezer, would you like to add anything?'

'No,' Minty replied rudely, head down and chin tucked into chest.

Anne looked at Sandra. 'Have you set contact?'

'Yes, for Tuesday and Friday at the Headline Family Centre. Mrs Mezer has asked for telephone contact as well. I suggest Wednesday and Saturday at six p.m. I'll give Cathy Mrs Mezer's mobile number.' Sandra had said she was going to discuss the arrangements for telephone contact at this meeting, but I guessed she felt there was little point with Minty being so hostile. I made a mental note of the days and time.

Anne finished writing and looked along the table. 'Well, if there's nothing further, that's it then. Well done.' She smiled at Tayo who grinned back.

Danuta Boyd immediately stood. 'I must go; I'm in another meeting. Thank you.'

Anne, Sandra and I got to our feet. Normally I would have made myself available to talk to the parents with the social worker present but given Minty's refusal to acknowledge me, that was going to be a little difficult to say the least. I hovered, looked at Sandra, then at Minty, then at Tayo.

'Mrs Mezer,' Sandra said, in a soft, neutral voice that couldn't have upset anyone, 'would it be helpful for you to have a chat with Cathy? It might allay some of your worries.'

Minty looked up. 'Fuck off the lot of you,' she snarled.

So I took it that she didn't.

We left pretty quickly after that. Without being asked, Tayo stood up, gave his mother a quick peck on the cheek, and said, 'See you tomorrow, Mum.' He bounded to my side. Sandra motioned for us to go, and I went out with Tayo, passing the security guard still posted in the corridor.

Chapter Nine

Hunger

We were crossing reception on our way to the exit.

'Will my dinner be ready when we get home?' Tayo asked.

'No, but don't worry, you won't be hungry, I'll do something quick.' I glanced at my watch. 'It's only a quarter to five.'

'I don't like being hungry,' he murmured.

'No,' I agreed absently. He appeared to have recovered from his encounter with his mother far more quickly than I had. Perhaps I'm a coward or of a delicate disposition but I loathe verbal and physical aggression of any kind, and am easily upset by it. Tayo was probably used to his mother's volatile nature, which was why he seemed so unruffled, but it chilled me to think that I was going to have to work with Minty for the best part of a year. There would be more meetings at Social Services, and I would see her twice a week when I took Tayo to contact, and I'd have to speak to her when I made the two telephone calls each week. It was a long time since I'd met with such open hostility at the first meeting, and yet again I wondered how Tayo had remained comparatively normal. With his good manners and amiable disposition, he was so unlike his mother in every way that I could well have believed there'd been some mix up and that he was really someone else's child.

'Have you got a snack in the car?' Tayo asked as we got in.

'No. But you had lunch, didn't you? You'll be all right until we get home.' I started the engine and pulled out of the car park, which was quickly emptying at nearly five o'clock. Two minutes later Tayo asked again about a snack. 'Look, love,' I said, trying to concentrate on turning right in the rush hour traffic, 'I haven't got anything, and we'll be home in twenty minutes. Could you sit quietly please? I'm driving.'

'I don't like being hungry,' he moaned five minutes later.

'Tayo, did you eat your lunch?'

'Yes.'

'What was it?'

'Chicken dippers, chips and beans.'

'And for pudding?'

'Jam tart and custard.'

'Well, you'll be fine until we get home then.' I would probably have stopped and bought something if he'd said he hadn't eaten his lunch, but I was sure that he couldn't be that hungry after a full meal at one o'clock, so I thought he was simply agitating, perhaps because he was unsettled after seeing his mother.

He was quiet for another few minutes, then said, 'I might be.'

I glanced in the mirror. 'Might be what, love?'

'Hungry.'

I felt a niggle of irritation and was about to tell him, more firmly this time, to sit quietly and think about something else, when something occurred to me. 'Tayo, were you often hungry when you were with your mother?'

He met my eyes in the mirror. 'Yes. And I didn't like it. It makes me panic.'

I could have kicked myself. Come on Cathy, I silently admonished myself, you should have picked that up. How many years have you been looking after children who've had no idea where their next meal is coming from?

Those of us who have never really experienced true hunger cannot fully appreciate the all-consuming fear of not knowing when or how you're going to get your next meal. It's not unknown in children who come into care for food to be linked to anxiety and vice versa. Tayo had just seen his mother and it had triggered those same feelings of worry and deprivation. He must have been reminded of all the times he'd gone to bed or woken up with that gnawing hunger in the pit of his stomach, and panicked.

'Tayo,' I said firmly, 'listen to me. You will never ever be hungry with me, I promise you that. You will always have regular meals. I've looked after other children who hadn't been fed and I know the feeling you're talking about. Those children felt the same thing.'

'Did they?' he said. 'I thought I was the only one.'

'No, love, unfortunately not. It's more common than people think.'

He thought about this for a while then said, 'It was OK when I stayed with friends, they gave me food, but when we were in rented, Mum didn't have the money. Once I went for two days without anything, then the woman at the hotel gave me a cooked breakfast.'

Cooked breakfast, I thought. That probably explained his feelings of being deprived when I hadn't made him a cooked breakfast and why he'd wanted to mention it to his teacher. Then I thought over what he'd just said. 'Did you and your mum live in a hotel?' I wondered how Minty would have had the money to stay in a hotel.

'Yes, you know – they're called guesthouses sometimes, or B&Bs. If we stayed in them, we had to leave early before the owner got up. Otherwise they asked Mum to pay and there was a scene because she never had the money. It was easier in rented because the owner didn't live there – but then there was no one to ask for food.'

'That sounds dreadful, Tayo, no wonder you panicked.'

I imagined the two of them, Minty and her schoolboy son, surviving on their wits and living like criminals on the run, a few days here, a few days there, then taking off before the owner demanded payment.

'Those two days when you didn't have any food – can you remember what Mum was doing?'

'Working,' he said, his face anxious with the recollection. 'I don't know where. She went off in a taxi. Sometimes she left food for me like bread rolls, which I ate in the room, but she didn't that time so in the end I had to come out of the room and ask someone for food. I didn't know when she was coming back.'

'So you were alone in the room for two days, without food?'

'Yes,' he said.

I felt anger and pity rush up inside me as I imagined him in some low-grade hotel room, desperate for something to eat but too frightened to open the door until eventually he was forced to, probably because he didn't know if his mother was ever coming back. I kept my voice neutral. 'Do you know where that hotel was?'

'South London, I think. It wasn't a nice area. There were lots of fights outside.'

'And do you know how long you were living like that? In guesthouses and rented, and moving all the time?'

He sighed. 'It's always been like that. We once stayed in a house for three months but there was no electricity, and the windows were boarded up. There were lots of people and I didn't like them. They drank a lot and stuck needles in their arms. There wasn't any water to wash with so we had to go to the toilets in the shops.'

'It's called a squat,' I said, horrified that Minty had taken her son to live among drunks and addicts in filthy, unsafe conditions. 'That's no way to live and you shouldn't have been taken there. It's bad enough for an adult, let alone a child. And it was wrong of your mother to leave you alone for two days. It will never happen again.'

I needed to make it quite clear to Tayo that he wouldn't have to suffer like that anymore. Perhaps he felt that now I had seen his mother and her temper, he could open the door a little bit more and let me peep in, and that he could start to tell me the truth. And again I wondered how Tayo had survived all this and remained apparently unscathed.

When we arrived home, I told Tayo about the Saturday morning football, and gave him the Adidas bag with the pen, pencil and crayon set in it. He was very pleased on all counts, though not as pleased as when he sat down at the table and tucked into the fish and chips I'd picked up on the way home. I don't rely on takeaways very often but every now and then it was a treat to have grease-laden but delicious fish and chips with oodles of tomato ketchup and white bread.

I finished first, and left the children at the table while I set about some housework. There was laundry to be folded and put into the airing cupboard upstairs. I was just tucking some sheets away when Paula suddenly ran up the stairs and dashed past me, in floods of tears.

'Whatever is the matter?' I called. I left the sheets and followed her.

She rushed into her bedroom and flung herself on her bed, sobbing uncontrollably. 'I hate him! I hate him! I wish I was dead.'

'Who? What's the matter?'

'I hate him!' she cried again.

'Who?'

'Tayo!'

'What's happened?' I asked, sitting on the bed. Paula was face down, hands over her head, beside herself with grief. I took her hand and tried to ease it away so I could see her face, but she snatched it back. 'Paula, love, what's the matter. Is it something he's said?'

But she didn't answer, her body wracked by sobs. Then Lucy appeared in the doorway.

'What's happened?' I asked her. 'Do you know why Paula is so upset?'

She nodded. 'Tayo's been very rude to both of us.'

I was astonished. I couldn't imagine softly spoken Tayo being so rude he could reduce Paula to this state. 'But what's he said?'

Lucy came further into the room and looked anxiously at her sister. 'Don't worry, Paulie,' she said gently. 'He's a prat.'

I stared at her aghast. What on earth had Tayo done to make Paula so upset, and for Lucy to turn against him so quickly? I'd only left the table five minutes ago. I stroked Paula's hair, and looked at Lucy. 'What did Tayo say?'

She perched on the bed next to her sister. 'He called me yellow because of my skin colour, and told Paula she was ugly because of her spots.'

I was shocked. 'What? Just now?'

Lucy nodded. 'I'm not bothered by what he said to me. He's just a silly little boy. But it was horrible to say that to Paula.'

'Where is he now?'

'Still at the table, eating.'

I was furious. When I'd spoken to Tayo about respecting differences in appearance, I'd used Lucy as a positive example, and he'd turned it round and used it against her. But worse was his remark to Paula. She'd had acne for two years, and I knew how she suffered because of it. Despite all the prescriptions from the doctor, and every potion available from the chemist or the Internet, it had stubbornly refused to go. All I had been able to do was to reassure her that it would pass in time, and constantly tell her how nice she looked, and what an attractive girl she was, but her confidence had suffered nevertheless. Tayo couldn't have picked a crueller weapon to attack her with – but presumably he'd known that, which was why he'd chosen it. Lucy was that bit older, proud of her ethnicity, and with a boyfriend in tow, so she could bat Tayo's remark away without being hurt by it.

'Look after Paula, please, love,' I said to Lucy. 'I'm going down to see Tayo now.'

I stormed down the stairs and into the breakfast room where Tayo was busy finishing off the chips the others had left.

'Tayo!' I demanded. 'What do you think you're doing?' He looked up, wide-eyed and innocent. 'Whatever made you say those hurtful things to Lucy and Paula? And please don't try to deny it!'

He shrugged, and popped another chip in his mouth with the kind of defiant and aggressive manner I'd seen in Minty that afternoon.

'Well? I'm waiting. I'd like an explanation, please. You've been very cruel and hurtful to two people who've done nothing to you, and that hurts me too. Why?'

He finished chewing and swallowed, then just looked at me, still defiant.

'Right, Tayo. You've lost your television for tonight. I will not have cruel remarks said by anyone or to anyone in this house. I am ashamed and appalled and very disappointed. It must never happen again, do you understand? When you're ready you can apologize but for now go to your room.'

Tayo began to look unsure of himself. I'm usually quietly spoken and when I do raise my voice it is all the more effective.

'Go to your room now,' I said sternly. 'And do not put the television on.'

He got up and walked past me with his gaze lowered, then went upstairs. I hated dishing out punishments, preferring talk

118

and cooperation, but Tayo's offence was serious and I had to be strict with him. Hurtful personal remarks that bordered on racism could not be tolerated, and he had to know that.

I returned to Paula, although there was little I could say to make her feel better. I cuddled her until she stopped crying and I left her talking with Lucy. In many respects a cruel and spiteful remark, designed to hit where it really hurts most, is far worse than any kick or thump. Not for the first time, I blamed myself for bringing a child into the house who had caused upset, and wondered what damage it was doing to my family.

An hour later, I knocked on Tayo's bedroom door and told him it was time to have his shower. He was quiet and subdued as he gathered together his pyjamas and went off to the bathroom. I was in my room when he knocked on the door, clean and ready for bed, and asked if he could speak to the girls. We went to Paula's room, where she and Lucy were still together. I knocked on the door and put my head round it.

'Tayo's got something to say to you,' I said, hoping they'd find it within themselves to listen.

Paula shook her head. 'I don't want to speak to him tonight.'

I couldn't blame her, and it wouldn't do Tayo any harm to know how badly she was hurt.

'I'll see him,' Lucy said, and went to the bedroom door.

I watched Tayo as he spoke. 'I'm sorry I said those hurtful things to you and Paula,' he said. 'I didn't mean them. I won't do it again.' He did look genuinely sorry.

'All right,' Lucy said, still a touch cool with him. 'I'll tell Paula. We accept your apology.'

Tayo went to his room and I followed. I drew the curtains and saw him into bed. 'See you in the morning,' I said. 'And remember, I don't ever want a repetition of that.'

'No,' he said. 'I won't. I know it hurts. I don't like it when my mum calls me smelly.'

'Exactly,' I agreed. Perhaps it was his mother's remark about him smelling that had sparked the verbal attack on Lucy and Paula: a small example of the abused going on to abuse.

'Cathy?' he said, with big eyes looking up from under the duvet. 'I don't suppose you want to give me a kiss tonight, do you?'

'Tayo,' I said, 'another thing you will learn about living in this family is that we forgive each other. Of course I'll give you a kiss.'

I leaned forward and planted the kiss on his forehead. 'Goodnight,' I said. 'See you in the morning.' I wasn't quite ready for the intimacy of our bed bugs routine, even if I had forgiven him.

It had been a long day. Tomorrow would be a fresh start.

Chapter Ten

Responsibility

Paula avoided sitting at the breakfast table with Tayo the following morning. She came down early while Tayo was getting dressed and ate her toast before he arrived. Their paths didn't cross until Paula, Tayo and I were in the hall, unhooking our coats from the stand, and getting ready to leave.

'Morning, Paula,' Tayo said normally.

I watched as Paula glanced in Tayo's direction and nodded. This was her way of saying she was almost ready to forgive him, and I hoped by the evening we would be back to normal. I hated having an atmosphere in the house.

Tayo and I arrived at school at eight forty-five, and he got out of the car and then spent some time adjusting his new school bag on his back. I could tell he was very pleased with it.

'Have a good day,' I said. 'And make sure you are ready when the bell goes. You've got contact.'

'OK. Oh, Cathy, I forgot to tell you yesterday, I had home-work, but I left it at school.'

I raised my eyebrows. 'All right, it's a bit late now. Apologize to Mrs Gillings, and tell her you'll do it over the weekend. And make sure you remember to bring it tonight.'

He nodded, then looked past me and down the road. I turned and saw his friend Sam coming. I waited until Sam drew close then watched as the two of them walked the short distance to the school.

Whether Tayo had genuinely forgotten his homework or not, I wasn't sure. His thoughts had no doubt been occupied by the placement meeting yesterday and seeing his mum, so it was quite possible, and I would give him the benefit of the doubt. Whether he would apologize to Mrs Gillings and offer to do the missed homework over the weekend was less certain, so I would check.

When I arrived home, having made a detour via the supermarket to stock up on essentials, I telephoned the school and asked if it was possible to speak to Sonya Gillings, or leave a message for her. It was morning break and I was put through to the staff room.

'I'm sorry to disturb you,' I said when she came on the line. 'I wanted to make sure Tayo had told you about his homework.'

'Yes, he did. He came to me first thing and apologized. He said he hadn't done it because there was nowhere quiet for him to study.'

As this sank in, I gasped and was about to say very vigorously what I thought of that, but Sonya Gillings was still talking.

'I said that was rubbish, and then told him off for lying again. He didn't deny it.'

'Thank you,' I said, relieved. 'Thank you very much indeed. Let me assure you there most certainly is a quiet place for Tayo to do his homework. My house is geared up for studying. One of my children is at college and the other is in her GCSE year. They have a lot of homework, regularly.'

'Don't worry, I didn't believe him for a second. I'll make sure he has his English homework from last night in his bag, and also the science for the weekend.'

'Thank you,' I said again. 'I've told Tayo to be ready at three-fifteen as he has contact.'

'I'll make sure he is. They've found his mother then?'

'Yes. He'll be seeing her every Tuesday and Friday.'

'OK, Cathy, I'll make a note of that. And by the way, he loves his school bag.'

'Good. I just hope he'll remember to put his homework in it.' She laughed.

It was reassuring to know that Sonya Gillings wasn't easily taken in, but worrying at how easily the lies slipped from Tayo's lips. It was hard to understand why he did it when it gained him so little and cost him in the way of our trust – he was clearly intelligent, so he must understand that. Still, I reminded myself, this little boy had been living on his wits with his mother for five years; lying and deceit had probably been an everyday occurrence, part of their survival. I would need to remain understanding but at the same time teach Tayo that this kind of behaviour was destructive and wrong.

I made a mug of coffee, brought my log up to date, then tackled the housework. I had been out of the house for most of the day before, and had some catching up to do. Adrian and Lucy, still on holiday, got up at eleven, made themselves toasted cheese sandwiches and then decided to go bowling together. Lucy was returning to college the following week, and said she'd better make the most of her last days of freedom. Adrian still had another ten days to go before returning to university, and I had already made a note in my diary to take him, a week on Sunday. I'd decided that Tayo would be coming with us. Although I could leave him with the girls in charge, I would be away from the house for the best part of five hours and, in view of recent events, I didn't feel comfortable with that. There would be room in the car as most of Adrian's things had stayed in his room on campus over the Christmas holiday, and it would do Tayo good to see inside a university and what awaited him if he worked hard and did well at school.

I collected Tayo from school without any trouble. He was ready and waiting for me besides Mrs Gillings' desk, his coat zipped up and his school bag on his back.

'Tayo's had a good day, and he's got all his homework and knows what to do,' said Mrs Gillings.

'Excellent,' I replied. 'Thank you very much. Come on then, Tayo, we've got to be quick.' He hopped to my side, and we both said goodbye to Mrs Gillings, and I wished her a good weekend.

In the car, Tayo was quiet. We were going straight to the Headline Family Centre, and the meeting with his mother was no doubt playing on his mind. I knew the feeling – I was not looking forward to this second encounter with Minty. Although it would only be brief – I would take Tayo into the centre and hand him over to Minty and the supervisor – I still had to meet her. Sometimes I chatted for a few minutes with the parents if they wanted to, but this wasn't likely with Minty. And whereas the Social Services offices had security guards, the family centre did not.

'Have you been to the centre before?' Tayo asked from the back seat.

'Oh, yes, lots of times,' I said. 'Though not for a couple of years.'

'Will there be other children there?'

'Yes, but in separate rooms, seeing their parents. It's very nice, they make it like home.' I'd already explained quite a bit about the family centre, and how he and his mother would be in a large room decorated like a lounge, with curtains, and carpet, lots of toys and books, a sofa and a television. I also explained that there would be a supervisor present who would sit to one side and make notes. There would be tea, coffee, fruit juice, biscuits and a microwave oven in the shared kitchen where parents could heat up or make simple dishes so the family could eat together. Everything was done to make the atmosphere as homely as possible – but the families were supervised all the time.

It could not be easy trying to be normal where one's words and actions were being noted down and interpreted by a third person, who would then write a report detailing the time spent with the child, the success of the relationship and parenting skills. It must be unsettling and intimidating, although supervisors tried their hardest to keep their role as neutral and unobtrusive as possible. But there are good reasons why the supervision is necessary; apart from assessing the parent, the supervisor also made sure the child was protected from any further abuse.

When we arrived, I saw Tayo glancing anxiously at the tall security controlled gate as I parked the car. 'Don't worry,' I said. 'It's to stop the little children from running into the road.'

'Can I show Mum my new bag and crayons?' he said, as we got out of the car. He'd taken off his bag when he'd got into the car and it was still on the rear seat.

I hesitated. Was it diplomatic to have this purchase thrust in Minty's face when she hadn't even been able to buy the essentials, let alone an Adidas bag? But then again she'd already seen him at the placement meeting in his new school uniform, coat and shoes, so I thought it wouldn't matter. 'Yes, OK.'

He reached in and pulled out the bag, then swung it over one shoulder. We went up to the centre together, up a short path, flanked by lawn, and to the main door which was security locked. A large terracotta tub containing a colourful display of winter pansies was to one side.

'They look nice, don't they?' I said as I pressed the buzzer. 'Cathy Glass with Tayo Mezer for contact,' I said into the intercom, and the doors clicked open. We went into reception and a man in his mid-thirties came out to meet us.

'Hi,' he said, in a very friendly manner. 'I'm James, the manager. I won't be supervising, my colleague Aisha will be. She's with Mum now.'

'I'm Cathy Glass, Tayo's carer,' I said. The staff had changed since I'd last brought a child here two years before.

'Yes, Sandra informed us,' he said. 'And she's booked an escort to take Tayo home.'

Good efficient Sandra, she'd organized and informed. While she was only doing her job, it was surprising how often I'd turned up with a child for an appointment to find they didn't even know my name.

'Minty would like to speak to you,' James said.

'Would she?' I was surprised in view of her attitude at the placement meeting, and not a little concerned. Tayo looked worried too.

'You know about yesterday?' I asked James.

He nodded. 'She's a lot calmer now, but I'll see you through and stay. It'll only take a minute. Are you all right with that?'

'Yes.' I could hardly refuse to speak to a parent when she'd asked; it wouldn't be professional. Tayo and I followed James out of reception, past the kitchen, where another worker was washing up mugs, and down a short corridor. It was a single-storey building with the six contact rooms leading off the main corridor. There was a well-equipped play area outside at the back for the children to use in good weather. The décor hadn't changed much since my last visit, only the staff were new. The doors to the six contact rooms were painted different colours, and the rooms took their names from that colour.

'You're in Yellow Room today,' James said to Tayo, and stopped outside the door. It was closed. James peered through the glass panel, knocked and entered.

'Tayo and his carer are here,' he said, standing in the door-way.

I heard a voice say, 'Fine,' but it wasn't Minty's. I hoped James's assurance that Minty was calmer remained true.

'Come in,' James said, leading the way. Tayo and I followed. Minty and another woman were on the sofa. 'This is Aisha, who's supervising,' James said. He turned to me. 'You've already met Mrs Mezer, haven't you, Cathy?'

'Yes, hello again. Nice to meet you, Aisha.' I smiled over at them.

Minty did look calmer and her face had lost the taut anger of yesterday, but her long tangled hair was even more dishevelled and didn't appear to have been brushed in the interim. She was wearing a pair of pink hipster jogging bottoms with a white, cotton, almost see-through top. She wasn't wearing a bra and her nipples were obvious through the material. The top was short and there was a gap between this and the jogging pants. Her belly button was pierced and a large red stone hung from a gold ring. As she bent forward, it disappeared into the roll of fat round her middle. Not only was it unsightly but completely inappropriate attire for contact. I felt sorry for Minty. This wasn't going to create a good impression – she looked liked she'd come straight from a hard night on the town.

Minty had delved into a large shopping bag by her foot and was now pulling out a box of After Eight Mints. She came towards me with the box held out. 'Here. Take these,' she said, thrusting them at me. 'You're looking after my son. You caught me on a bad day yesterday.' She spoke English with only a trace of an accent.

I smiled and took them. 'Thank you, but there was no need to do that.' James hovered to my right while Tayo went over to the sofa and sat in the place his mother had vacated. 'Thank you,' I said again.

'It's nothing. But those buggers yesterday wound me up a treat. It's not your fault. Just make sure you look after my son. I'll have you if you don't.' She didn't say it in a threatening way, but the matter-of-fact coldness unsettled me even more than if she had shouted and blustered.

I saw James make a little movement to my right. I wasn't sure what to say to Minty. On the one hand she'd given me chocolates, and apologized (sort of) but on the other she had issued a veiled threat. 'I'll look after Tayo very well,' I said. 'And thanks again for the chocolates.' It crossed my mind to ask her if there was anything she'd like to discuss about her son's care, but I didn't think I'd push my luck. I had the feeling that her calmer mood could quickly evaporate, and be replaced by something I didn't particularly want to witness.

I took a step towards the door. 'See you later,' I called to Tayo. But he'd found the remote to the television and was engrossed in trying to make it work. 'Nice to see you again,' I said to Minty. She shrugged and, turning her back, walked away. James held the door open for me, then followed me out, closing it behind him.

'I can't accept these chocolates,' I said to James as we walked back to reception. 'Would you like to share them amongst the staff?'

'Sure. We'd be glad to take them off your hands,' he said, and I gave him the chocolates. He knew the reason why. It was all right to accept a small gift from a parent at the end of a placement, when the case had been to court and the decision on the child's future made, but anything before that could be interpreted as collusion, possibly leading to a misplaced loyalty. And while a small box of chocolates was hardly going to influence anything I wrote about what Tayo told me about his mother, it was better to be safe than sorry and accept nothing.

'Enjoy,' I said to James as he saw me out.

'Will do.'

I returned to the car and breathed a sigh of relief. Given the state Minty had been in yesterday, this encounter hadn't been too bad. The fact that she'd recognized her behaviour the day before was not acceptable and had made the gesture of an apology with the gift, was promising. Although I would be on my guard in my dealings with her, I hoped that if Minty's attitude continued to improve, I would be able to work with her in the future.

Chapter Eleven

Loss of Trust

With an hour and a half before Tayo was due to return home, I decide to stop off at the shopping mall quickly. Lucy and Paula had been agitating for some time about buying a Skype phone. They'd downloaded some software that would enable them to talk to their friends through the Internet for nothing. All they needed now was the phone for the computer, which they said would only cost £20. I had been won over. My telephone bill was on the up, and their continuous use of the line meant that the phone was blocked for most of the evening, almost all week. And although all three of them had pay-as-you-go mobiles, I appreciated the high cost of calls made it impossible for them to use their mobiles for extensive chats, apart from any health concerns I had about the level of radiation. So I'd agreed.

I parked in the multistorey and nipped down in the lift. Thirty minutes later I was back in the car with the Skype phone in a bag. I drove to the exit barrier and fed in the ticket. The minimum charge of £1.00 popped up on the machine and I reached down to take the coin from the plastic well in front of the gear stick. It was empty. I switched on the interior light and peered in, running my fingers round the inside. Damn! I thought. I quickly opened my handbag on the passenger seat and pulled out my purse. A car drew up behind me. I rummaged through the change section of my purse and found a collection of coins that the machine would accept. With relief, I fed them in, as the car behind tooted. The barrier lifted. I snapped my purse shut, threw it on the passenger seat, and drove out.

I knew for certain that there had been change in the car. I always kept change there, not only for car parks but also for the parking meters that now littered all the roads in the town. My stock of coins never ran dry as I replenished it regularly from the loose change in my purse. I'd used it that morning when I'd stopped off briefly at the supermarket. I remembered I'd taken out two 20p coins, and there had been plenty left, probably over £4.

My stomach contracted, and an unpleasant taste settled in my mouth. Tayo knew about the money. I'd pointed it out to him after our shopping trip the day before yesterday, when he'd been concerned that I wouldn't have the cash for the car park. Had he taken it? I didn't want to consider the possibility but, if I was honest, there was no other explanation. No one had been in the car besides Tayo and myself, and if any other member of the family had urgently needed change they would have asked me, and I would have given them the car keys and told them to help themselves. But they hadn't, not for months. My heart sank. Tayo had stolen it.

We'd had children living with us before who'd stolen, and it had created a very unpleasant and unnatural situation in the house. It was not the value of what had gone missing that caused the upset and anxiety, but the strain of living on a daily basis knowing we did not dare leave anything of value unattended. Adrian, Lucy and Paula often left their mobiles and money downstairs, and I'd dump my handbag in the hall. My digital camera was always on hand in the lounge to take a picture that might go into the album. But that had to change when someone dishonest was about. Even worse, I had to ask any visitors to make sure their valuables were kept with them, particularly handbags, which were easy pickings for a thief.

How I hated the word thief with all its connotations – but if Tayo had taken the money, then that was what he was. I dearly hoped I was wrong, however slim that chance might be.

When I got home, Adrian, Lucy and Paula were in their respective bedrooms. I went to each of them in turn and asked if they'd borrowed the loose change from the car. 'No,' they each said, and Lucy added, 'I would have told you.'

'I know, love.'

I went downstairs, and quickly checked each room for items that could have disappeared, but I couldn't see anything missing. Then I went back upstairs with a heavy heart. This bit was more difficult, and I loathed what I had to say. I went again to each of the children and explained that the money had gone from the car, and they should keep their valuables with them, or in their bedrooms, for now. They knew what I meant, and I also knew they felt as uncomfortable as I did with the situation.

Adrian said, 'Sure, Mum. We had someone nicking stuff at uni last term.'

'Did you?' I asked, surprised. 'You didn't say.'

'No. I wasn't targeted. We're supposed to keep our doors locked at all times, but you don't. It's just impossible to remember all the time, especially if you're just popping along the corridor to the kitchen or to a mate's room. Someone had been going into the rooms and taking their stuff – money, cards, MP3 players, DVDs, anything that was easy. They caught her. But it took a while. It wasn't anyone on my floor.'

'What happened to her?' I asked, dismayed at the thought of a university student stealing from her fellow students.

'They threw her out. They're pretty strict with that sort of thing.'

'Poor girl – what a stupid way to destroy your future.'

Downstairs, I made dinner, unable to think of anything else but what I'd have to say later. This wasn't like university – throwing Tayo out certainly wasn't an option. I would have to deal with it, and try and alter his behaviour, but in the meantime we would all unfortunately have to be vigilant.

What really upset me was the loss of the trust we'd had between us. It was such an important part of everyday life and without it, things would be a great deal less comfortable. Once lost, it took time to regain.

The clock on the cooker ticked along. At five-thirty I knew Tayo would be saying goodbye to his mother and leaving the centre. The traffic would be heavy so I wasn't expecting him until six, then we would all sit down to eat. After that I would speak to him, though exactly what I would say I couldn't think.

Sure enough, just before six o'clock, the doorbell went. Wiping my hands on the kitchen towel, I went down the hall and opened the door. Tayo was on the doorstep, accompanied, to my surprise, by Aisha. 'Hello. I didn't know you were bringing Tayo home,' I said.

'The escort didn't turn up.'

I raised my eyes. 'Thank you.' I knew James could have phoned me at the last minute and asked me to collect Tayo. 'That's very kind of you.'

'No problem.'

Tayo came in and Aisha hovered. I could tell she wanted to talk to me.

'Tayo,' I said, 'hang up your coat, then you can have a wash. Dinner's nearly ready.'

Aisha waited while Tayo hooked his coat onto the stand and then disappeared upstairs. 'I thought I should let you know,' she said. 'Minty was pretty upset and angry for most of the contact. I'm not sure how it affected Tayo.'

'I see. She seemed quite calm at the start. Was it anything in particular?'

'No, not really. To be honest, I couldn't always understand what she was saying. I don't think Tayo did either. She was very confused and went from one subject to another. I couldn't smell alcohol but I wondered if she'd been drinking. Tayo spent most of the time watching the television. Oh yes, but she did say she was going to bring in food next week, so to tell you there was no need for you to give him anything.'

'OK, that's fine. But he hasn't eaten tonight?'

'Apart from the plate of biscuits, no.'

I smiled. 'Well, thanks for letting me know and for bringing him home.'

'You're welcome. It might become a regular thing. I pass the end of your road on my way home and Tayo's is the last contact session. James has asked me. It would give Tayo continuity and save the cost of the escort. I could give you feedback at the same time.'

'That would be great.'

'See you Tuesday.' She smiled. 'Have a good weekend.'

'And you.'

What a lovely, helpful person, I thought as I closed the door.

We sat down to eat shortly before six-thirty. Tayo didn't seem upset by his mother's behaviour at contact, but ate with his usual hearty appetite. Adrian, Lucy and Paula, to their credit, chatted normally with Tayo, although they knew I would have to speak to him later. For my part, it hung over me, and I went through the motions of eating and asking Paula and Tayo about school, but my heart wasn't in it. I was pleased when we'd finished and I could clear away. The moment had arrived but at least that meant getting it over with.

'Tayo,' I said. 'Before you do your homework, I need to have a chat with you.'

He looked at me. Was it my imagination or could I detect a hint of guilt in his eyes?

'Let's go through to the lounge,' I said. 'We won't be disturbed in there.'

He trotted behind me. 'Can I watch *The Simpsons* after?'

'As it's Friday, yes. On a weekday you'll do your homework before television. But on a Friday, there's always the weekend.'

'And I've got football tomorrow,' he said excitedly. Seeing him so happy made my task even more difficult.

'Sit down,' I said. He sat next to me on the sofa and looked at me questioningly. There was no trace of guilt in his eyes now as I met his gaze. 'Tayo, what I have to say is very difficult for both of us, but it's something I have to deal with. I'm going to ask you a question in a minute and I want you to give me a truthful answer. If you do, we'll speak no more of it and I will respect you for your honesty. If you don't, I'll have doubts, which will make us both feel uncomfortable. Do you understand?'

He nodded, still looking at me.

'Do you remember when we went shopping together and I explained to you about the money I kept in the car for the car park? I showed you where it was?' He nodded again. 'Well, Tayo, that money has gone missing. All of it. Did you take it? I'm not going to be angry with you but I want a truthful answer.'

'No—!' he began almost indignantly, then stopped and seemed to gather his thoughts. He went on calmly, 'When could I have done that? You haven't left me in the car alone.'

I knew for certain then that he had taken it but that he'd only admit it if I could prove he'd had the opportunity.

'You're quite right, Tayo,' I said slowly. 'You haven't been left in the car. But you would have had time to lean forward and take it when I got out and went round to open your door to let you out.'

He said nothing, and while his gaze still held mine, some of his self-assurance seemed to have gone.

I continued. 'You've been in that position twice today. The second time was when I took you to contact, and that's when I think it happened.'

'How can you be sure?' he asked, obviously taken aback.

'Because the money was there after I'd taken you to school this morning. I used some of it.'

'Someone else might have taken it.'

'No one else has been in the car today, apart from you and me.'

'Perhaps *you* took the money and forgot,' he said, wide-eyed and innocent.

I smiled sadly. 'Tayo, do you really think I could be that daft?'

For the first time he dropped eye contact and looked down. 'It wasn't much,' he said. 'Why make all the fuss?'

'It doesn't matter how much it was. It's the principle of taking something that doesn't belong to you. It's stealing, Tayo.' I paused, but he didn't say anything. I took a breath. 'If you needed money, why didn't you ask me? I told you I give you pocket money on Saturday but you could have had it early if you'd needed it.'

He said nothing and I saw his gaze flick to the clock and I knew he was calculating how much of *The Simpsons* was left. I felt my irritation build. 'Tayo, please pay attention. This is serious. It doesn't matter if it was four pounds, forty pounds or four hundred pounds. It's wrong to steal. Why did you need the money?'

'I didn't,' he muttered.

'So why take it? Have you still got it?' He hadn't had a chance to spend it – we'd gone straight from school to contact, then home.

'No,' he said. 'I gave it to Mum. She didn't have any.'

'You're sure about that?' I asked, not altogether surprised.

'Yes!' he said vehemently. 'Cut my throat and hope to die.'

'I think that's a bit drastic. I just need to know you're telling me the truth. That's the most important thing for me.'

'Yes, Cathy, honest.'

I felt certain he was. 'I believe you, Tayo. Thank you for being honest. Now listen.' I turned sideways so that I was fully facing him and chose my words carefully. 'I know you've spent a long time looking after your mother and worrying about her. I think you probably looked after her better than she looked after you.' A flash of recognition flew across his face. 'You're not the first child I've fostered who's been in that position, and you certainly won't be the last. In a perfect world, parents should look after their children but I know sometimes that doesn't happen. You are ten, Tayo. Your mother is an adult. She is not your responsibility. Sandra will give her all the help she needs, and now your mum just has herself to look after, it will be easier for her. I think she found it very difficult trying to look after you as well, didn't she?'

He nodded sadly, clearly identifying with what I'd said.

I went on. 'I once looked after a girl who was the same age as you, and she used to save up her pocket money and give it to her mum. That's how worried she was. I only found out after a few months because I couldn't understand why she never had any money when she wasn't spending it. I know you love your mum and still worry about her, but you must believe me when I say that stealing for her is not going to do anyone any good.'

'She didn't know I'd stolen it,' he put in quickly, still protective of her. 'And it was for food.'

'All right, but do you think I would accept money from Adrian, Lucy and Paula for food, unless it was a short loan until

I got to the bank? And what about your friend Sam – do you think he has to give his mother money for food? One of the things about being a responsible adult is that you learn how to manage money. You make sure you don't run out, particularly if you have children. It's an adult's responsibility, not a child's.'

It needed to be said. Tayo would grow up to become an adult one day, and possibly have children of his own. What sort of role model had he had on which to base his own parenting skills?

He sat listening to me in silence. I hoped that some of it was sinking in. 'Do you understand what I'm saying, Tayo?'

He nodded.

'If your mum needs anything, she can ask Sandra. There's no reason why she should go hungry. Sandra will help her apply for benefit if she hasn't got enough money.'

'Mum can't apply for benefit,' he said firmly.

'Why not?'

'Because no one knows she's in this country.'

So that confirmed what we'd all suspected – Minty and Tayo were here illegally. 'I understand,' I said. 'Even so, Sandra will make sure Mum has help. It's up to your mum to ask.'

'I'll tell her,' he said, easing up a little, and glancing again at the clock.

I decided to put him out of his misery. My point had been made and I felt that he had taken it in. 'Well, I'm pleased we've had this little chat, and in a minute you can watch the rest of your programme. But first I want you to promise me you won't ever take anything again that doesn't belong to you. Either from here or anywhere else.'

'Yes. I promise,' he said.

'Good. Now, because you've taken that money, I won't be giving you your pocket money this week. It will be your way of paying me back. I'll explain why to Sandra.' I wasn't being vindictive. Tayo might have promised to be good from now on, but he needed to understand that his actions had consequences. As a set part of the fostering allowance had to be given to the child for pocket money, I would have to clear it with Sandra.

'Does she have to know?' Tayo asked.

'Yes. She's your social worker, and we don't have secrets from her. But I know that when I tell her how sorry you are, and that you have promised it won't happen again, she'll feel the same as I do. We'll say no more about it.'

He nodded.

'OK. Off you go and watch your programme. And remember, if you don't do your homework this evening you must do it after football tomorrow.'

He grinned. 'I'm really excited about football.'

'Good. You'll have a great time.'

As I watched him run off, I was glad it was all over. He wasn't really a bad child, or a thief. I didn't believe that it came naturally to him at all – but the life he had been living had taken its toll. I hoped that he had been rescued from it in time to allow the good child inside him to flourish.

Chapter Twelve

A Past

Everyone had a lie in on Saturday morning, including me. With Tayo's football club starting at ten o'clock, I thought I'd better wake him at eight-thirty, which would give him enough time to wash, dress and have his (cooked) breakfast before setting off at nine-thirty.

I knocked on his bedroom door and he called me in. He was already wide awake, staring at the ceiling.

'Cathy,' he said, the moment I entered. 'I can't go to football. I haven't got any kit.' His face showed abject disappointment but resigned acceptance. He clearly believed he was not going.

'Yes, you can,' I said. 'I have—'

Before I could get any further, he said, 'No. I can't use my new joggers, they'll get ruined. And you're not allowed to wear trainers for football.'

He'd obviously been awake for some time considering the situation and running through all the possible solutions. As usual, he'd taken on the responsibility of the problem and tried desperately to solve it. I thought of Adrian who, at the same age, had never had such worries. Like most boys, he'd assumed his football kit would be washed and ready whenever he needed it.

I went over to open his curtains. 'How long have you been lying there worrying about this?'

He glanced at the wall clock. 'An hour, I guess.'

'Well, don't,' I said firmly. His big eyes opened wider, uncertain how he should interpret my insistence. 'I've already thought of all this. I knew we wouldn't have time to shop for your kit so I've found some of Adrian's that he had when he was your age. It's washed and ready. That'll be fine for today, then I'll get you some of your own.'

He propped himself up on one elbow and grinned as though I was his fairy godmother, waving a magic wand and making all his problems vanish. 'You're great, Cathy!'

'Thank you. I aim to please.'

'But what about the boots?'

'I have your size, four, virtually brand new. Adrian grew out of them fast at your age. There's even a sports bag to put them in. So get dressed and please stop worrying.'

He leapt out of bed and planted a kiss on my cheek. I gave him a hug.

'Good boy. Now get ready. I take it you'd like a cooked breakfast before you go?'

He grinned sheepishly. 'Yes, please.'

'OK, get yourself clean pants from the drawer, and your joggers and top from the wardrobe, then go through to the bathroom. The kit is in there, apart from the boots. Put it on under your clothes then when we get to the field you can slip out of your fleece and joggers and leave them in the car. That's what the other boys do.'

I came out, adding that he should be quiet as Adrian and Paula didn't want to be woken at eight-thirty on a Saturday. Lucy had already left for her Saturday job at Boots. Fifteen minutes later, just as I'd finished cooking his breakfast (egg, bacon, sausage and mushrooms), he appeared with the kit on, and his fleece and joggers in his hand. 'It fits great,' he said. 'I thought I would show you.'

'Excellent. You look terrific, just the part.'

'But can I still have my own for next week?'

'Yes, of course.' I set his breakfast on the table, and Tayo sat down to tuck in. I went back to the kitchen to make his black tea with one sugar.

As I returned a few minutes later with the mug, I suddenly noticed an ugly scar on his left arm. His elbow was sticking out as he used his knife and fork, and the scar, about three inches long, ran along the soft flesh of his underarm from the elbow towards his wrist. It wasn't the fine pink scar of a neatly mended and healed wound, but a jagged, taut mish-mash of white tissue. I stared at it as I set the mug on the table. I had never seen a scar like it – it was a real mess. The two edges of the wound looked as though they hadn't knit-ted together properly, and the new skin that had formed over the top had the appearance of stretched gauze. I hadn't seen it before because Tayo had always been in long sleeves, but someone at the school must have seen it surely, when he'd changed for PE.

'I bet that hurt,' I said, lightly touching his arm.

'It did. And it was bleeding for ages.'

'Did you go to the hospital?'

'No. Mum and her friend stuck it together with plasters. But every time they took the plasters off it opened up, and started bleeding again.'

Yes, I thought, horrified, a three-inch-long gaping wound, stuck together with plasters, would tend to do that! No wonder the scar looked so angry – it was incredible it had healed at all. What on earth had Minty been thinking of?

'How long ago did it happen?' I asked.

Tayo was more interested in his breakfast than my questions and shrugged. 'A year, I guess. Maybe more. It took a month to stop oozing. My mum and her friend were getting worried. There was blood and yellow stuff coming out. It smelt horrid.' And as if to demonstrate, he squirted tomato ketchup onto the yolk of his egg. I was so pleased I wasn't eating.

'It sounds like it went septic – that means it got an infection in it. Who was this friend of Mum's?'

He shrugged again. 'Some bloke we lived with for a while.'

'And you didn't see a doctor?'

'No. But I stayed in bed for a few days and I didn't have to go to work.' He stopped, suddenly aware he'd just let something slip. 'I used to help Mum clear up the house, and she'd pay me,' he explained. 'Anyway, it's fine now, and I make sure I don't knock it.'

It was on his underarm, so not in the most vulnerable place, but he would have to be very careful. The new skin was so thin it wouldn't take much to make it burst open again. I would mention it to Sandra when we next spoke, and show the doctor when Tayo had his medical, although I doubted much could be done, other than to reopen the wound and sew it properly.

'How did it happen, Tayo?' I said lightly, removing his empty plate.

He was silent as he concentrated on sipping his tea, then he set it down and said, 'Cathy, I promised you yesterday I'd try and tell the truth. But I can't tell you the truth about this, not yet. So please don't ask me.'

I was taken aback, both by the maturity and sincerity of his response. For a boy of ten it was unheard of. I looked him in the eye. 'All right, Tayo. I respect that, but when you can tell me, I think you should. I have a feeling that it's important and I should know. Agreed?'

He nodded, finished his breakfast and then went upstairs to clean his teeth. I went to the front room, took a log sheet from my desk and quickly noted what Tayo had just said. I would mention it to Sandra the next time we spoke and also ask the school if they knew anything about the scar. Perhaps he'd said something at school, for surely it couldn't have gone unnoticed.

When we arrived at the field where the football club met, there were already half a dozen boys kicking a ball around in a warm-up. The coach, who was carrying a clipboard, watched them from the side. I left Tayo in the car to take off his fleece and joggers, and change into his football boots, while I went over to the coach, introduced myself and gave him the cheque for the term's fees as arranged on the phone.

The coach ticked Tayo's name off the list on his clipboard, and then handed me a medical questionnaire together with a consent form for emergency medical treatment, should it be necessary. As a parent, I completed and signed forms like this all the time without a second thought, but as a foster carer (and therefore not Tayo's legal guardian) I was not allowed to.

'Tayo is a looked-after child,' I said, out of earshot of the other boys. 'I'll have to ask his social worker to sign this. Can I bring it with me next week?'

'No problem,' the coach said. 'Let me check your contact details.' He flipped over a page on his clipboard, and read out my name, address and telephone numbers, which I'd given him over the phone.

'Yes, that's right,' I said. 'Tayo's a good boy, and loves his sport. He won't give you any problems.'

Tayo bounded over, looking the part in the football kit.

'Right, lad,' the coach said. 'Join in for a warm-up while the others arrive. Do you know any of the boys here?'

Tayo looked across the field. 'Is that Dean?'

'Dean Emmory. He goes to Meadway School,' the coach said.

'He's in Year Five!' Tayo exclaimed, happy to see a familiar face. He jogged towards the boys, and I saw Dean look up, recognize Tayo and wave, while another boy kicked the ball in his direction, instantly including him in the game.

'Thanks,' I said to the coach. 'See you at twelve.'

I returned to the car and drove away. None of the other parents had stayed to watch, and Tayo certainly wouldn't want me to be the only one. I bought a newspaper on the way home, and when I got there, I made coffee and sat down to read it.

Ten minutes later, I realized I was reading without taking in a word. My thoughts were firmly on Tayo and the mysterious comment he had made about work. It was very unlikely that Minty had paid him for helping her – she barely had the money for a pint of milk from the sound of it and if she had, I very much doubted she would have given it to Tayo. Had he done some casual cash-in-hand work to bring some money into the house? At nine he would have been well under the legal age – even to have a paper round a child must be thirteen, but he looked older than his age. I knew some of the traders in the food market used lads to pick up fruit and vegetables that had fallen from the stall, and generally help clear up. While, strictly speaking, it was illegal, it was unlikely to do any great harm, and if that's what Tayo had been doing, then the money would probably have been a vital part of his and Minty's income. It was all conjecture, and I hoped that in time Tayo would feel he could tell me.

I arrived to collect Tayo from football ten minutes before the end. Other parents had done the same, and we stood on the side-line and cheered on the boys in the final minutes of their five-a-side. The coach blew his whistle, signalling the end of the match, then called everyone together. The boys sat on the ground in a circle at his feet, while the parents grouped around the edge. It was clearly the way he ended every session as the other lads had gathered round him without prompting. The coach talked about the game they'd played, highlighting any areas that needed improving, and congratulating the boys on their individual skills and achievements. Everyone got a mention.

'Tayo Mezer,' he said, glancing at his clipboard. 'You're a very good shooter; just make sure you don't hog the ball. Teamwork is the key.'

Tayo glowed and nodded, then glanced proudly at me. 'Well done,' I mouthed. I felt proud too. When the coach had mentioned everyone, the parents clapped. Then we were dismissed. Tayo bounded to my side.

'I did so well, Cathy. It was great. Can I come next week?'

'Yes. You said you wanted to, so I've enrolled you until Easter.'

'Terrific! Thanks!'

He continued to talk about the game non-stop as we walked to the car, while he changed out of his muddy boots and into his trainers, then on the drive home. He whistled in the shower, then when he came out, still glowing from having had such a good time, he told Adrian all about the match, then Paula, then Lucy. Then he bolted down a huge lunch, ravenous from running around all morning.

Perhaps it was his euphoria from enjoying the football so much, or perhaps because he felt he owed me something for arranging and paying for it, but after lunch, he came to me while I was still sitting at the table and said, 'Cathy. I can tell you about the scar now.'

'Yes?' I said. I thought that I already knew what the answer would be. I was sure he was going to say that he'd had an accident at home and that he'd been sworn to secrecy by his mother; he hadn't told anyone before, I thought, because he knew that it would look bad for his mum if Social Services found out that she'd let something like that happen to him and then not taken him to hospital.

But it was absolutely nothing like that.

'I got it at work,' he said.

'Work? You mean when you were helping Mum?'

He shook his head. 'No, when I went out to work. At the factory – only we weren't allowed to call it that.'

I was puzzled. 'Factory? What sort of factory?'

'It was a place where we made clothes and bags. It was a big old building in a really rough area. The windows didn't open and it was hot and dusty inside. It made me cough. That's when my asthma started. I was collected at six in the morning by a man in a van and brought back after dark so no one saw me.'

I had stopped what I was doing and was now staring at Tayo. 'Which country was this in? Nigeria?'

'No. England.'

He must be mistaken. 'Are you sure?'

He nodded. 'There were other kids there too, about six usually, and lots of women, and teenage girls about Paula's age. Lots of them were Asian. We had to stitch the clothes and bags with big machines. I was working on a bag when it happened. The machine for the bags had bigger needles than the one for clothes. It was my fault, I wasn't concentrating, I was so tired. I fell asleep and the needles ran over my arm.'

I cringed and held back a gasp.

'The man in charge was so angry. He said I was a liability and couldn't work there again. Mum was furious because the money had stopped.'

'Did she work there as well?'

'Not often on the machines. She came in sometimes but Mr Azzi, the man in charge, said he had other work for her. She used to go with him. I don't know where. Sometimes for an hour. Sometimes longer. Then she would go home and I'd stay. I didn't go to school.'

I gaped at him. If all this was true, it sounded like a scene from Dickensian England. But I had no grounds for doubting him, and his now sombre manner and sudden dejection at what he was remembering, suggested I had every reason to believe him. 'Are you *sure* the factory was in England?' I asked.

'Yes. London. I don't know the address. We stayed at a man's flat while we were working there. I know the flat was near Spitalfields and Shoreditch and Whitechapel because I some-times caught a bus with Mum and it went to those places.'

The East End of London, I thought. That seemed to ring a bell and I started to remember hearing something about East End sweatshops on the radio. They were places where people were paid a pittance for long hours and hard work, but I'd always thought they were proper factories even if they did employ cheap labour – not like the sweatshops of the Third World that set children to work for the equivalent of a few pence a day in appalling conditions. Surely that kind of place did not exist in London, in the twenty-first century?

I didn't want Tayo to see how appalled I was by what he was telling me in case he clammed up again, so I reined in my shock and asked, 'Did they pay you?'

'Mr Azzi gave money to Mum. I don't know how much.'

'And what happened after the machine ran over your arm?'

'I don't know. Mum said I passed out, I don't remember anything. I woke up in the flat where we were staying, and Mum and the man who owned it were standing over me. I was on the settee. It was also my bed. The man was angry, and he said we had to get out as soon as I was able to walk. Mum and he argued and he hit her. I couldn't walk because each time I moved, the towel round my arm got soaked with blood. The man gave me a tablet to make me sleep but it made me have weird dreams where things were moving, so I didn't take them anymore. I hid them under the cushion on the settee. I couldn't even go to the toilet, I had to pee in a pot, because if I tried to stand the blood started oozing again, and I felt dizzy. After a week or so, Mum found another friend for us to live with, another man. He and Mum put lots of bandages on my arm and got me in his car. I had a bed at his place, and we stayed there until it had stopped bleeding.'

'Who was the friend?' I asked. 'Do you know? Your mum seems to have a lot of friends.'

'Dave. He was Irish. He and Mum drank a lot, but he was OK to me.'

'And this happened when you were nine?'

'Yes. I was eight when I started in the factory. I remember because I'd just had my birthday and I didn't get any presents.'

'So you worked there for a year?'

'Yes, until the accident. I would probably still be there if the machine hadn't stitched my arm, so maybe it was good that it happened.'

I didn't comment. 'And you can't remember the name of the road the factory was in?'

'I never knew it. The van that took us and brought us back didn't have any windows in the back. It was one of those white vans builders use. It was horrible. It made me feel sick, bumping around in the dark.'

I looked at him carefully. We were still in the breakfast room adjoining the kitchen. 'Tayo,' I said slowly, 'you are telling me the truth, aren't you? You wouldn't make it up to protect your mum, would you?'

'No! Honestly. Cut my throat and hope to die.'

'So why tell me now? Have you told anyone else before?'

'No. I haven't.' He looked down. 'I'm telling you, Cathy, because you're the first person I could tell, and you might be able to help. I made a friend when I was working in the factory. A proper friend, I mean, not one of Mum's men. Her name was Angie and she and her sisters worked there. I promised her I would help her and that if I ever found an adult I could trust I would try and get her out.'

Although I had only known Tayo for a short while I didn't think he was a fantasist and what he'd said with its childish detail did make sickening sense. If I didn't believe Tayo when he was telling me the truth, he'd never trust another adult again. 'Do you know Angie's surname?'

'It sounded like Tenjaby but I don't know how to spell it.'

I nodded. 'You realize I'm going to have to tell Sandra all of this so she can help?'

'Yes. I want you to.'

'And you're not worried about what your mum will say when she finds out you've told me this?'

He shook his head. 'No. She never helped me and I'm safe now.'

I felt a great wave of pity and respect for Tayo. He was so strong and mature in many ways, yet still only a child, vulnerable in his request for help and keen to assert that he wasn't worried. I believed what he had told me.

I stood up and went to him, putting my arms round him to give him a big hug. 'You've done well telling me this, and I'll do all I can to help. But once Sandra has told the police it will be up to them. We might have to make a statement to the police, I don't know. But it's nothing to be scared of. You're not the one who's done anything wrong.'

If I'd had any remaining doubt about the validity of what he was saying, it vanished now as he said emphatically, 'Good. Will they arrest the owner?'

The mention of the police would have made him back down if he was inventing it, I was sure, but he only looked satisfied that the man who had forced him and the other children to work those long hard hours might be punished.

'I hope so. If they can find him. What he's been doing is certainly illegal, and immoral. He should be stopped.'

'I hated him. He used to make Angie cry. He seemed to enjoy seeing her cry.'

I looked him in the eye. 'There are some horrible adults around, Tayo, as you've no doubt discovered, but fortunately there are even more nice ones. Now, I think you should get going on your homework while I make some notes about what you've said.' I paused. Once again, I felt the niggle of the unexplained. Perhaps, with all the honesty in the air, now was the time to ask Tayo about what had been puzzling me. 'Tayo, you haven't been to school much, have you?'

'No.' He shook his head. 'Not much.'

'Why are you so clever then?' I smiled. 'You can read and write well, and have a good general knowledge, and you speak beautifully. Where did you learn all that?'

'I went to school before I came here when I was four and five.'

'In Nigeria?'

'Yes. It was a very good school and they taught me to read and write. Then since I've been here, I've used the libraries because they're free. And when I stayed with families, I read the books and magazines they left lying around. And newspapers. I learned from the television as well. I like the documentaries. My dad said it was important to learn and have a good education. So I try to do it.'

I thought of all the children in this country who wasted their excellent and free education while Tayo had surpassed many of them on discarded magazines, the library and television. He was quite a boy, there was no mistake about that.

'Your dad was right,' I said. 'He sounds like a very wise man. Where is he now?'

Tayo shrugged. 'I don't know. I thought he would come and find me but he hasn't. I don't think he cares.'

'Tayo, do you know anything else about your father that might help Sandra to trace him? Is his surname Mezer?'

He looked blank. 'I don't know.'

'And where does he live?'

He travels a lot for work, or he used to. His home is in Nigeria, near Lagos. I don't know the address.'

'And did you and your mum live with him as a family?'

'Only when I was a baby and I don't remember that.'

'Is there anything else you can tell me about him? Do you know how old he is? When his birthday is? Anything he could recall might help us trace this mysterious father.'

Tayo frowned with the effort of trying to remember. 'I'm sure his birthday is in June. I guess he's about thirty-five. It's a long time since I've seen him, Cathy. I remember he was tall with big muscles. And he's black.' He cocked his head to one side. 'Is it OK to use that word?'

'Yes, in this context. It's correct.'

Tayo's big brown eyes filled with hope. 'Do you think he can be found, Cathy? I'd really like to see him.'

'Oh, love, I don't know,' I said honestly. I wished so much that I could promise him that we would find his father, but Tayo's description of a tall, black, muscular man living in Nigeria was hardly going to refine the search. 'But we can try. I'll speak to Sandra on Monday, and tell her how much you would like to see him again.'

'Thanks, Cathy.'

I smiled at him. 'Now, homework. Off you go.'

When he'd gone, I sank into my seat at the table again, stunned by everything he had told me, trying to take it all in.

Chapter Thirteen

Clutter

While Tayo set about his homework at the desk in his bedroom, I set about writing up everything he'd said, using his words whenever possible. His account of the 'sweatshop' had to be as near verbatim as possible if it was ever going to be used in a prosecution – and I hoped it would be. The talk we'd had about home and his dad, I paraphrased.

When I'd finished writing, I typed up my notes and emailed them to Sandra ready for her to find in her Inbox on Monday morning. I also emailed a copy to Jill – whoever was covering her work would collect it at the office. Then I opened my Internet browser and typed 'sweatshops' into the search engine. An hour later, when Tayo had finished his homework and come down to find me, I was still scrolling through the results and reading the various articles. I was convinced now that what Tayo had told me was not only feasible, but also highly probable. There were accounts that described factories similar to Tayo's and supported the details of what he'd said. Some were written by young adults who had escaped these sweatshops and were describing their experiences. Others were newspaper articles – investigative journalistic pieces. There was even a photograph of the inside of one such 'factory'.

So why, I thought angrily, are these places still in existence? Why haven't they all been shut down? What are the police doing about this?

'Hi, love,' I said, as Tayo came in. I closed the site window – I didn't want him to see what I was looking at – and turned to him. 'Would you like a game of cards now you've done your homework?'

'Yes, please. I'm good at cards.'

He wasn't wrong. We played for over an hour and he was at least as good as I was. When we added up the number of games each of us had won, it was fortuitously a draw.

'Ah!' he said, competitive to the last. 'Next time I'll beat you.'

'Don't be too sure of that,' I laughed.

Adrian, home for the afternoon, then gave Tayo a game of chess, and although Adrian won, Tayo played well and could plan his moves and strategy well in advance. The afternoon passed happily and at six o'clock I called Tayo into the lounge. 'We need to phone your mother,' I said.

Interestingly he hadn't mentioned the phone contact. Children usually get quite excited at the prospect of phoning their parents, not only because they want to speak to them but, with younger children particularly, because of the novelty of using the phone.

We sat down together on the sofa next to the phone in the lounge. 'Sandra's asked that I make the call and then stay while you speak to Mum,' I explained to Tayo. I looked in my file for Minty's mobile number.

'Do you have to listen?' he asked.

'Yes, I do, love.' It crossed my mind that he might have wanted to tell her that he'd told me about the scar and work, and put her on alert. Tayo's loyalty and sense of responsibility for his mother wouldn't evaporate overnight, not after five years of looking out for her, even if he was starting to realize how little she had looked out for him in return.

I keyed in the number and it rang for some time, then the call went through to her voicemail. I glanced at the carriage clock on the mantelpiece. It was exactly six o'clock. 'That's strange, there's no answer.'

'Perhaps she can't hear it ringing?' Tayo suggested.

I tried again and the same thing happened. I looked down at Tayo. 'I'll try one more time then if she still doesn't answer, you can leave a message on her voicemail. OK?'

He nodded but looked quite dejected.

I pressed redial, it rang, and she answered immediately. 'Who is it?' she demanded. There was a lot of noise in the background that could have been the sound of a busy pub.

'Minty, it's Cathy, Tayo's carer.'

'Hello, Cathy,' she shouted over the noise. 'Hang on and I'll go in the toilets.'

I waited as doors banged and the noise subsided. 'All right now?' I asked when she came back on.

'I'm at work. Is Tayo there?' she said tersely.

'He is.' I passed the phone to him.

'Hello, Mum,' he said, his voice immediately dropping to a monotone, where it stayed for the rest of the call. He didn't say anything, but only mumbled the odd no and yes in answer to her questions.

159

I don't usually take notes during phone contact unless there are real concerns and I'm asked to put the receiver on speaker-phone. I listen and make notes afterwards of anything the social worker should know. I really don't like monitoring phone contact and feel quite uncomfortable at this eavesdropping, even though it is necessary and I had been instructed to do it. Minty was still talking ten to the dozen but Tayo had the phone pressed close to his ear and I couldn't hear much of what she was saying. Eventually, after his third 'nothing' said in the same flat and emotionless voice, I whispered, 'Tell her about football.'

'I went to football this morning,' he said, about as excited as a wet lettuce.

I glanced at him. I knew what he was doing – I'd seen children do it before. He wasn't going to admit to having had a good time because he didn't want his mum to be let off so easily. He wanted to punish her by making her think he was unhappy and thereby twisting her conscience and increasing her feelings of guilt. I had to hand it to Tayo – with his intelligence and skills at manipulation, he was doing an excellent job. Five minutes later, after he'd grunted another couple of 'nothings' and a few 'don't knows', he handed the phone to me and said, 'She wants to talk to you.'

I took the handset and before it was to my ear, Minty had started. Once started, she didn't stop, lambasting me for not looking after her son, telling me how she was going to report me to Sandra, and threatening that I'd better watch out because she had *friends*. I tried interrupting but it was hopeless, I couldn't get a word in. The deluge could have been exacerbated by drink, but after another five minutes of condemnation and what she planned to do about it, I cut her off.

'Well, you certainly know how to wind your mother up,' I said to Tayo, not best pleased. 'She's in a right state.'

'She's a waster,' he said fervently. 'She's not interested in what I'm doing. She's pissed.'

I couldn't deny that she'd sounded drunk. Her words had been slurred and most of what she'd said was incoherent nonsense. I doubted she got that way at work, whatever her 'work' was.

'All right, but you needn't have made the situation worse. Next time you can answer her questions properly and tell your mum some of the things you have been doing, and reassure her you're OK. She is your mother after all.'

'My bad luck, isn't it,' he answered grumpily.

'Tayo,' I said firmly, 'if you don't want telephone contact I can tell Sandra and she will stop it. No one will force you to speak to your mother on the phone. But if we are phoning her, then you can try your hardest not to upset her. You could try answering her questions and not sounding so depressed. Look at you, you're fine now.'

He shrugged. 'Can I watch some television now?'

'Yes – but remember what I've said.'

'Will do!' He went off, happy as Larry, while I settled down to write yet more notes in anticipation of the phone call I was sure Sandra would make on Monday, after Minty had complained.

* * *

On Sunday Lucy, Paula, Tayo and I went to a car boot sale. Adrian and Paula were going to see their father but he'd unfortunately had to cancel at the last minute. Adrian wasn't interested in shopping of any kind so we left him in bed.

There was a huge car boot sale, with over a hundred stalls, held on the site of an old airfield, about a mile from where I lived. I went about three times a year. Lucy, Paula and I liked to rummage around and we usually came away with a bargain each, though not necessarily something we needed. I had suggested going today because at the back of my mind was the thought that I might be able to pick up some things for Tayo and his room. Apart from the few models I'd put out, there was nothing in his bedroom other than the clothes in his wardrobe. I wanted to get him some 'clutter' – the personal belongings that by the age of ten children have normally acquired to display in their bedrooms. Tayo had arrived with nothing and there didn't seem much chance of retrieving any of his possessions from the numerous places where he'd stayed. He'd had his birthday, and Christmas had gone, so there wouldn't be another opportunity for some time to shower him with presents and help fill the void. Adrian, Lucy and Paula's bedrooms, like most teenagers', were overflowing with their personal possessions, so much so that every so often I insisted they cleared out, and we bagged up and put in the loft what they had outgrown or weren't using for the time being. The loft contained numerous bags of soft toys, pre-school games and toys, none of which I was allowed to give away for sentimental reasons. Tayo's shelves and cupboards by contrast were completely bare, and while I couldn't afford to replace ten years of lost possessions new, I hoped to go some way with good second-hand.

Tayo had never been to a car boot sale before, which surprised me as they would have been a good source of inexpensive items for Minty's limited budget. From the moment we entered, he was enthralled. We walked between the rows of tables, stalls, open car boots and traders' vans, looking at what was on offer.

It was a cold, but bright and dry day, and the market was very busy. I'd explained to Tayo that if we got separated he should go to the hotdog stand by the entrance and wait for me to find him. I hadn't actually told him the main reason for us coming, not wanting to disappoint him if there was nothing suitable to buy, but I couldn't have chosen a better day to visit, for many people were using the market to sell unwanted Christmas presents, and the commercial traders were having a New Year sale.

Tayo spotted the latest Harry Potter book, never opened, together with a boxed set of miniature toy soldiers. There were over a hundred pieces, including rifles, tanks, camouflage nets and tiny waters bottles in survival packs, which I thought would block up the Hoover a treat.

'Would you like them?' I asked.

He looked at me with big doleful eyes. 'Yes, but I don't have any money. I've lost my pocket money for this week.'

'I know, but I'll treat you. You weren't here for Christmas so we'll call it a late Christmas present. All right?'

To say he was excited was an understatement. He watched me pay the woman the nine pounds she was asking for the two items, then clutched the box and book tightly to his chest, as though he thought they could be spirited away like all his other things. Further along, in the next aisle, he stopped and looked at a twenty-piece boxed car set, similar to the old Matchbox cars. It was six pounds, so again, I asked him if he'd like it and then bought it. Lucy and Paula had stopped at a stall selling silver jewellery – hundreds of earrings, necklaces and bracelets. I wasn't sure they needed any more jewellery but gave them five pounds each to treat themselves and continued along the aisle with Tayo. Presently he saw a set of model dinosaurs – a dozen pieces, each four inches high and painted very realistically in dark green and brown.

'Wow!' Tayo breathed as he looked at them. It was four pounds for the set, so I bought that too and carried it, as his arms were full.

'Tayo,' I said, 'I've spent nineteen pounds so far. So we'll say another eleven pounds to spend, which will make it up to thirty, and we'll call it a day.'

Quarter of an hour later, with the girls in possession of yet another pair of earrings each, Tayo spotted a six-piece Thunderbird model set for five pounds.

'Good heavens!' I said. 'It's not back in fashion, is it? I used to watch *Thunderbirds* on television when I was a child.'

The girls looked at me, unable to imagine me as a child, while Tayo and I went in for a closer look. I picked up the red rocket, the drop-down pod, and then the pink FAB 1 car. So nostalgic was the recollection that if Tayo hadn't wanted it I'd have bought it anyway. But he did.

'Six pounds left,' I said to Tayo, who was now fully into the swing of this buying. We continued to wander up and down the aisles for another twenty minutes and I knew Tayo wanted to spin out and make the most of his last purchase. It was twelve-thirty and I was starting to get hungry; we'd been here for the best part of two hours. The sun had gone and the temperature was starting to drop. 'You don't have to spend the six pounds,' I said. 'It was just the limit I set on it.'

This intensified his search, and two minutes later he'd found a wooden chess set. It wasn't new, in fact it had been quite well used, but when I examined the pieces I could see they were good quality and had stood the test of time.

'Are you sure you want a chess set?' I asked. 'We have one at home you can use any time.' I wondered if it was more a matter of spending the six pounds than the actual acquisition.

'Yes, I've always wanted one of my own,' Tayo said imploringly.

'OK, let's see how much it is.' I asked the owner and he said nine pounds, which I thought was enough given that they'd obviously had good use from it.

'It's hand-carved mahogany,' the man added as I admired the pieces.

'Can I have a look at the board please?' I asked.

The owner lifted it out of the box, and although obviously used, it wasn't split or torn and was generally in good condition.

'Cathy,' Tayo said, 'I know it's three pounds more than you said, and I haven't got my pocket money this week. But how about if you keep next week's as well? Then we can afford to buy it.'

That sealed it – if he wanted it that much, of course he could have it, without the deduction of the following week's pocket money.

I paid and we returned to the car, with Tayo's possessions now being carried by all four of us. I stored them in the boot, apart from the Harry Potter book, which Tayo wanted to start reading on the journey back.

Once home I made us a hot chocolate and then prepared dinner while Tayo set about organizing all the newly acquired possessions in his room. He called me up an hour later to admire the display, and as I entered I was pleased to see his shelves were now 'cluttered' like everyone else's. The miniature soldiers were doing battle on the top two shelves, all one hundred of them, while the twelve dinosaurs roamed on the shelf beneath. The Thunderbirds were exploring the moon landscape on the fourth shelf, while the Matchbox cars raced a circuit at the bottom. The book was positioned spine outward on the desk, next to the chess set, which remained in the box.

'I won't take all the chess pieces out,' Tayo said. 'I'd like to play with it downstairs later.'

'Good idea.' I admired the arrangements on the shelves. 'When you've read that book, we can get you some more. Second-hand books are very cheap compared to the price of new ones. I often buy mine from the Oxfam shop.'

Tayo frowned. 'My mum won't go in a charity shop. She says it's for poor people, and she wouldn't be seen dead in one.'

I marvelled at Minty's perverse snobbery. It was inverted logic to avoid a cheap shop when she had been unable to provide the basics of life for her son.

'I don't consider myself poor,' I said, 'and in any case, poverty is nothing to be ashamed of. But I do like a bargain as much as the next person, because it means there's more money for other things.'

'Yes. I agree,' he said, and set about rearranging his tiny army on the top shelf.

'I was thinking of meeting Peter tonight,' I said later to Lucy and Paula. 'Can you babysit Tayo please? I won't be going out till after eight, so he'll be in bed.'

'No problem,' Lucy said. 'It must be strange having a boyfriend at your age.' Paula smiled in collusion.

'Thank you for the vote of confidence, ladies,' I said tartly. 'And he's not a boyfriend, more a companion, or good friend.'

They raised their eyebrows and giggled, and I couldn't help but laugh. 'And don't forget Tayo's light goes out at eight-thirty. It's a school night tonight. I won't be back late.'

Going out in the evening was a fairly new thing for me. When the children were younger and I was newly divorced, I didn't attempt much of a social life outside the family beyond the odd lunch or coffee date with friends. To be honest, I didn't have the stamina after a busy day looking after the children, running the home and working part-time, or much enthusiasm for the whole idea. Now the family was older, though, and I'd completely recovered from the divorce, I tried to go out in the evening once a week. Lately, it had been to see Peter, a widower five years my senior with two grown-up children. Six months before I'd stopped for petrol and had been struggling to remove the petrol cap from the tank of my car when the man waiting in the car behind offered to help.

'The key's jammed,' I explained, feeling somewhat hot and flustered. I was proud of my ability to cope and didn't enjoy looking like a helpless woman.

He came over to lend a hand and the petrol cap was off in seconds. 'Aren't you Adrian Glass's mother?' he asked as he handed back my keys.

'Yes, that's right.'

'I thought I recognized you.'

His son had been in Adrian's year at school and he remembered me from parents' evenings, sports days and prize givings. I thanked him for his help and we went our separate ways, only to bump into each other a week later in the supermarket. This time we went for a coffee and ending up sitting for an hour in the supermarket café, chatting away while my frozen food gently thawed out. I had enjoyed it hugely, and had felt like a teenager again when he asked me for my telephone number as we said goodbye.

The next day Peter called and we arranged a dinner date. His kindness and warmth appealed to me, and it was delightful to know that someone was obviously interested in me and keen for my company. Since then, we'd been seeing each other regularly, though both of us were happy to keep things moving very slowly. I was the first woman Peter had been out with since his wife's death three years before, and he was the first man I'd dated since my divorce, which was longer ago than I cared to admit. The demands on my time suited us both – it kept the pressure off and allowed us to take our time as we got to know each other. Nevertheless, I enjoyed his company and looked forward to our evenings together.

I made a light supper of quiche and salad just before seven, then explained to Tayo that I would be going out in the evening once he was settled in bed. It was best to prepare him, as he'd obviously ask where I was when Lucy went to turn his light off and I didn't want him to think I'd sneaked out and left him.

'What time will you be back?' Tayo asked, a touch of anxiety in his voice.

'Not late. About ten-thirty. You'll be sound asleep by then. Lucy and Paula will say goodnight tonight, and they'll be here if you need anything at all.'

He seemed happy with this but when I went in to say goodnight to him as he sat up in bed reading his Harry Potter book, he frowned and said, 'Do you *have* to go out?'

'No, I don't *have* to. But I like to, and it's only once a week.'

'I don't want you to go,' he said in a small voice.

'Why not, love? I'll be back in a couple of hours.'

'I don't like being left on my own.' His brow furrowed deeper.

'You won't be alone. Paula and Lucy are here, and Adrian's still downstairs. They'll look after you and you're going to sleep in twenty minutes anyway.'

He put down his book and appealed to me with his big, sad eyes. 'Please don't go,' he begged. 'I'm worried you won't come back. My mum used to go out and not come back.'

'I know, Tayo, but this is different. I never spend the night away, and Lucy, Paula and Adrian are here.' I could see he wasn't convinced, and while I was loath to cancel my arrangements, I recognized he'd been with me for barely a week and was still learning to trust me. He was feeling some of the fear and anxiety that must have overwhelmed him during the last five years, when he'd seen his mother disappearing off in a taxi and not known if she was ever coming back.

I gave him a hug. 'Listen, I'll tell you what I'll do. I'll wait until you're asleep before I go, then when you wake up I'll be in the house again and you won't know anything about it. How about that?'

He thought for a moment and decided this was a good second option, put the book on the table and snuggled down. I gave him the usual kiss on his forehead, and we swapped our usual refrain:

'Goodnight. Sleep tight.'

'And don't let the bed bugs bite.' He managed a smile.

I came out of his room and then phoned Peter to rearrange our meeting time. I sat downstairs with the girls until quarter to nine, then checked on Tayo and found him sound asleep.

'I'm off, girls!' I called as I put my coat on in the hall. 'Now, don't forget, call me on my mobile if there's any problem at all ...'

'Yes, yes,' sighed Paula as she came to see me out. 'Don't *fuss*. We know what to do. It'll be fine.'

I grinned. Fussing was second nature to me – or at least, being alert to any possible problems and dangers. It was part of my job, after all.

'Now off you go and have a good time,' she said, for all the world as if she was the mother and I was the teenager heading off for a night out.

By nine o'clock, I was sitting with Peter in a warm, comfortable pub, enjoying a drink and a chat about all the news of the previous week. As we talked, I realized what a lot had happened since I'd last seen him. I couldn't tell Peter much about Tayo, as it was confidential but what I did say about fostering in general left him amazed. Like many people I knew, he was in awe of my work, and sometimes appeared to be in danger of seeing me as some kind of martyred saint.

'I don't know how you do it, Cathy. You're incredible,' he said, shaking his head.

'I know it sounds demanding, and it is sometimes, but I wouldn't do it if I didn't want to,' I said. 'There's no great sacrifice or altruistic motive. I love doing it and the rewards are endless. If I can make a small difference to a child so there's a chance they might have a better future, then not a single day has been wasted. I don't ever remember feeling like that when I worked in the civil service.'

'No. OK. But I still think you're wonderful,' he said with a warm smile.

'Thanks. You're not so bad yourself.'

If Peter was able to understand fostering and feel the same way I did about it, then perhaps there was a chance that we could have a future together. But all that was a long way off, and there was lots of work to do before then.

Chapter Fourteen

A Hectic Week

Tayo had forgotten all about my going out by the following morning when I woke him and told him it was time to get dressed. Only when I dropped him off at school did he remember. 'Did you have a good evening, Cathy?' he asked.

'Yes, thank you, nice of you to ask.'

'You're welcome,' he said with one of his cheeky grins, then jogged off towards the school gates.

Well, he hasn't been too traumatized, I thought as I watched him go. I'm glad I didn't cancel.

Within fifteen minutes of returning home, I was on the phone to Sandra. She'd received my email detailing what Tayo had said about his scar and the factory, and had called at once, genuinely shocked.

'The poor kid has really been through it,' she said. 'I can't believe how he's coped. It must be such a relief for him to be looked after now, and share all this with you.'

'Yes, and he *has* coped very well. Too well in my opinion. He's so calm and controlled. You know, even when he described how the machine cut his arm, he was very removed, almost emotionless.'

'I suppose he's had to be in control of his feelings with Minty being as she is. There's no way he could ever rely on her. He's the one who has been in charge and had to remain calm.'

'Yes. Which reminds me, Minty was pretty incoherent and angry on the phone on Saturday.' I told her about Minty's tirade and that she was going to report me.

'Don't worry. I'll deal with it if she phones. She still hasn't given me her address, and her mobile was off all last week.'

'It took three attempts for me to get through on Saturday,' I confirmed. I paused. 'Sandra, do you think Minty would really have put her eight-year-old son to work in a factory?'

'It's a possibility,' Sandra replied grimly. 'If she's in the grip of addictions and needs to fund them ... well, it's by no means out of the question.'

'But have you ever previously come across a child who has been forced to work in one of these sweatshops?'

'I haven't dealt with one personally but a colleague of mine had a case a few years back where a twelve-year-old girl ended up in one. It made the national press because she'd been brought into the country illegally then kept prisoner in a house somewhere in South London and forced into prostitution. The owner of the house had sold her on to work in a sweatshop when he could no longer pass her off as a virgin. She was fourteen when she escaped from the factory.'

'God! How terrible! That poor girl. Did they get those responsible?'

'I believe the police arrested the owner of the sweatshop and the owner of the brothel. It was part of an international people-smuggling ring. Apparently her parents in Pakistan had been told she was going to be given good lodgings and educated in England in return for some light housework. They'd handed over all their life savings, believing their daughter was going to have a better life here. They traced her parents and she was repatriated to them. The feeling was that her case was only the tip of the iceberg.' She paused. 'Tayo hasn't said anything about being put to work sexually, has he?'

'Struth! I hope not. He's only ten.' I felt a shiver of fear; I knew only too well that children much younger than that were abused. 'Although from what Tayo said, it sounds like Minty was giving sexual favours to the factory owner, Mr Azzi.'

'Yes, but she's an adult,' Sandra said bluntly, 'and I haven't got an awful lot of sympathy with her right now. Cathy, I'll inform the police of what Tayo's said. The name of this owner might help. I'll also approach the Nigerian Embassy again about his father. I'm going to get back to the Home Office as well. It's occurred to me that if Mum is going to attend contact, they might like to interview her there about her immigration status.'

We talked a little about what had happened over the weekend, and about the disappearance of the money and Tayo's pocket money being stopped.

'If he thieved for Mum, he'll have learned that behaviour from her,' remarked Sandra. 'Thanks, Cathy. I'll phone you later in the week.'

I was really impressed with Sandra; she was so thorough that she made it appear as though Tayo's case was the only one she had to deal with, whereas in fact she'd be working on fifteen or more. All of them would require home visits, meetings, court appearances, telephone calls, emails, and endless paperwork and form filling, not to mention dealing with the emotional and often difficult parents. Social workers have said to me in the past that they couldn't do my job, but I certainly couldn't do theirs.

The week continued to disappear in a hive of activity. Apart from the school run, housework and a day's training, I had Tayo's various appointments. The beginning of a placement is always hectic, particularly when a child first comes into care.

After school on Monday, Tayo had his dental check-up; the dentist said his teeth were fine, very strong and healthy, and needed no fillings. On Tuesday I drove him straight from school to Headline contact centre. Minty was late so I left him with Aisha who was supervising and was also going to bring him home. I came away concerned that Minty hadn't turned up on time: it's such a disappointment for the child if their parents are late or miss contact – they see it as another rejection.

When Aisha returned Tayo at six o'clock she said Minty had been nearly an hour late, which meant that they'd seen each other for only thirty minutes. Tayo, true to form, shrugged off his disappointment and, without being asked, set about his homework.

On Wednesday Lucy returned to college and needed a big prompt to get her out of bed and back into the routine. After school I took Tayo for his optician appointment and his eyesight was fine. At six that evening I had to make the contact phone call to Minty again. With Tayo seated beside me on the sofa, ready to speak to his mother, I keyed in Minty's mobile. Once, twice, three times; on the fourth I passed the phone to Tayo so he could leave a message on her voicemail.

'Hello, Mum,' he said sombrely. 'It's Tayo. Where are you?'

That was all he said and I felt his disappointment and rejection. Why on earth couldn't she be ready with her mobile switched on? It was almost as if she had set him up for being let down, as she was the one who'd requested phone contact in the first place.

'Perhaps she's working,' I said.

Tayo shrugged despondently.

'What exactly does Mum do?'

'She works in a bar. That's all I know.'

'OK. I just wondered.'

We said no more about it.

On Thursday Tayo had his Looked-After Children medical, which had been fast-tracked as he hadn't seen a doctor for so long. All children have a medical when they first came into care but sometimes the paperwork takes months to arrange. Sandra, with her usual efficiency, had made it a priority.

Tayo, unused to doctors, was pretty worried about the whole business, although I'd explained that morning what to expect and that there was nothing to worry about. We arrived for our five-thirty appointment and were asked to sit in the waiting room until a doctor, Dr Page, was ready to see us.

Tayo kept shuffling uncomfortably as we waited. 'Why are those people here?' he whispered, glancing at the man and woman seated opposite.

'They're waiting to see a doctor too,' I said, feeling that I was stating the obvious.

'Will they still be here when I have to take my clothes off?'

I looked at him puzzled. 'I'm not sure I understand …?'

He tutted. 'When I have my medical, you said the doctor will examine me.'

'Yes.'

'So will they still be here watching?'

Then I twigged and I didn't laugh. 'Tayo, this is the waiting room. When it's our turn, we'll be called through to Dr Page's surgery down that corridor. You don't have your medical here!'

He nodded, relieved. Tayo had never been in a doctor's surgery, so he wasn't to know. Five minutes later the receptionist called us through, and Tayo had his medical. For a LAC medical, the doctor receives a ten-page booklet form from the Social Services, which has to be completed. Sandra had attached a note to the form explaining that Tayo had no medical history as it was thought he hadn't been registered with a doctor before.

'And Tayo's been here for five years?' Dr Page asked, unable to believe what he'd read.

'As far as we know, yes.'

'And you've never seen a doctor?' he asked Tayo.

'Once at the hospital when I fell off my bike and banged my head.'

The doctor made a note and then had to write 'unknown' across vast tracts of the form relating to medical history. 'What about immunizations?' he asked.

'Nothing in the last five years,' I said. 'And before that no one knows.'

'I'll recommend that Tayo starts the childhood immunization programme straightaway.'

I nodded. It was a sensible idea. If Tayo was totally unprotected against all the childhood diseases he was very vulnerable. 'We'll need to get a consent form signed by Tayo's social worker or his mother. He's on an interim care order, so I can't sign it,' I said.

Dr Page nodded and made a note.

Tayo's heart, lungs, ears and eyes were fine, as was his height and weight. I mentioned the possible asthma and the doctor said Tayo's chest was clear but if I had any concerns, particularly if he caught a cold which could trigger an asthma attack, to come back straightaway. The doctor saw the scar on Tayo's underarm and I briefly explained that Tayo had caught it in a machine about a year ago and hadn't been to the hospital.

'What sort of machine?' Dr Page asked as he lifted Tayo's arm.

'One for stitching bags,' I said.

'Whatever was he doing near one of those?' He glanced at me.

'Working.' I gave him a significant look that warned him not say anything further while Tayo was with us.

He shook his head with a sad expression, then ran his finger lightly over the scar tissue. Tayo winced. 'Does that hurt?'

'Not really,' he said. 'It's just a bit sensitive.'

'It would be. It's healed but the skin is very thin. Does it cause you a problem?'

Tayo shook his head. Dr Page returned to his desk and wrote on the form, then looked at Tayo. 'When you're older you can have cosmetic surgery on it if you wish, although I understand scars are considered quite macho now.'

Tayo grinned.

Then to me Dr Page said, 'It's obviously tender but it shouldn't open up unless he injures it again. If he does, they'll close it properly at the hospital.' He looked back at Tayo. 'Why didn't you go to the hospital at the time?' he asked.

Tayo shrugged.

The last part of the medical was to examine Tayo's genitals to make sure his testicles had descended and he was developing normally. The doctor asked Tayo to lie on the couch, which was behind a screen to my right.

'I'll wait here,' I said to the doctor. 'As a female carer with a male child, I have to be careful not to compromise myself or embarrass the child.'

He understood. 'That's not a problem as long as I have someone in the room with me.'

It's a sad reflection on our society, I thought, that even a doctor needs a chaperone now.

The rest of the examination was fine and everything was normal. All that was left then was for Tayo to give a urine sample, so we went off towards the toilets, thanking the doctor as we left. Tayo was a tiny bit embarrassed at having to fill the little sample pot but when I explained to him about the laboratory where it would be sent for examination, he grew quite interested.

'I want to be a scientist when I grow up,' he declared as we handed in the sample at reception.

'Well, you're certainly clever enough. All you have to do is work hard, and you can do anything you want. Come on. You've been very good. Let's go home.'

It was Friday already. I was in the car taking Tayo to school that morning and I congratulated him on having had a really good week. 'Football tomorrow,' I said, 'and pocket-money day. Are you going to save or spend it?'

'Save it,' Tayo said, without hesitation. 'For a plane ticket to Nigeria.'

I glanced in the rear-view mirror. 'Would you really like to live in Nigeria?' I asked. 'Or is it because your life in this country has been so bad?'

'I want to go there and live with Dad and Gran like I did before,' he said.

'Do you actually remember living with them, Tayo?' I asked, hoping he might reveal some more details that would help us trace these people.

'Yes. I can just remember it. And I remember I was happy then.'

I glanced at him again in the mirror. 'Can you remember anything else that might help Sandra to trace your dad and gran? Do you know Gran's name? Is she your dad's mother?'

'Yes. I only have one gran. I used to call her Gran – I don't suppose that helps?'

I smiled sadly. 'Not really, sweet. And she never wrote to you in this country? Or phoned?'

'No. She didn't know where I was. Mum took me away when I was at school one day and I never saw Dad or Gran again.

I had to leave behind all my things, and that's what's happened ever since. I don't think Dad knew I was being taken away or he would have helped me.' He stared miserably out of the window.

My heart went out to him. His story had the ring of truth, but how much of his sad tale was what Tayo really remembered, I couldn't know for sure.

Sandra phoned later that Friday morning and I told her what Tayo had said in the car about leaving Nigeria.

'It sounds as though Minty might have snatched him,' I concluded.

'It certainly does,' Sandra agreed. 'But I'm not sure it's going to help. The Nigerian Embassy assured me they have no record of Minty, Tayo, or his dad, whose surname may or may not be Mezer. Not only is Mezer a common name like Brown or Jones here, but people can and do change their surnames. Mezer can also be used as a first name, and you can alternate your first and second names if you want. It's not like here, where everything is well documented and you keep the same surname, unless you marry or change it by deed poll. It's similar in my country – my surname is my grandmother's, not my parents'.'

'I see,' I said, appreciating the explanation, but realizing it was going to be virtually impossible to trace Tayo's family; I felt hugely disappointed on his behalf.

'The Home Office showed even less enthusiasm,' Sandra continued. I could tell she was coming to the end of a particularly difficult and frustrating week. 'They weren't interested in interviewing Minty, even when I said she would be at the

Headline Family Centre on Tuesday and Friday. I find their attitude a bit strange given all the recent figures on illegal immigration.' She paused. 'Now, I've also been in touch with the police with Tayo's account of the sweatshop. I was told that they are aware of such places existing, they've even raided some of them in the past, but unless Tayo knows the exact address they can't even start active surveillance. Do you think there's a chance he might remember the address?'

'He says he never knew it. He might recognize the building if he was taken to the area. It was only a year or so ago, and he's very good at memorizing places and streets, or he has been round here.'

Sandra paused. 'Hmm. Well, it's a thought. I'll run it past my manager and see what she thinks. Would you take Tayo into London if we went ahead?'

'Yes, we could have a day out.'

'OK. Leave it with me. I'll get back to you. Have a good weekend.'

'And you.'

That evening when I took Tayo to contact after school, Minty was already there waiting in Yellow Room.

'Hello,' I said brightly as I went in with Tayo and Aisha. 'How are you, Minty?'

She was sprawled along the sofa, feet up, head resting back, looking absolutely knackered. Her full cleavage and stomach were exposed and she was wearing a flimsy cotton top and short skirt, another outfit completely inappropriate for contact, let alone the cold weather. Again, in dress and attitude Minty wasn't doing herself any favours. She heaved her feet down with a sigh to make room for Tayo on the sofa. He bounded to her side and picked up the remote for the television.

'How are you, son?' she said, ignoring me. It didn't take great insight to realize she was cold-shouldering me today.

'Have a nice time,' I said. 'See you later.' And I left. It was their contact time and there was no requirement for Minty to speak or acknowledge me beyond courtesy.

When Aisha returned Tayo at just gone six, she had been instructed by Minty to tell me that Tayo smelt and to ask why I wasn't letting him have a shower.

'Of course he showers,' I said to Aisha as she stood on the doorstep. Tayo was inside hanging up his coat. 'Every day. And he wears deodorant. He doesn't smell.'

'I know,' Aisha said apologetically. 'But I have to pass it on.'

If parents complain about the care of their child, the person supervising contact usually notes it and mentions it to the carer, acting as go-between. It's an awkward role – they have to be objective while at the same time establishing a good working relationship with parents, so that the child doesn't sense any hostility in the atmosphere during contact.

'And Minty didn't bring in any food,' Aisha continued. 'So Tayo's only had biscuits and a drink. She said she didn't have any money for food.'

'Did Tayo hear that?' I asked.

Aisha nodded.

'That's a pity, I'm trying to help him let go of responsibility for his mother. Now he'll be even more worried.'

'I'll keep an eye on it next time. Sandra told me about the money he gave to his mother.'

'Has he given her any this time?' It didn't seem likely but I thought I should check.

'No. Only a cake he had in his school bag. He said it was from lunch. It was rather squashed.'

'Did she eat it?'

'No.'

'OK, thanks Aisha. I'll try and persuade Tayo not to feel that he has to find food for his mum. He's got football tomorrow. That'll take his mind off it for a while, at least.'

Saturday football repeated the success of the previous week, and when we made the contact phone call to Minty that evening, Tayo managed to tell her a bit about it before she began a diatribe of abuse. This time it was against her most recent landlord who, according to Minty, had thrown her out without reason or warning after three days. She was shouting down the phone so I could hear most of what she said despite Tayo having the phone pressed to his ear.

'I haven't got the fucking money. I told the bastard I'd have him. Bloody sex pervert. Who the hell does he think he is?'

It was always someone else's fault, never Minty's.

After a few minutes of this, Tayo sank lower and lower in his seat, weighed down with his mother's problems. When I took the phone from him, he didn't resist.

'Minty,' I said, over the noise of her tirade. 'Minty. Minty, it's Cathy.'

Eventually she realized Tayo had gone and I was on the line. 'Yes? What do you want?' she demanded.

'Minty, Tayo doesn't need to hear all this, can you please talk about something—'

'Get the fuck off the line, you fucking cow! You've got my fucking son!'

'Minty,' I tried again, but there was only a stream of more abuse, so I hung up.

Tayo looked at me in awe.

'Sorry, Tayo,' I said. 'It wasn't a good phone call and you don't have to listen to that.'

'You're brave,' he said. 'I wouldn't dare do that.'

I suddenly realized that although he'd cared for his mother and looked out for her he was also scared of her. That wasn't surprising – dealing with Minty made me, with all my adult outlook, confidence and experience, feel very uncomfortable. Her volatile, unpredictable and hostile nature made her difficult to be around. It was impossible to know what Minty would do next.

On Sunday I took Adrian back to university and Tayo came along for the ride. He enjoyed the journey and the experience of seeing where Adrian studied.

'I'm going there,' he announced on the way home, impressed and excited by what he'd seen.

'I'm sure you could if you work hard. But there are lots of different universities, and you have to choose one that best suits the subjects you want to study. Adrian goes there because it has a good reputation for engineering which is what he wants to do. Nottingham, on the other hand, is very good for law.'

'I'll go to Nottingham then,' Tayo said. 'I want to study law.'

'Do you? I thought you wanted to be a scientist.'

He thought for a moment. 'No. I think law would be more useful, then I can change everything that's wrong in the world.'

'That's a lovely thought, Tayo,' I said, glancing in the rear-view mirror. 'I wish it were that easy.'

'I can't do it on my own,' he conceded. 'But if everyone makes a little bit of a difference then it will produce a big change over all, won't it?'

I smiled at him in the rear-view mirror. 'I wish more people thought like you. I think that's a philosophy we could all do well to live by. The world's always a better place when people try to do their best for others.'

The coming week would make me realize the truth of that more than ever.

Chapter Fifteen

Threats

'Cathy,' Tayo said at breakfast the following morning. 'What will happen to me?'

I took my coffee and sat opposite him at the table. The girls weren't down yet so it was just the two of us. 'Do you mean about being in care?'

'Yes. I don't think I'll be going back to Mum, will I?'

'It's early days yet, love, we don't know and we won't know yet for a little while. You'll stay here till then.'

He took a bite of toast and thought while he ate it. 'I don't want to live with Mum.'

'All right. The judge will bear that in mind when he makes his decision.'

'I don't want to stay in foster care either,' he said.

My heart sank. This was more difficult. For the moment, he didn't have any choice. 'It's nothing to be embarrassed about; lots of children are in care. And it's far too early to start worrying about it. Try not to look too far ahead.'

He gazed at me. 'I want to go and live with my dad and gran.'

'I understand, sweet. But you lived with them a long time ago, and situations change. The memories you have may not be what things are like now.'

'If my dad knew I was in foster care, he'd come and find me. He'd be furious,' he said solemnly.

'Would he, love?' I felt so sorry for Tayo. It was difficult sometimes for a child to adjust to being in care, particularly an intelligent and thoughtful child like Tayo. Like many children before him, he had built up unrealistic expectations and ideas of an absent parent, seeing him or her as a knight in shining armour, ready to rescue them in a second as soon there was the opportunity. In reality, Tayo had left Nigeria five years ago and neither his father nor his paternal grandmother had contacted him. I didn't want to sound harsh but neither could I let him build up his hopes, only to have them quashed.

I said carefully, 'I've told Sandra everything you've told me about your father and where you lived, but there isn't enough to trace him. There's no way we can track him down with so little information. And you've got to consider the possibility that even if he was found, his life might have changed in the last five years — he might be married with a family and it might not be possible for him to look after you. Once you're an adult, it's different — you can go looking for him if you want. But at the moment, the judge will say you must be looked after while you're a child. If your mum can't do that, you might be in long-term foster care.'

'What — stay here?' he asked.

'Well no, not necessarily. If we get to the point where it looks as though Mum isn't able to look after you, then the Social Services will hold what's called a Family Finders meeting.

They'll think about the best place for you. It might be that they decide this is the best place for you, and your stay becomes what's known as permanency, like Lucy's. Or they might decide you'd be better looked after in a different sort of family, maybe one with two parents so you'd have a father.'

'I've got a father already,' he said adamantly.

'Yes, I know, love, a natural father. But wouldn't it be nice to have someone there all the time, someone who could play football with you, and do all the things that fathers and sons do?' This touched a raw nerve with me. That kind of relationship was something Adrian had missed out on, even though he'd seen his father once a month.

Tayo shrugged despondently and pushed his toast away. 'I don't want another father, I want my own.'

'Look, love, you've only been in care a short while and we've got a long way to go yet. Lots of things can happen, but it's not going to help worrying about them. Trust me. I've seen plenty of children go through this and it all works out in the end.' I kept to myself the thought that while every situation was always resolved, it wasn't always as the children wanted – sadly, children aren't always right about what is best for them. 'Please, Tayo, try not to worry. There are lots of people working with you on this. We all want to see you happy.'

He edged his plate towards him and began eating again. 'But they are trying to find my dad, aren't they?'

'Yes.' It wasn't exactly a lie – Sandra had tried her best but with nothing more to go on, the search was at a dead end. What else could I say to him? 'In the meantime, let's take it a day at a time, and enjoy the little things in life. Time goes so quickly, before you know it, it will be Easter, and I'm hoping we'll all go away for a short holiday.'

'Really?' His eyes finally lit up. 'Where? Africa?'

'No.' I smiled. 'I can't afford that, although it would be nice. Have you ever heard of CenterParcs?'

'Yes. Sam went there for New Year.'

'Did he? Well that's a coincidence. So you know all about it.' I hadn't intended saying anything yet but I'd booked us all in for a five-day break, and if it helped Tayo feel better, he could know now.

'Can I have a bike there?' he asked, excitement sparking in his eyes.

'Of course. We all will.'

'And go swimming, and bowling, and everything else they do?'

'Absolutely! And that's something you can look forward to when you're feeling down, isn't it?'

He nodded, grinning.

I knew I'd have to get Sandra's permission nearer the time to take Tayo, and that she'd have to ask Minty as technically they were both legally responsible for Tayo. I couldn't see a problem though; social workers appreciate foster children taking full advantage of any new experiences, and his mother was hardly likely to object to her son being taken on an all-expenses-paid holiday, was she?

The house was quiet with everyone at school, and I was wondering if I should try my hand at another Italian recipe after the success of the last one, when the phone rang.

I went through to the lounge and answered it. 'Hello?'

There was silence.

'Hello?' I tried again.

More silence. The line was open, someone was on the other end. 'Hello? Who is it? Is someone there? If there is, I can't hear you.'

Nothing. So I hung up.

I pressed 1471 but the caller had withheld their number. Nothing unusual in that, many people keep their telephone number private to stop canvassing calls from companies. I had a permanent block on my number coming up because of the contact phone calls the foster children made.

I waited by the phone for a moment in case someone was having difficulty getting through, in which case they would probably try again straightaway. They didn't, so I returned to the kitchen and the recipe book I'd left open on the table. I'd hardly got back when the phone started ringing again; I hurried back.

'Hello?'

Nothing, but the line was open.

'Hello?' There was still no answer, so I hung up. Before I had reached the kitchen, it rang again.

'Yes?' I said, snatching it up as I got to it.

'Mrs Glass?' It was a deep male voice with a heavy East End accent.

'Speaking.'

He cleared his throat. 'You have Minty's son.' It was said as a statement rather than a question although he waited for a reply. I wasn't about to divulge details to a stranger.

'Who is this?' I asked.

He ignored my question. 'This is a warning,' he said. 'If you know what's good for you, you'd better do as I say. Do not make up lies about Minty, you'll be sorry if you do. She has friends and we know where you live. You have a nice family, keep it that way. Make sure Tayo goes back to her.'

Before I could say anything he'd hung up.

I sat down heavily on the sofa and slowly replaced the receiver. My heart was pounding and I suddenly felt cold. What he'd said didn't need any explanation – he was clearly threatening me and my family. *You have a nice family.* How did he know? Were he and Minty watching us? But how did they get the address? It was surely too early in the proceedings for Social Services to have sent documents to Minty, which was how in the past parents had sometimes acquired my address when they weren't supposed to. Apart from that, Sandra didn't have an address for Minty to send documents to. Perhaps this thug didn't know where we lived and it was a bluff to frighten me. But – I turned even colder – he knew my telephone number. How had he got that?

My stomach tightened and my throat went dry as my usual calm demeanour vanished. At contact, Minty had threatened me with her 'friends'; I'd brushed it off as bravado but she had clearly kept her word.

My mind raced as I started to think through all the ramifications of this threat. As well as the immediate worry about the safety of my family and myself, there were dire implications for Tayo. If Minty knew the address, then there was a good chance Sandra would want to remove Tayo and place him with other carers, which would be terrible for his stability. He'd had

so many moves in the past, the last thing
uprooted again.

With all these thoughts chasing round in
up the phone and dialled Sandra's extension.
was at her desk and I quickly explained what h

Sandra, normally so calm and contained, swo.
'That's all we need. Are you sure your telephone nu
show up when you dial out?'

'Positive. I've got a permanent block on it. Chec
phone display.'

'Yes, you're right, it's anonymous,' she said. 'So how t
have they got it?'

'I take it my contact details couldn't have gone out on pa
work from your end?'

'No documents have left the office, apart from the ICO an
that certainly didn't have your address on it. Anyway, I still
haven't got an address for Minty. Remind me who placed
Tayo?'

'Brian Williams,' I said.

'I doubt he's let it slip but I'll check. Hold the line, Cathy,
his manager is across the office.'

I waited as the phone was put down. It was Brian who had
originally told me Minty wouldn't be given the address of
where Tayo was staying, but with the best will in the world,
mistakes happen, especially with all the endless chasing
around that goes on in these cases.

'Cathy?' Sandra said returning to the phone.

'Yes?'

'Binta is certain Brian knew not to give it out.'

'So how's it happened?' I asked lamely.

andra paused and then asked, 'I've just thought, is your
phone number on any of your phones?'

'No.'

'Not even handwritten on those little bits of plastic-covered
ardboard?'

'No. I've never used them and we haven't got digital display
phones.'

'It's just the only person I can think of who might have given
Minty the number is Tayo. Do you think he found it somewhere and told her?'

I thought. 'It's possible, I suppose. But why would he want
to do that?'

'I've no idea. I'm just trying to think how it's happened.'

I tried to think of a time and place when Tayo could have had
access to my telephone number. 'I really don't know, Sandra,
we're pretty careful. My children know our contact details
mustn't be given out.'

'I think we need to have a chat with Tayo and see if he knows
anything about it. This is serious. Are you collecting him from
school at the normal time this afternoon?'

'Yes. Three-fifteen.'

'Can I come to you at four then?'

'Yes, of course.' I was pleased Sandra was treating the
matter so seriously and as a priority. When my address had
been inadvertently divulged before, the social worker had had
a very cavalier attitude, and said the parents probably wouldn't
turn up and if they did I was to send them away.

'Don't say anything to Tayo about why I'm coming,'
Sandra added. 'I don't want him to be on his guard. We've
seen how smart he can be at bending the truth, so if he is

responsible, the less time he has to invent something, the better.'

'No problem. I won't say a word.'

'And, Cathy, I'm sure what the man said was just an idle threat, but be careful for now. Mum has lived underground for a long time and doubtless knows plenty of undesirables – these so-called friends of hers.'

'Yes, I was thinking the same thing.'

'I'll see you at four then. And I'm so sorry this has happened.'

'It's not your fault,' I said. 'Thanks for everything, Sandra. See you later.'

I'd lost enthusiasm for cooking an Italian meal, so I took something out of the freezer instead. I checked the back door was locked and then went to the front room where I looked out of the bay windows, up and down the street.

If that man had my address then he could be watching right now. I had to take this very seriously. I'd had threats before from emotional parents at contact and meetings, but they'd been the vague 'you'd better watch out' kind of warnings with no real substance or intention, and there'd always been a social worker or a security guard present. This was different. I had no idea who this man was, except that he sounded like exactly the kind of person Minty could have associated with.

I felt another chill of fear. This threat was very real. His words about my 'nice family' still rang in my ears; the implicit suggestion was that, unless I did as instructed, my children wouldn't stay 'nice' for long. Images of Paula and Lucy being slashed with a razor flashed across my mind. They were vulnerable, walking to and from school and college, and we didn't even have Adrian here with us now … what if someone burst in while we were here in the evening? What if they were armed …? I quickly stopped myself; I had to keep calm.

Tayo's future with us certainly didn't look good. If Minty and her 'friends' did have my address, then I couldn't risk our safety by continuing to look after him. I shouldn't have anything to fear – after all, I'd only ever told the truth and would continue to do so. It was completely outside my powers to ensure Tayo was returned to his mother even if I wanted to. I had no clout. I simply recorded what Tayo said about his past, and his telephone conversations with his mother. Was I being asked to doctor what Tayo said or fictionalise his phone calls to Minty so that he could go back to her? It was ridiculous.

But this was no joke. If Minty had my address, then I would be locking doors and windows at all times, looking over my shoulder every few minutes when I left the house, and taking Lucy and Paula to college and school in the car, never letting them out of my sight. And, much as I hated the idea, Tayo would have to be moved, and quickly, for all our sakes.

I couldn't settle that afternoon. I was half expecting the phone to ring again with more threats. I was on edge the whole time. When the letterbox snapped shut as a flyer was delivered, I nearly jumped out of my skin. Before I left the house that afternoon to collect Tayo from school, I propped a big note on the hall table:

PAULA
DON'T ANSWER THE DOOR.
WILL EXPLAIN LATER
LOVE MUM x

Paula would be in from school first and alone in the house before I returned with Tayo, and I didn't want to take any chances.

I opened the front door, glanced up and down the virtually empty street, then Chubb-locked the door and got straight in my car, which was parked on the driveway. After locking it from the inside, I reversed out. I looked up and down the street again as I pulled away, then checked in my rear-view mirror that I wasn't being followed. As far as I could see, it was all clear.

With a sad and heavy heart, I went into the school to collect Tayo from his classroom. He was ready and waiting, and Mrs Gillings said he'd had an excellent day.

It's just a shame it won't end the same way, I thought, but said only, 'That's good. Your social worker is coming at four, so we'd better hurry.'

Tayo didn't ask any questions. He knew Sandra would be paying regular visits and I guess he assumed this was one of them.

Five minutes later, when he noticed I wasn't my usual chatty self, he asked, 'Are you OK, Cathy?'

'I'm a bit preoccupied,' I said and left it at that. Not only was I thinking about the conversation Sandra, Tayo and I would have shortly and its repercussions for Tayo's future with us, I was also keeping a watchful eye in my mirrors. Minty knew where Tayo went to school, as it was the same one he'd attended when he'd last lived with her, so the threat from her 'friend' would just as easily apply on the school run as at home. It would be a simple matter to follow me home. But the car behind me had changed twice since I'd left the school so I didn't think we were being followed.

It was three forty-five when we arrived home and Paula was already in and had removed the note from the hall table. While Tayo took off his coat and shoes, I went up to Paula's room to tell her that Tayo's mother had somehow found out our contact details and that his social worker was coming at four. I wasn't going to scare her with details of the threat until I knew more from Sandra about what precautions would need to be put in place.

'If the phone rings while she's here, I'll answer it,' I said. 'I'm expecting a call,' I added, seeing Paula's surprised expression. I usually asked not to be interrupted when social workers were here.

Sandra arrived at ten past four. Tayo had had a drink and a snack and was reading Harry Potter in the lounge.

'All right?' Sandra asked me as she came in. 'No more phone calls?'

'No. Tayo's in there.' I nodded to the lounge so that Sandra was aware he was within earshot.'

'I think we'll go straight through then.'

'Do you want a drink?' I asked her.

'No, thanks. Let's get on with it.' She walked swiftly down the hall and I could tell she thought Tayo was responsible and that she would quickly get to the bottom of it. 'Hello, Tayo,' she said as she entered the lounge. 'How are you?'

He looked up from his book. 'Fine, thank you.'

Sandra and I sat down just as the phone started ringing. We exchanged a pointed glance and I reached over to answer it. We both looked at Tayo, wondering if he had knowledge of the possible caller, but he looked back innocently.

'Hello?' I said. My heart gave a couple of loud thumps of anxiety, but I felt slightly reassured now that Sandra was with me.

'Cathy.'

'Hi, Jill.' I breathed a sigh of relief. I saw Sandra relax too.

'I'm back at work part time,' Jill said. 'And you're on my list of people to phone. How's the new placement going?'

Until today, I would have said good. 'Look, Jill, I've got Tayo and his social worker here now. Can I call you back later?'

'Of course. Hope it's not too bad. I'll be in the office until six.'

'OK. If we haven't finished by then I'll call you tomorrow.'

'Fine. Speak later.'

'Jill's my link worker,' I said to Sandra.

She nodded. Tayo was still sitting happily on the sofa, his book now closed, looking expectantly at Sandra.

'How's school?' she asked him.

'Good.' He smiled.

'Are you getting all your homework done?'

'Yes.' He looked at me for confirmation.

'Tayo's been doing very nicely,' I said.

'Excellent. Well done.' Sandra twiddled at her little finger and I could tell she felt as uncomfortable as I did about what she had to say.

'Tayo,' she began, direct and forthright, looking straight at him, 'we've got a problem. A rather big one. And I need to ask you about it.'

His eyes widened to that practised childlike innocence and I knew then that he felt guilty about something, though, of course, it could be unrelated to what Sandra was about to say.

'You remember when you first came here,' Sandra continued, 'and Brian brought you in the car?' Tayo nodded. 'Do you remember Brian saying to you that your mother wouldn't have the address or telephone number of where you were saying?' Tayo nodded again. 'I understand you asked Brian if your mum would be visiting you here at Cathy's, and Brian explained that it had been decided it would be better if she didn't.'

Clearly Sandra had spoken to Brian since our telephone conversation and had all the details to hand.

'We made that decision,' Sandra went on, 'for very good reasons. Your mother was told you were in the area and being well looked after. That was all she needed to know.' Tayo nodded again. I watched him carefully for any change in expression, but there was none. He continued to look at her, interested and expectant, maintaining his wide-eyed innocence. 'Unfortunately it seems that your mother has somehow found out where you are, and I'd like you to think carefully and tell me if you have any idea how it happened.'

'She knows my address?' he asked, surprised.

Sandra nodded. 'And the telephone number.'

Tayo opened his mouth as if to speak and then closed it again quickly.

'Yes?' Sandra said. 'Have you thought of something?'

Tayo looked from one of us to the other. Clearly he had thought of something and his brain was working overtime on the gap between what he'd thought of and what he was going to say.

'I need to know,' Sandra said firmly. 'This is important and serious.'

Tayo thought some more and then appeared to choose his words very carefully. 'I don't know how she found out about the address,' he said slowly.

'No?' Sandra asked.

'I didn't tell her, honestly. I didn't tell her the address.' His voice had risen to protest his innocence, but Sandra and I had both noticed he had omitted to mention the telephone number.

'Did you tell your mother the telephone number here?' Sandra asked. 'Please be honest, it's very important that we know the truth.'

Again, he looked between us, then settled his gaze on me. 'Yes,' he said in a small voice, 'but only the telephone number.'

'Are you certain of that, Tayo?' Sandra asked.

'Yes. Honestly. I don't even know the address.'

Sandra said what I was thinking. 'I'm sure you do know the address. This house has the number on the door, and the street name is on a sign at the end of the road. You know which town you're living in because you've been in the area for some time. You're a bright boy, Tayo, and I'm sure it wouldn't be too difficult for you to put all of these together and come up with an address.'

Tayo shrugged, unable to deny it. It was clear to all of us that he would have guessed the address at once. 'But I didn't give it to her, I promise,' he said.

Even though Tayo had been less than honest in the past, I started to believe him and I thought that Sandra did too.

'So how did she find out?' Sandra asked.

'I don't know. Really, I don't. Why? Has she been here?'

'No. But Cathy received a phone call today, a threatening phone call, from a man who said he was a friend of your mother's.' Tayo visibly paled. 'It was not a nice phone call and it shouldn't have happened. That's why we make the decisions we do – to keep everyone safe.'

I could see that Tayo was now as anxious as I had been, although I was now feeling a good deal better since hearing that he hadn't passed on the address.

'I gave her the phone number,' he said. 'But I didn't give her the address. Even if I knew it I wouldn't. I don't want her and her friends coming here. Really I don't.'

Sandra looked at him. 'I hope you're telling the truth, Tayo.' But I could see she believed him as well.

'Yes I am, honestly,' he said. 'I am, Cathy, cross my heart and hope to die.'

'OK, Tayo,' Sandra said. 'So why did you tell your mother the telephone number when you knew she wasn't supposed to have it?'

He lowered his gaze for the first time. I knew Tayo well enough to see he was genuinely embarrassed, upset, and even remorseful for what he had done. 'She made me,' he said at last.

'How?' Sandra asked. 'She's not here.'

Tayo looked up. 'At contact. She said she had to have it.'

Sandra and I exchanged a glance, and Sandra said, 'Aisha is with you at contact, Tayo, and she didn't mention it in her report. I read them very carefully.'

'When we were in the kitchen on Tuesday last week,' he said. 'Mum was late because she'd bought sausages and chips for tea and we heated them in the microwave. Aisha went to the toilet while we were in the kitchen, that's when Mum said I had to find out and tell her Cathy's telephone number. She gets very angry and upset if I don't do what she says. So I found out and told her on Friday at contact. I wrote it down and gave it to her so Aisha wouldn't know.'

It seemed that Aisha, an experienced contact supervisor, hadn't anticipated quite how devious and manipulative Minty could be when it came to her son.

'Did your mother ask you to find out the address as well?' Sandra asked.

He nodded. 'But I didn't give it, honestly. I didn't want her friends coming here. I like it at Cathy's, I've got food and clothes and my own room, and it's safe, away from all that lot.' He began to cry.

I was sure they were genuine tears of fear and remorse so I immediately went over, sat beside him and rubbed his shoulder lightly. I looked at Sandra who clearly agreed with me.

'All right, Tayo,' she said. 'Don't worry. If you haven't given your mum the address we'll assume she hasn't got it, so you're still safe here. I shall be speaking to her tomorrow, after contact. I'll also speak to Aisha to make sure you're not left unsupervised again, although I'm not blaming Aisha. You're a big lad for your age, Tayo, and I think you could have walked away from your mum if she was demanding the number, or maybe even made up a telephone number. I'm sure you could have done that if you'd thought about it. Sometimes you're good at making up things.'

I wondered if this was a bit harsh as Tayo was still crying, but I was leaving it to Sandra to deal with and so far she had done a very good job at getting to the truth.

I passed him the box of tissues. He blew his nose. 'If I'd lied to her she would have found out,' he said. 'And then I'd be in for it at the next contact. She scares me when she's in a mood. She shouts and screams and hits people.'

That was true enough; I'd witnessed it firsthand at the placement meeting.

'Did she hit you?' Sandra asked.

'Sometimes,' he said glumly, 'when she'd been drinking.'

'As I said, Tayo, I'll make sure you're not left alone with her, not even for a second. All right?'

Tayo sniffed and nodded.

'Now dry your eyes, love,' I said. 'There's nothing to be worried about.' I could say that now I knew that Minty and her 'friends' didn't have my address, but it had been a different matter half an hour ago when I'd felt Tayo's fear of what his mother and her associates were capable of.

Sandra smiled. 'Tayo, one more question before I go, and I know Cathy wants to hear the answer to this as much as I do. A truthful answer please.' Tayo looked from one of us to the other and nodded. 'How did you get Cathy's telephone number? She never says it when she answers the phone, and it's not on any of the handsets.'

'I heard her say it in the car on Thursday,' he said, without hesitation. 'Her mobile went off and I didn't know who she was talking to, but she said, "Would you call the landline when I have my diary to hand, please." Then she gave the number and I remembered it.'

'What? Eleven digits?' Sandra asked. 'I doubt I could remember eleven digits after hearing them once.'

'I knew the first five already,' Tayo said. 'It's the area code, so I just had to remember the last six.' And to prove it he rattled them off.

I looked at Sandra and nodded, then added dryly, 'Tayo's good with numbers. His maths is excellent.'

'Obviously,' Sandra said.

With a final warning to Tayo about not releasing the address to his mother, Sandra asked Tayo to read his book in another room so she could talk to me. He went out and I closed the door. We both had smiles on our faces, a mixture of relief that my address was safe and Tayo wouldn't have to be moved, and also an acknowledgement that Tayo was a pretty smart cookie.

'I'll have to go shortly,' Sandra said. 'I've got another child to see who's been up to mischief.' I glanced at the carriage clock, it was after five. Sandra worked well beyond the call of duty. 'I'll speak to Aisha first thing in the morning and make sure Mum can't get at Tayo again. I also won't pull any punches with Minty when I see her. If there's another phone call like the one this afternoon I'll have her arrested for harassment. Hopefully there won't be after I've warned her. I'll take a security guard with me to emphasize the point. Are you happy about continuing the placement?'

'Yes. I'm pleased we can.'

'Thanks. Just be a bit careful with answering the phone until I've had a chance to see Minty tomorrow.' I nodded. She stood ready to leave. 'The phone contact Tayo is having with Minty – are you able to put it on speaker phone?'

'Yes.'

'Do it then, please, from this Wednesday, I'll have to tell her we're doing it, and I'll make it clear why, when I see her tomorrow.'

'No problem.' I walked with her to the front door.

'Thanks for all you're doing,' she said. Then she called, 'Bye, Tayo.'

A small and chastened voice replied from his bedroom. 'Bye, Sandra. Sorry.'

We said goodbye and she went off into the night.

Tayo was very quiet and, apart from coming down to eat, stayed in his room all evening.

'Don't worry,' I said, as I kissed him goodnight. 'We all make mistakes.'

He nodded, managed a smile, and then pointed to his forehead for another kiss.

'Two?' I said with a smile.

'It's to make up for all the ones I didn't have before I came here,' he said. 'D'you know, Cathy, my mum never kissed me goodnight. But my gran used to, I remember.'

'That's a nice memory then, isn't it?' I said and gave him the second kiss on his forehead. 'Goodnight, sleep tight.'

'And don't let the bed bugs bite.'

I came out and closed the bedroom door. Could Tayo really remember his gran kissing him? Or was it a made-up memory

– a snapshot from the album of a perfect childhood he'd never had?

I thought of the mother who never kissed her son goodnight, and went downstairs.

Chapter Sixteen

Hidden Children

Although our address appeared to be safe, I still looked both ways, up and down the street, as I left the house the following morning to take Tayo to school. It was all clear, and there had been no threatening phone calls so I was starting to relax.

Tayo had obviously been thinking along the same lines because once we were in the car, he said, 'I'm so pleased Mum's friends can't come to the house.'

'Me too,' I agreed, as I concentrated on starting the car and turning on the heating. There had been a heavy frost during the night.

'Most of her friends were horrible,' he went on. 'They were horrible to me. I don't know what she sees in them.'

I sat with the engine running as the lines of melted frost slowly etched their way across the windscreen. 'How were they horrible, Tayo?'

'They used to get drunk and shout at her and me. Sometimes they walloped me or told me to get the fuck out. So I had to leave the room. They used to hit her as well.'

'This was when you were staying in rented bedsits? Not with families like the one you stayed with over Christmas?'

'No, they were proper friends – well, Mum didn't really know them, but they were nice to me. If I stayed with families they were nice; it was all the others, the men.'

'Were your mum's friends all men?' I asked. Tayo was clearly in the mood for talking and I'd have to make a note of all this in my log when I returned home.

'Yes,' he said. 'She never had any women friends that I knew.'

'They don't sound much like friends to me. How long had she known these men?'

'Not long. She'd go out at night and bring one back, sometimes more than one. Different men, sometimes three a week. They'd bring loads of booze with them and start drinking and laughing and then shouting and hitting each other. Sometimes they were still there in the morning. I hated that. They were in a right bad mood and would swear, and then have a go at me.'

I flipped the windscreen wipers to clear the melted frost. 'What do you mean by "have a go" at you?'

'You know – ask me what the fuck I was looking at and then belt me round the ear.'

'Where was Mum?'

'In bed, asleep, with a hangover. She never gets up until the afternoon.'

I turned to face Tayo. 'Did any of these men try and touch you in a sexual way?' It was a direct question but Tayo was old enough and intelligent enough to know what I meant and give a direct answer.

'No, not really. Well, one wanted to come in the bathroom with me and watch me pee. But I locked the door each time

I went. He was there for a week, drunken pervert. Another kept trying to stroke my leg when we sat on the sofa but I got up and went out.'

'But no one actually molested you?'

'No. I'd have kicked him where it hurt.'

Thank goodness, I thought, at least Tayo had escaped the added trauma of sexual abuse, apparently because of his intelligence and quick thinking. I put the car into gear and pulled out of the drive.

'They were mostly ex-cons,' Tayo continued, looking out of the side window as I drove slowly down the frost-heavy road. 'They used to brag about what they'd been banged up for, banged up means going to prison.' I nodded. 'Some of them carried knives. They'd flash them around when they got drunk or high. They thought they looked big.'

'High on what?'

'Drugs. You know, they'd either inject it or sniff it, crack mainly, I think. One bloke, John, even had a gun. It was loaded, he showed me the bullets and kept pointing it at me. He was laughing because I was scared, Mum laughed too, but I didn't think it was funny. When he passed out from the booze, I thought about taking it from his pocket and shooting him. But I didn't want to get banged up too.'

'That was sensible,' I said, struggling to picture this underworld existence of drink and drug-fuelled violence. Tayo's loyalty to his mother was quickly evaporating and his anger was showing through. Was that because Tayo recognized that, by passing our telephone number to one of these men, his mother had jeopardized his safety yet again? Perhaps the idea of being sent back to her was too terrible to contemplate now that he'd lived another, safer and more secure life for a while.

And how many other children, I wondered, were living in this twilight zone that Tayo described, struggling on, in a hand-to-mouth existence, fending off advances, party to things that the average person only ever saw depicted on late-night television? If there was no record of these children entering or being in the country, and they weren't on any medical, education, or Social Services databases, they were completely hidden; no one could help them because no one knew they even existed.

'Can you remember a time when you lived in this country and things were normal with you and your mum?' I asked.

'No. It was always like that – moving, stealing food from shops, Mum going out at night and bringing back drunken blokes. It was only with the families when things were normal, nice, like they were with my dad and gran. I wish I was still with my dad and gran, they were the happiest days of my life.'

I met his gaze in the rear-view mirror and smiled an acknowledgement. 'I hope you're happy now, Tayo,' I said. 'I know it's not easy but as you said to Sandra yesterday, you've got plenty of food and clothes, your own room, and you know you're safe.'

'Oh yes,' he said. 'I don't mean to be ungrateful. And I like football too. I just wish I was with my dad.'

'You don't have to be grateful, you're only getting what you should have had all along.' Again I marvelled at the huge gap between the person Tayo was now, and what he could have become, living that existence for five years. I admired his character and his tenacity. He'd been determined not to be destroyed by what was happening to him, and he'd succeeded. It was his victory.

The phone rang three times during the afternoon and each time I answered I was on edge, aware that Sandra wouldn't have spoken to Minty yet. But I needn't have worried. The first call was from the Guardian Ad Litum, appointed by the court to represent the child's interests for the duration of the case. This was her first contact and she asked how Tayo had settled in, then said she wanted to come and see us. I fetched my diary and we agreed on Thursday at four. Her name was Alison Hemming-Sanders, which I thought was a bit of a mouthful. She said she hadn't had a chance to read Tayo's file yet but hoped to have done so by then. I hoped so too.

The second phone call was from Jill, checking that everything was running smoothly between her visits. As I was an experienced foster carer she knew that I could be left to get on with it, and that I would ask for help and advice if I needed it. I updated her and then fetched my diary and penned in the day of her next visit.

Jill hadn't long been off the line when Sandra rang to confirm that she had spoken to Aisha at the Headline Family Centre, and that Aisha would be extremely vigilant in future and was sorry for what had happened. Sandra, with her usual efficiency, had also spoken to the Head at Meadway school and asked them to be vigilant too, as Tayo could be approached by one of his mum's associates or even snatched.

'I'll be at contact tonight to see Minty – but don't tell Tayo,' Sandra said. 'It's best if he doesn't know in case he feels he has to warn his mother. She's already avoiding my calls.'

'I'm not so sure he would do that,' I replied. 'He's quickly losing his loyalty to her.' I told her what he'd said to me in the car about his life with his mother.

'We're starting to build up a picture,' Sandra said. 'If only Minty would overcome her hostility and start talking to me, I might be able to help her, but I can't until she does.'

'No,' I agreed. I told her that the Guardian had been in touch and was visiting later that week.

'Good. And, Cathy, I've asked my manager about Tayo going to have a look at the area where he thought he worked in London, but she's not keen.'

'Oh?'

'She feels it would be too unsettling for him especially when it might not lead to anything. So I'm afraid it means we can't take this aspect of the investigation into his past any further. And without an address the police can't act.'

'I understand,' I said.

'I'm disappointed.'

'So am I. I won't tell Tayo. He's hoping something will be done to rescue his friends.' I had to accept the decision of Social Services, although I wasn't convinced it was the right one. I'd have thought having his disclosures acted on would have given Tayo a boost even if it didn't come to anything.

'I'll be in touch later then, Cathy, after I've seen Minty,' said Sandra.

'OK. Thanks.'

* * *

I collected Tayo as usual from school and took him to the contact centre. I was relishing the prospect of seeing Minty even less than usual. Not only was I fast losing all sympathy for her plight as a mother, but the threats she'd issued had been terrifying, and her attitude towards me had obviously become personal and vindictive. I was determined not to show her that I was afraid, though. Bullies, for that was what she undoubtedly was, thrive on seeing their victims scared.

Tayo chatted about school and football during the twenty-minute journey but when we turned into the road to the Headline Family Centre, he fell silent.

'I hope my mum isn't too angry about me snitching on her,' he said.

'It wasn't snitching, Tayo, you did what was right. You know that it was your mother who was in the wrong. Aisha will be keeping a watchful eye from now on, so if your mum does try and say anything like that to you, Aisha will stop her.' And anyway, I thought grimly, Minty doesn't yet know she's been caught out.

Tayo was still subdued as we got out of the car and went through the security gate and into reception. James, the centre manager, was waiting for us. 'Hello, Tayo, Cathy,' he said brightly. 'How are you?'

'Fine, thanks,' I said.

Tayo looked at him and nodded.

'Mum's here with Aisha. You're in Blue Room today, Tayo. I'll show you through.'

We followed James down the short corridor and stopped outside the blue door. James knocked and opened it. 'Tayo's here,' he said.

We followed him in, Minty was already on her feet coming towards us, or rather towards James. 'Why did you put us in here?' she demanded.

I looked about. Blue Room was smaller than Yellow, but was still well equipped with a sofa, television, small table, three chairs, and plenty of games, toys and books.

'As I said earlier, Minty,' James said patiently, 'Yellow Room is needed for a large family today. This is fine for the two of you.'

Minty's eyes flashed with anger and her face set. This was obviously an argument that had begun earlier.

'Well? I'm waiting!' Minty shouted, clearly unmoved by James's explanation.

'Don't, Mum,' implored Tayo.

Her eyes flashed again, then her gaze fell on me.

I smiled. 'Hello, Minty, how are you?' My voice was light and even.

'I'm good. Thank you for asking, Cathy.' She smiled back. 'And I'd be a damn sight better if these bastards stopped pissing me around, wouldn't I?' She glared at James.

I said nothing. James was evidently the object of Minty's wrath today; perhaps he'd be getting a nasty phone call later instead of me.

'Minty,' James said, 'as I explained when you first came in, I can't guarantee the same room each time. I do my best to keep change to a minimum but I can't promise any more than that.'

She rolled her eyes upwards.

'Mum!' Tayo said again and went towards the sofa. I headed for the door.

'Everything all right?' James asked Aisha, who was sitting at the table with her notebook in front of her. She nodded. 'I'm in my office if you need me.'

Without further ado we came out and James closed the door. He hovered outside for a moment, looking through the glass panel to make sure Minty didn't turn and vent her anger on Aisha, while I continued down the corridor, through reception and let myself out.

Does Minty have mental health problems? I wondered as I headed for the car. She wouldn't be the first parent I'd met who had done themselves real damage with drug and alcohol abuse. Those chemicals attacked the brain and central nervous system, and I remembered reading that excessive and long-term substance abuse could lead to irreversible brain damage. Minty's ability to function as a person and as a parent would be assessed as part of the court proceedings when she would spend about six sessions with a psychiatrist. From what I'd seen so far, I wasn't very convinced of a positive outcome.

Back home I prepared dinner for the girls and myself, making sure there was extra in case Minty didn't bring Tayo's dinner into contact. It hadn't seemed prudent for me to ask her when I'd seen her.

Tayo was returned by Aisha at six, and he was in very good spirits. 'I saw Sandra,' he said, as he bounced in. 'She came at the end of contact, and she had the biggest bodyguard you've ever seen! He was massive. Over seven feet tall! With huge muscles, and body armour, and a great big motorbike! I'm going to be a bodyguard when I grow up!'

'Are you?' I said, and smiled at Aisha. 'This morning he wanted to be a lawyer.'

'Our security guard isn't quite seven feet tall — more like six feet two,' she said with a grin. 'Sandra is with Minty now.' As Tayo disappeared down the hall, she added, 'Minty was very confused again. At first I thought she might be drunk, but there was no smell of alcohol and she seemed more bewildered than intoxicated.'

'I'm beginning to wonder if confusion and temper aren't just her normal state,' I said unkindly.

'I'm so sorry for what happened with your telephone number,' said Aisha, reddening. 'I didn't leave them unattended even for a second today, and noted down everything Minty said.'

'Don't worry about it,' I reassured. 'It was OK in the end.'

'Minty wanted to play noughts and crosses at one point, but when I sat so that I could see what was being written, she suddenly lost interest.'

'Do you think she was trying to exchange written messages with Tayo?' I asked.

'I'm sure of it. But apart from that, Tayo spent most of the time watching television. Oh yes — Minty didn't bring any food again, so Tayo hasn't eaten.'

I thanked Aisha for bringing Tayo home, wished her a pleasant evening and went inside. When I served dinner for the four of us, Tayo said, 'How did you know my mum hadn't brought food in?'

'I didn't,' I said, 'but I'll always do extra just in case. Don't worry, you won't ever go hungry here.'

'I know that now,' he said.

* * *

At nearly half past seven in the evening, with the meal finished, and Lucy, Paula and Tayo ensconced in their bedrooms doing their homework, the phone rang.

It was Sandra, and I could tell immediately something was wrong. Her voice quivered unsteadily and normally she was so calm and composed.

'I've only just got away from Minty,' she said breathlessly. 'I thought she was going to hit me!'

I could hear background noise and knew she wasn't in the contact centre. 'Where are you?'

'On the bus. Going home. She waited for me after we'd finished, round the corner from Headline.'

'What? Are you OK?' The idea of Minty lying in wait for me was terrifying. No wonder Sandra was in a state.

Her voice quivered again. 'Yes, thank God she didn't follow me onto the bus.' I heard her take a deep breath. 'We didn't finish at Headline until nearly seven. Minty left first, in a rage. I waited until she'd gone, then dismissed the security guard and left. When I turned the corner and started walking towards the bus stop, she appeared from nowhere. She was so angry, Cathy, and there was no one around. She kept screaming at me, ranting and raging and making no sense at all. I tried to calm her, but it was hopeless, she just wouldn't listen, so I started walking away. I got all the way down Pallin Road with her a few steps behind screaming obscenities.'

Pallin Road, where Headline was situated, was a quiet and secluded side road. The only other building was a block of council-owned retirement flats, whose occupants were hardly likely to venture out and intervene if they heard a disturbance.

'I kept trying to calm her down,' Sandra went on, 'but she wouldn't listen. I threatened to call the police a number of times, but it was only when I actually dialled the number that she backed off, so I cancelled the call and got to the bus stop with her following a short way behind. I could hear her talking to herself non-stop, some of it was about me and what she was going to do, but a lot of it was gibberish. She waited about five yards from me while I was at the bus stop. She was watching me the whole time, and her mouth kept moving as if she was talking to herself. I decided that if she followed me onto the bus I would have to call the police again, but she didn't, thank goodness.' Sandra gave a heartfelt sigh, relieved to have unburdened herself. 'It was the weirdest thing,' she said. 'And I'll admit I was frightened. I've obviously dealt with angry parents before but this was something else – she seemed deranged. If I have to see Minty again at Headline, I'll leave by taxi and have the security guard see me to it. Sorry, Cathy,' she said, at last recovering from her ordeal, 'I'm in a bit of a state. I couldn't think of anyone to call at this time.'

'Don't worry,' I said. 'As long as you're safe. So how did the actual meeting go?'

'Minty wasn't so angry to begin with, but I had Bob the security guard with me then. She was very confused though, and kept starting sentences but not finishing them. I tried to explain I wanted to help her but she kept saying I'd be sorry for taking Tayo. She wouldn't give me her contact details even when I explained it was so I could send the paperwork, and also for her assessment. She said she was staying with friends and it was none of my effing business. I can't assess her with no home address, and if she's not assessed then there's no way she'll get Tayo back.'

I knew Sandra meant the assessment she would be doing, which was separate from the assessment the psychiatrist would make. The social workers focused on Minty's home life and whether she could provide a stable and suitable environment for a child of ten.

'I hadn't said anything to her at this point about the telephone call,' Sandra continued. 'I'd left it until the end in the hope that I'd have won her trust and cooperation, but there was no chance. I asked her about Tayo's father and pointed out if he could be found, and if he was willing, he could also be assessed with a view to looking after Tayo. I didn't tell her that Tayo had said he wanted to live with him – I thought that would incite her further. She said it was none of his effing business and he wouldn't be interested in Tayo anyway.' Sandra paused. 'Yet I had the feeling that she thought if he knew Tayo was in care, he would be angry with her, which suggests there was a relationship between Tayo and his father.'

'Tayo said the same thing – that if his father knew he was in care he'd be furious.'

'Yes, I saw it in your report, but as there's no way of finding his father I can't explore that avenue any further, unfortunately. I finally told Minty about the phone call and warned her off. She was livid, as you can imagine. First she denied getting the number from Tayo and passing it on, then she said she could phone who she effing well liked. However I did manage to get her to hear that if it happened again I'd have her arrested and stop her from seeing Tayo. She screamed at me that I couldn't do that. So I said I could, and to watch me. She stormed out, screaming obscenities, so I suppose I should have guessed she might have been waiting for me. God, Cathy. She was so angry, I've never seen anything like it, her face was crimson and her eyes bulged.'

'She's a very frightening person when she loses control. I know Tayo's been very scared.'

'Anyway Cathy, I've done my best,' Sandra said. 'And I made it clear to Minty that I wouldn't tolerate her putting the frighteners on Tayo either. Hopefully when she's had time to reflect on this she'll realize that if she wants to keep seeing him, then she'll have to toe the line. I don't like using a child like that but it was for her own good and nothing else was going to get through to her.'

We said goodbye, and I sat mulling over what Sandra had said. I decided to play safe and remain vigilant for a few more days. Minty had obviously been enraged by the whole thing and might well confide her fury in her 'friend'. I wouldn't relax my guard just yet.

Chapter Seventeen

Falling Out

Tayo had settled easily and comfortably into family life, partly because he was so adaptable and partly because he was delighted to have a secure and safe place to stay at last. Unlike some of the children I looked after, he hadn't pined for his mother and he now seemed at ease with being Lucy's and Paula's younger foster sibling. We hadn't had any repetition of his manipulative behaviour or lying, or any resentment of what the girls had compared to himself.

I didn't sit back and congratulate myself though, because I knew it wasn't that simple. Whatever had happened to him in the past, and the experience of living a life of lying, stealing and fending for himself, wasn't going to disappear in weeks – but, I felt, it was all looking very positive.

Jill visited as planned on Wednesday, and over coffee and biscuits I updated her on everything that had happened with Tayo in her absence. I also asked her about her family and she said her son was in rehab and doing well.

Tayo had to phone his mother on Wednesday evening. This was the first time we'd have contact using the speakerphone. I'd explained to him what we were going to do and he didn't object, clearly now able to see that such precautions were necessary and put in place for his safety.

I sat him closest to the phone, pressed the hands-free button and keyed in Minty's mobile number. We sat side by side on the sofa and listened to the ringing, then the automated message as it switched through to her voicemail. On the third attempt I said, 'Do you want to leave a message if she doesn't answer this time?'

He shrugged. 'No. If she can't be bothered to answer, I won't bother to leave a message.' Which I accepted.

I wondered why Minty didn't make it a priority to answer the phone, particularly when it had been she who had asked for the phone contact. Apart from disappointing Tayo, it wasn't helping her chances of having him back, assuming he wanted to go. We had just heard that the final court hearing had been set for 20th October and, although that was still months away, every time Minty let Tayo down, it would be viewed as a further sign of her unreliability and lack of commitment. Added to her volatile and aggressive outbursts, it meant that I had to admit it wasn't looking good for Minty, although I had seen parents turn their lives around in less than nine months, and then, with help and monitoring, have their children returned to them.

Apart from not doing herself or Tayo any good, every time Minty let down Tayo, it strengthened the idealized picture he had of his father, who was fast becoming faultless in his eyes. For Tayo, his father was turning into the pinnacle of respectability and good fatherhood, a wonderful hero who was out there somewhere waiting to rescue him.

'My dad would always be there if I phoned,' he said. 'I'd wish he'd hurry up and find me.'

I didn't say anything. One rejection an evening was enough, and I wasn't going to squash Tayo further. It was obvious that he was starting to rely on the dream of his father as an emotional crutch, and I would have to make it my job to guide him gently to a realization that his long-term future was most likely to be in foster care until he reached adulthood.

Alison Hemming-Sanders, the Guardian Ad Litum, was due for her first visit at four on Thursday. I'd told Tayo she was coming, and explained her role: she would visit every couple of months and talk to him (as she would all the other parties), then draw all the information together and present it to the judge with her recommendation as to what was best for Tayo.

'Will she visit my dad?' Tayo asked.

I should have predicted that, I thought. Tayo was mentioning his father more and more. 'No, darling. No one knows where he is. But when she visits, you must tell her how you feel about him, as you've told me.' It was the best I could offer.

Alison Hemming-Sanders didn't arrive at four. She phoned at four-thirty to say she had left the office late and was now stuck in traffic. She phoned again at five to say she was still stuck in traffic. Then at five-thirty she phoned to say that she'd abandoned the visit and was now driving home as it was too late. She said she'd phone me the following day when she had her diary to hand to arrange another visit.

I thought an apology wouldn't have gone amiss, particularly as Tayo had been unsettled as he waited for her arrival and I'd been on tenterhooks each time the phone had rung. I'd also delayed the preparations of the evening meal because I was expecting her at any moment. Sometimes professionals involved in a case appeared to think that foster carers had nothing better to do than wait for them. Guardians Ad Litum, like social workers, varied in their professionalism, conscientiousness and efficiency; I'd had an excellent run so far with Brian, Sandra and Aisha. Perhaps Alison Hemming-Sanders was going to balance this out.

By Friday, when there hadn't been another threatening phone call, I dropped my guard on the phone and allowed the girls to start answering it again, with the caution that if it was anyone they didn't know, to call me immediately. Tayo had had another good week at school, despite all the upset surrounding the phone call on Monday. However when I breezed into Tayo's classroom later that afternoon to collect him for contact, I knew at once that something was wrong. Tayo was ready with his coat on, bag on his back, standing by Mrs Gillings' desk but he had a face like thunder.

'I need to have a word,' Sonya Gillings said ominously. She waited until the rest of the class had left in their Friday afternoon bubble of delight, then turned to me.

'I'm sorry to say that Tayo was involved in a nasty incident at lunchtime,' she said gravely. 'He verbally taunted a boy in the playground then, when the boy ran off, chased him and hit him.'

I looked at Tayo and he stared back. I could see before he spoke that he was going to stand his ground.

'He called me names,' Tayo said dismissively.

'That doesn't give you the right to hit him,' I said.

'And actually the boy didn't call Tayo names,' Sonya Gillings put in. 'I couldn't get to the bottom of it but from what the other lads said it was Tayo who did the name calling and it was very personal.'

'Well, he is fat,' Tayo said, in his defence.

I glanced at Sonya Gillings and she was clearly looking to me to reprimand Tayo.

'That doesn't come into it,' I said sternly to him. 'You don't call people names and then hit them. It's bullying, Tayo. And it's not nice.'

He shrugged. 'He started it.'

I could see we could go round in circles and I was conscious of the time ticking by. 'Tayo has contact tonight,' I reminded Mrs Gillings. 'I'll stop his television as a punishment and try and find out more later.'

She nodded. 'He lost his break this afternoon, and I made him apologize to the boy.'

'All right. Thank you,' I turned and began towards the door with Tayo following. 'I'm sorry you've had to deal with this,' I said to Sonya Gillings before we left. Then to Tayo, 'I'm not pleased with you. You've let me down.'

He followed in silence as we left the building and then walked to the car. Once inside he said, 'She overreacted.'

'Mrs Gillings? I doubt it. Bullying is not tolerated in school or at home Tayo, rightly so.'

'I didn't bully him. And we're friends again now.'

I glanced in the rear-view mirror as I pulled away from the kerb. 'Well, I'm pleased you're friends again. Did you tell Mrs Gillings that?'

'Yes, but she wasn't listening.'

I could understand that, with thirty children on a Friday afternoon, she wouldn't be hanging on Tayo's every word. 'Who was the boy involved?'

'Sam.'

'Your best friend Sam?'

Tayo nodded.

Perhaps Mrs Gillings had overreacted, I thought. It sounded more like friends falling out than cold, calculated bullying.

'But what happened for you to hit him? And I want the truth, Tayo.'

'He said my mum was a waster, and he's not allowed to say that, Cathy. I know she is but it's not for him to say.' His voice was full of hurt.

While this explanation didn't justify him hitting Sam, I could see only too clearly how it had happened. We are often happy to acknowledge the flaws and failings in our own families, but let someone else try to point them out and our loyalty and defences kick in at once.

'I see,' I said. 'And you've made up your quarrel?'

'Yes, straightaway, even before Mrs Gillings made me apologize.'

'OK. But you've still lost your television because you should-n't have hit Sam, whatever the reason.' And I left it at that.

Although we were ten minutes late arriving at Headline, Minty wasn't there. Another let down, I thought, as I saw Tayo's face set in a mixture of disappointment and anger.

Aisha was very kind and said Tayo could wait with her in Yellow Room so that I could leave, adding that if Minty was more than half an hour late, contact would be abandoned because it wasn't fair for Tayo to be kept waiting indefinitely. I knew that was normal policy because, as with the phone calls, the onus was on the parent to make sure they were available at the set times and therefore reliable and committed.

I went straight home and began preparing dinner. Three-quarters of an hour later the doorbell rang – it was Aisha with Tayo. Minty had phoned the centre and said that she couldn't make contact but didn't give a reason, so Aisha had brought Tayo straight home.

After I'd said goodbye to Aisha and closed the door, I turned to Tayo who was obviously very disappointed.

'Not the best day,' I said, and gave him a hug. 'But on the bright side there's football club tomorrow.'

'Sam was right,' he muttered vehemently. 'She *is* a waster.'

I looked at him carefully. It was very difficult when a child had a really low opinion of a parent. Harbouring negative feelings for a parent can have a knock-on effect on a child's self-esteem, making them feel worthless; they seem to feel that if their parent is useless then they must be too. By the time a child can talk, they've formed strong attachments to their parents, except in the most serious cases of abuse, and when a parent is demonised the child is thrown into confusion and even self-loathing. There was a lot written on the subject and I had attended many training sessions dealing with it, so I knew enough to be sure that it wasn't going to help Tayo by calling his mother names and that it was time we had a little chat.

'Tayo, come with me.' I said, and went through to the lounge. Lucy wasn't home yet and Paula was in her bedroom listening to music. 'Sit down, love, and stop looking so worried. You haven't done anything wrong.'

Tayo perched on the sofa next to me, still dejected. I took his hand and gave it a little squeeze. At least I could talk to him on a reasonably adult level. It was far more difficult dealing with these issues with younger children or those who had learning difficulties.

'Tayo, we both know that your mum has a lot of problems and doesn't always behave as she should. Sometimes she's happy, sometimes she's angry, and often she's confused. It must be very difficult for you to see your mum like that.' He nodded. 'But despite everything, she is your mother and I think you're going to have to be very patient and forgiving, just as you've been in the past. You're your own person, you're talented and intelligent, and you have your whole life ahead of you. It may not seem like it now but very quickly you'll be an adult and able to make all your own decisions, and all this will be just a memory. But for now, I think you must accept that you're going to be disappointed by Mum not doing what she's supposed to, and just enjoy what time you spend with her. Don't forget, I'm always here if you want to talk or let off steam. But I don't think calling your mother a waster, or rejecting her by watching television for the whole of contact, is going to help.'

He nodded.

'Good boy.' I didn't want him to feel responsible for her as he used to, but I did want him to have a bit of empathy for her, and not nurture negative feelings of anger and resentment. When all was said and done, Minty hadn't been born like that, she had been shaped by her experiences just as everyone is, and she'd obviously had a rough ride. 'OK?' I asked him.

'OK,' he said, and planted a big kiss on my cheek.

If I hadn't known better, I might have suspected that Minty had been party to this conversation and decided to give it her best shot.

When we phoned on Saturday evening with the loudspeaker on, she answered immediately and then asked Tayo how he was, and if he had enjoyed football.

Tayo seemed unable to believe his good fortune: here was Mum, coherent and interested. He talked ten to the dozen about football, school and his life with us. And when he asked her how she was managing, she didn't quite hide her problems from him but said, 'Not bad, son. No money as usual, but don't you worry. I'll get by somehow, I always do.'

I was impressed. This was a vast improvement on the previous litany of hysterical complaints. She apologized for missing contact and when it was time to go said, 'Love you, son, see you Tuesday.' She also asked to speak to me.

I lifted the handset and put it to my ear. Although I had to listen to Minty and Tayo's conversation there was no need for Tayo to listen to whatever Minty wanted to say to me.

'Hi, Cathy,' she said. Tayo hovered.

'Hello, Minty. How are you?'

'You know because you've been listening,' she snapped, and for a moment I thought she was going to lambast me, but she changed tack again. 'I'm sorry I missed contact but I had to see a solicitor. He's going to get Tayo back for me. In the meantime, I want you to look after my son properly.'

Her tone wasn't threatening, so I said soothingly, 'Of course, Minty. Please don't worry. Tayo is settled and doing very well.'

'I guess you know what you're doing.'

As there appeared nothing more she wanted to say, I finished the call politely, saying how much Tayo was looking forward to seeing her on Tuesday and wishing her a good weekend.

She scoffed at that, and then was gone.

I smiled at Tayo. 'That was better, wasn't it?'

He beamed back with a nod, and went off to his bedroom to play with his army of toy soldiers.

While it seemed that Sandra's words had had an effect on Minty, I doubted that she had missed contact because she was seeing a solicitor. I'd never known a solicitor book a client with a contentious case to discuss at four o'clock on a Friday afternoon, and if he had, then Minty would have known of the appointment beforehand, and had time to rearrange contact. I also knew that a solicitor dealing with a care order would never have said he would get the child returned – it would be highly unethical, particularly so early in the case.

Dealing with Minty was like dealing with a big child – the excuse of seeing a solicitor was probably the first thing that popped into her head and sounded important enough to merit missing contact. But, on the positive side, I was pleased she hadn't given this excuse to Tayo, and doubly pleased she had managed to control herself reasonably well and have a sensible conversation with him. It was a step forward, and if she continued in this manner, the future of their relationship looked a lot brighter.

Chapter Eighteen

Review

Under the Children Acts, every child in care has a series of regular reviews. These are meetings for those immediately involved with the child, to look back over the child's life since the last review and see what has happened – good and bad – and plan future work. It is also a monitoring system to make sure everything is being done for the child, and that the adults involved are doing what they should under the Acts. The review is usually held either in the foster home or in the Social Services offices.

Tayo's first review was scheduled to take place at Social Services. Invited along were Tayo, his mother, his social worker, the Guardian Ad Litum, a representative from his school, and myself as his foster carer. A senior social worker unconnected to the case would be chairing the meeting.

Although Tayo was old enough and intelligent enough to be present, he declined because it would have meant him missing PE (and therefore football). Instead, he was sent a small booklet to fill in with his views, wishes, and any grievances. It was returned to his social worker so that his perspective could be brought to the meeting.

We began the meeting fifteen minutes late, at quarter past eleven. Roberta de la Haye was the representative from Meadway, as I'd expected, as she was the designated person for looked-after children. Sandra and I were also there, along with Maureen Green, who was chairing. Minty hadn't turned up or sent a message to say she wasn't coming; neither had the Guardian, Alison Hemming-Sanders. Minty's absence and lack of apology was forgivable if disappointing, but the Guardian's absence with no apology was unacceptable.

'Has anyone heard from her?' Maureen Green asked a little crossly.

'No,' Sandra said.

I shook my head.

'I'm going to start then. We can't wait any longer.'

After introductions, Maureen asked Roberta de la Haye to start. She took a sheet of paper from a folder in front of her and began a résumé of Tayo's progress at school, which had markedly improved since his circumstances had settled. Not only was he now looking smarter and had more confidence, his academic work was going from strength to strength, and she supported this by giving some recent test results. Tayo was also less sly and less prone to using his intelligence to manipulate situations. She said that Mrs Gillings found him a likable and pleasant member of her class.

'That's it, really,' she concluded, running her finger down the sheet of paper. 'Except that we've noticed Tayo has begun to talk a lot about his father. We weren't aware that his father was on the scene ...'

'He isn't, I'm afraid,' Sandra said quickly. 'Tayo hasn't seen his father in over five years. He thinks he could be in Nigeria but we haven't been able to trace him.'

'I see,' Mrs de la Haye said. 'I'm surprised. From the way Tayo has been talking about him, we thought they were in regular contact with each other.'

I shook my head and looked over at Maureen Green. 'It's becoming a bit of a problem because Tayo is convinced that his father is going to come to this country to take him "home", and he's built up a picture in his head of what his father is like – a heroic figure who will suddenly appear and whisk him away. He has a vague recollection of living with his gran and dad when he was little. It's possible he did, but it's so long ago, we can't know for sure.'

'And he has no names or addresses or anything, so it's impossible to trace them. I've tried,' Sandra added.

'Does his mother know where they are?' Maureen asked.

'If she does she's not saying,' replied Sandra. 'She refuses to discuss the subject.'

'So there's no chance of Tayo going to Nigeria to live with them?' Roberta de la Haye asked.

'No, I'm afraid not,' Sandra confirmed.

'I see,' Roberta said. 'I'll tell his class teacher. Tayo was pretty convincing when he told her that's what he was going to do. Poor kid.' She looked at Sandra. 'I take it he won't be going back to Mum?'

'Highly unlikely,' Sandra said. 'Although the final court hearing isn't until October.'

Roberta nodded, then looked at me. 'It's a shame he can't stay with you for the long term, Cathy. He seems so happy and settled.'

'I know,' I said, feeling guilty even though I knew it wasn't my fault. 'But I'm a short term and emergency carer. I help children adapt to care before they're found permanent families. Besides, I think Tayo might be happier in a two-parent family. He would benefit from a strong male role model.'

'I understand,' said Roberta. 'You obviously can't keep all the children you foster, Cathy – but it's a shame he'll have to move again. Now, if you've finished with me, I'd better be getting back to school.'

Maureen Green thanked her, and Roberta de la Haye left.

'Cathy, would you like to go next?' Maureen said.

My report was brief and I didn't need notes. It was nearly all positive, although I touched on the problems we'd had earlier, with the incidents of lying and stealing. I said that Tayo's poor self-image in relation to his dual-heritage had greatly improved – in fact, I now found it difficult to get him away from the bathroom mirror in the morning, so busy was he preening himself. Sandra and Maureen laughed.

But I also stressed what I'd said about Tayo's unrealistic expectations of his father. 'I'm trying to guide him towards accepting that he's going to be in care for some time,' I added, 'but he's not there yet by any means.'

'Does Tayo talk about his father often at home?' Maureen enquired.

'Yes. I wouldn't say it's obsessive but it might become so. He's built up quite a detailed picture in his mind of what his father looks like, and the sort of character he is, including his likes and dislikes. We'll be out visiting somewhere or doing something and Tayo will say, "My dad likes that" or "My dad can do that" or "I'm going to show my dad that". Needless to say, in Tayo's eyes his father is absolutely faultless, and he ignores the fact that there has been no word from him for five years, and that as far as we know, he hasn't been looking for him.'

Maureen nodded and took notes. 'It's sad, isn't it?' she said, then looked up at Sandra. 'And you're sure there's no way his father can be found?'

'I'm certain. We're not even sure of his surname or if he is still in Nigeria.'

Maureen finished writing. 'Thank you, Cathy. Was there anything else?'

'Only that I'd like permission to take Tayo on holiday with us at Easter. I've booked us a short break at CenterParcs.'

'That sounds nice,' Maureen said and made a note. 'I take it there's no problem with permission?' she asked Sandra.

'Shouldn't be. I'll get Minty to sign the consent form at contact, nearer the time.'

'Excellent,' Maureen said. 'That's something for Tayo to look forward to. I don't suppose he's ever had a holiday before.'

'No,' I confirmed, 'he hasn't.'

It was Sandra's turn next and she covered the legal position, what was known of Tayo's background including what Tayo had told me, and then outlined Minty's volatile, confusing and threatening behaviour. She added that Minty still hadn't produced her contact details or any documents. 'There are no passports, birth certificate, or any evidence of either of them being in the country or existing at all for that matter.'

'Nothing at all?' Maureen asked, surprised.

'No. I don't think Minty has any of the paperwork and she won't cooperate so I can't even begin to try and get photocopies. She's very angry. I've spoken to her on her mobile once and I saw her at Headline Family Centre after the threatening call to Cathy. Minty did attend the placement meeting, although it was a bit of a disaster.'

Maureen wrote this down. 'Is she being assessed?'

'We hope so,' Sandra said, 'but she'll have to have an address. The court has ordered a psychological assessment as well, but that will rely on Minty coming to the offices, which she won't at present.'

'And did she know about this meeting?'

'Yes. I left a message on her voicemail.'

'I don't see there's any more you can do then. It's a pity.' Maureen paused. 'All that remains now is for me to read out what Tayo has said.'

She opened the small booklet, which Tayo had previously completed himself. I hadn't read what he'd written. With younger children or those who couldn't read, I help them answer the questions, but Tayo was quite competent and had completed it unaided and put it in the envelope. Sandra had seen it though, and she smiled as Maureen began reading the first question, which was about what the child thought of his social worker. Tayo had written: 'I like my social worker very much and I hope she finds my dad.' The next question was about me, and Tayo had written: 'I like Cathy and her family and I like all my new things and going to football. Thank you, Cathy.' Next was about how he felt about being in care and Maureen read: 'I don't like being in care. Other children aren't in care. They are with their mums and dads. I don't want to be with my mum. I want to be with my dad.' The last question was about how he saw his future, and predictably Tayo had written in large letters: 'WITH MY DAD AND GRAN!'

'I see what you mean,' Maureen said as she closed the booklet. 'He's an intelligent lad so hopefully he will adjust in time.'

Sandra and I agreed.

Maureen finished by setting the date for the next review, which would be in three months' time, then thanked us for attending, and added a special thanks to me for looking after Tayo. This was always done at the end of a review but is still nice to hear. 'I'll send a copy of the minutes to the Guardian,' Maureen said, standing. 'And, Sandra, will you make sure Minty has a copy? I hope Minty will feel able to come to Tayo's next review.' Then she added pointedly, 'I hope the Guardian Ad Litum will feel the same.'

The meeting was at an end.

Chapter Nineteen

Happy Holidays

The end of February turned bitterly cold. The temperature plummeted to minus four degrees centigrade at night and didn't rise above one degree during the day. Every morning Tayo helped me scrape the ice off the car windows while telling me they didn't have snow in Nigeria, and that his dad lived near the coast so when he had finished school each day he would be able to go for a swim.

I was becoming so used to his imaginary life in Africa that I rarely commented now. Only if the fantasy became too extreme did I draw him up and correct him. I felt that if this was Tayo's prop, his way of dealing with the uncertainty of what lay ahead, then he probably needed it; if I took it completely away, it could do more harm than good. In all other aspects of his life, Tayo was doing very well, functioning as a well-balanced and healthy ten-year-old. Considering his past, that in itself was little short of a miracle.

It was the half-term holiday and the weather obliged by snowing. I knew something was different even before I got out of bed and opened the curtains. There was that peacefulness, that muffled silence, as nature enfolded the streets, houses, trees, the very air, in its magical white cloak. Tayo must have felt it too because he was up at dawn. I heard his bedroom door open and, slipping on my dressing gown, I went out to the landing.

'Cathy! It's snowing!' he exclaimed, beaming.

'I know, isn't it lovely?'

We went into his bedroom and looked out over the garden. It had been a good fall, about four inches, and it was still coming down. Large fluffy snowflakes drifted steadily past the window.

'Can I make a snowman?' he asked.

'Of course, we all will. And go tobogganing.'

'Tobogganing!' he cried. 'What, with a real toboggan?'

'Yes. I have a lovely toboggan in the shed that my father made for me when I was a child. We used to have more snow then.'

'Wicked!' he yelled and literally jumped for joy.

'Tayo, it's only seven o'clock, and Paula and Lucy are still asleep. Could you do something quietly for an hour or so? Then I'll wake them. We'll go the park, that hill is terrific there for tobogganing. I'm sure the girls will want to come too.'

At nine o'clock, as the traffic struggled past in the icy conditions, the four of us headed towards the park, Tayo pulling the toboggan. With a decent fall of snow even walking was exciting, and we pelted each other with snowballs and left patterns with our gloved fingers on garden walls as we went. The air was so still, it was almost like a Christmas card scene. The snow had stopped falling now and a watery sun was rising in the frost-laden air.

The park was really no more than a grassed wide-open space with a magnificent slow-gradient hill that was the best slope for miles around. There were already a couple of dozen children and adults there when we arrived, with more arriving by the minute. Tracks of compacted snow were starting to form as the toboggans, trays, sheets of plastic and cardboard hurtled down to the bottom. We walked up the hill, keeping to one side, our wellingtons crunching into the soft snow.

Tayo admitted he had never used a toboggan before and I wanted him to take second go so that either Lucy or Paula could give him a demonstration first. I didn't want an accident.

'I know what to do,' he protested, eyeing the other lads speeding down. 'You just lie on it and go!'

'But this one goes very fast,' I said. 'You wait until you see the runners.' I turned the toboggan on its end and showed him the shiny metal strips my father had nailed on the wooden runners many years ago. They still shone. 'And it's heavier than the plastic ones,' I said. 'It gathers speed. That's why we have this rope for the steering. Watch first, then you can have next turn.'

We positioned the toboggan at the top of the hill where a line of us were waiting for those already at the bottom to get clear.

Lucy climbed on and sat with her feet on the footrest and took the rope in her hands. We gave her a push and off she went.

'Wow!' Tayo said, as she quickly gathered speed. 'Wow! Look at it go! It's the fastest one here! It's beaten all the others!'

I wasn't sure that was true, but it was fast. My father had made two exactly the same, one for my brother and one for me.

And although it didn't get as much use as it once did, especially with the warmer winters, when it did come out it was always a success. I was so pleased I'd kept it.

We stood back from the edge to allow others to take their turn while Lucy dragged the toboggan back up the hill. 'When you come back up,' I said to Tayo, 'make sure you keep well over to the side so you're not hit by the ones going down.'

'Yes, yes,' he said, unable to control his impatience. 'And I'm going to lie down on it.'

'Not for the first go. I want you to get the feel of it, and it's safer sitting so that you don't go head first into anything.'

Lucy returned with her cheeks glowing and eyes glistening from the cold. 'It's great,' she said. 'Can we do a double next time?' The toboggan was big enough to seat two, one behind the other, and Lucy remembered the last time we'd used it, when she and Paula had doubled up thus getting more turns and not having to wait so long.

'Yes, but let's all have single go first,' I said, wanting my turn.

Tayo edged the toboggan to the brow of the hill and sat on it, heels on the foot rest with his toes pointing up. He took the rope in his hands and I showed him how to take up the slack and steer. 'It's really like the reins on a horse,' I said. 'Pull right for right and left for left. OK?'

'Yes! Give me a big push off!'

The girls and I gave him the biggest push we could muster and off he sailed. We heard him shout 'Eureka!' as he gathered speed and raced down the slope, then came to a halt at the bottom. He did as I had told him and kept well clear of the down-coming toboggans as he made his way up. Five minutes later he was beside us again, out of breath, and brimming over with exhilaration.

'Terrific! Wicked! It was so cool!'

Paula had her turn next, and then it was mine. As I sailed down, with the air rushing past my ears, I was a child again and felt that buzz of excitement and risk.

'That wasn't as fast as me,' Tayo said on my return.

For the rest of the morning we sailed down the hill in various combinations and by one o'clock we were all exhausted, although Tayo wouldn't admit it, and hungry, and starting to get cold. I insisted we returned for some lunch, with the promise that we would come back in the morning if the snow held. I thought it would, as the temperature was dropping fast and the sky looked full of snow.

That afternoon Tayo and the girls made a giant snowman in the back garden and then followed it with a snowball fight. I took photos of the three of them covered in snow and hardly distinguishable from the snowman they posed beside.

As I tucked Tayo into bed that night, he could hardly keep his eyes open. I realized we had gone a whole day without him mentioning his father once.

'Night, night, sleep tight,' I said.

'And don't let the bed bugs bite,' he returned as he always did, and was asleep by the time I'd left the room.

That evening I phoned my parents and told my father of the superb day we'd had tobogganing thanks to his piece of craftsmanship, which we calculated was thirty-six years old.

* * *

It froze that night and another two inches of snow fell so that the four of us made a return trip to the park the following morning. We had another fine morning of tobogganing, and Tayo met a friend from school there and brought him home to play, which was a first.

By the end of the half-term week the snow was beginning to melt and what was left was dirty and grey and not suitable for tobogganing. I returned the toboggan to the shed and prepared for new half term that would see us to Easter and our holiday.

Minty had missed both contact sessions during the week, using the snow as an excuse, even though all the main roads had been gritted and the buses were running normally by Tuesday. Tayo didn't seem unduly upset, but I felt the rejection even if he didn't seem to. Was this Minty's way of beginning to separate from Tayo, without having to be assessed or go to court? That might be the easiest option for her, but it was the worst possible outcome for Tayo. I knew that children needed to see their parents fighting to have them returned to their care, even if there wasn't a glimmer of hope, otherwise the child would feel that they weren't wanted and not worth fighting for.

What was Minty doing? Wasn't she going to fight for Tayo? Sandra must have told her that she was entitled to legal aid and travel expenses. I wondered if it was something to do with Minty's immigration status. Perhaps it had occurred to her, as it had to Sandra, that each time she made an appearance at the contact centre, she was more likely to be apprehended and ultimately deported. After all, she wasn't to know that the Home Office hadn't the least interest in detaining or deporting her.

I suddenly realized that if Minty's attendance at contact was going to become sporadic or nonexistent, then Sandra needed to get her signature on the consent form to allow Tayo to come away with us at Easter sooner rather than later. We couldn't go without it and I had now paid the full cost of the holiday, over five hundred pounds, which I wouldn't get back if we had to cancel at the last minute – to say nothing of the family's disappointment.

As soon as everyone was back at school on Monday I telephoned Sandra, and after giving her an update on the excellent week we'd had at half term, I asked her about obtaining Minty's consent.

'Don't worry,' she said. 'I've left the consent form with James at Headline, and next time Minty is there, he'll ask her to sign it. I've also left a message on Minty's voicemail explaining about the holiday and the form.'

'Thank you,' I said. 'Minty must turn up for at least one contact this week surely?'

'Yes, most definitely. Because I've left another message on her voicemail saying that if she doesn't turn up, I'll apply to the court to have the contact terminated as it's unfair on Tayo.'

I should have known by now that Sandra was one step ahead of me and was not going to pussyfoot around. 'Thanks,' I said. 'Tayo doesn't need any more rejection or uncertainty. And he deserves a holiday – I know he's really looking forward to it.'

Minty heeded Sandra's warning and did turn up at the next contact session on Tuesday. This time she was absolutely furious. We could hear her storming and shrieking in reception before we got into the centre.

'She's got no fucking right! Who the fuck does she think she is? I'm going to get a solicitor on to her. The whole fucking lot of you!'

I wasn't sure if the 'she' Minty referred to was Sandra or myself and I could see that Tayo was unsure as well. He looked at me anxiously, almost protectively. We waited outside until James had led Minty out of reception and the furore receded.

I pressed the security buzzer and Aisha let us in. 'I'm afraid Mum's a bit upset with Sandra right now,' she said. 'It's nothing for you to worry about though, Tayo.'

'Is contact going ahead?' I asked.

'If Mum calms down, yes. You go, Cathy, I'll look after Tayo in the waiting room until James says we can go through.'

I left, hoping for Tayo's sake that Minty managed to get control of herself.

When Aisha returned Tayo at the usual time, she said Minty had calmed down enough for Tayo to have an hour with her, although once again she hadn't brought him any dinner. Aisha waited until Tayo was out of earshot before adding, 'And James said to tell you that she hasn't signed the consent form for the holiday. She says she doesn't think it's safe and won't sign until she knows more about it.'

That was a reasonable request when it was made by a reasonable parent, but coming from Minty, it seemed ridiculous, given her standard of care.

'All right,' I said. 'I'll speak to Sandra tomorrow and work out the best way to reassure Minty.'

'Thanks. And also Minty wanted to know why Tayo hadn't phoned on Saturday.'

'He did,' I said. 'But Minty wasn't there and Tayo didn't want to leave a message.'

'OK. I'll make a note because Minty was making an issue of it and said you were breaking the court order.'

'Did Tayo tell her we phoned?' I asked.

'Yes, and she accused him of siding with you against her. I don't think the poor kid knew what to say for the best – tell the truth or lie to pacify her.'

'No,' I agreed. Poor Tayo is caught between a rock and a hard place, I thought, as I closed the door. But Minty was so confused most of the time that I doubted she'd had the where-withal to check on her mobile for the list of missed calls.

The Guardian Ad Litum phoned later in the week, and with no apology for missing the review or not seeing Tayo, said she was too busy with other cases to visit Tayo at present and asked for a telephone update, which appeared to replace her visit.

We were busy too. Tayo had asked if he could join two after-school clubs, chess on Monday and gym on Wednesday. I had agreed, with the proviso that he found time to do his home-work, which he'd assured me he would. The weeks flew by in a cycle of activity, with contact on Tuesday and Friday, the school clubs on Monday and Wednesday, football club on Saturday, and me squeezing in a night out to see Peter on Sunday evenings.

Easter was fast approaching and I was now seriously worried that the consent form for our holiday still hadn't been signed. Although I'd left a CenterParcs brochure at Headline for Minty, and Sandra had left a number of messages on Minty's mobile reassuring her, she was still refusing to sign. It seemed that her stubborn refusal was more a matter of asserting what little bit of authority she had left rather than genuine concern for Tayo's safety.

Eventually, with only seven days to go before our holiday, Sandra went to Headline for the Friday contact session and came away with Minty's signature on the form.

'Well done!' I said, when she phoned to tell me. 'That's a huge relief, it really is. Our holiday was hanging in the balance.'

'I can't take all the credit,' she said. 'Tayo brought pressure to bear on his mother when he realized he might not be going.'

I hadn't told Tayo that our holiday was in jeopardy because his mother wouldn't give her consent, but Minty was unable to keep anything from Tayo and told him. He had ordered her to sign in no uncertain terms, according to Sandra. While I wasn't completely comfortable with the way her consent had been extracted – it really wasn't the child's responsibility, after all – I was just glad that we had her signature and could go.

School finished, I collected Adrian from university, the spring weather warmed up, and we packed our bags and left for Tayo's first holiday ever. The build up of anticipation, the journey, and our eventual arrival jettisoned Tayo into unbridled excitement as his cries of 'Are we there yet?' were replaced by 'We're here! We're on holiday!'

We unpacked, hired a bike each, then cycled to the Oasis swimming dome where we stayed until late evening. After a huge meal in the American Wild West themed restaurant we cycled back to our villa under the pine trees and stars and fell into bed, exhausted. The following day was action-packed as we took in ten-pin bowling, badminton (which Tayo had a natural flair for), archery, a long bike ride, an hour's swim, and another huge meal, this time Italian. And so the week continued, living up to everyone's expectations, with something new every day. The weather was kind to us and there was no rain, and although the evenings were chilly, a brisk cycle ride along the tracks in a hitherto unexplored part of the forest soon warmed us up. Everything we did was an adventure for Tayo, and it was nice that Adrian was with us, for he had a made a big impact on Tayo who followed him everywhere like a shadow.

There was one blot on the otherwise near perfect landscape, however, and I became increasingly concerned about it as the week progressed. Far from taking Tayo's mind off his absent father, the holiday seemed to have fuelled his imagination even more.

Tayo's previous comments of 'I wish my dad could see this' had been replaced by the more definitive: 'I'm going to show my dad this' or 'My dad likes this too'. And rather than three or four comments a day, he was now making three or four an hour. I began to feel that it was bordering on the delusional. We couldn't do anything without the invisible presence of Tayo's father and he was everywhere.

Adrian came to me at the end of the second day and asked, 'What's all this about Tayo's father? I didn't think he was seeing him.'

'He's not,' I said. 'And he's never likely to.' I explained what had been happening while Adrian had been away.

'Tayo talks as though he's in regular contact with him,' Adrian said.

'I know. Perhaps you could have a word with him, man to man?'

Adrian agreed. When the two of them cycled on ahead the following morning, he took the opportunity to chat with Tayo, using his own absent father as a starting point, as he thought Tayo could relate to that. It was obvious that Tayo had enjoyed their man-to-man chat when the girls and I caught up, but the effects were minimal. There was an hour's respite from Tayo's father over lunch at the Pancake House, then it began again when we played crazy golf.

'My dad can hit the best shot in the world. He plays golf every week and gets a hole in one. I'm going to play golf with my dad when I go home,' declared Tayo.

And so it went on. Adrian and I exchanged a glance and he shrugged. Later he said, 'Sorry, Mum, I did my best. I thought he'd taken it on board.'

'I know love, he might yet. He's excited at the moment. Hopefully it will lessen as times goes on.'

But it didn't. Despite a truly brilliant week when we took in all the activities the village had to offer at least twice, Tayo's talk of his father had become obsessive and compulsive, like an itch that had to be scratched.

We returned home refreshed and energized by our holiday. But once back, I decided I had to say something to Tayo about his dad. I explained that while he most definitely had a father, and it was possible he liked and could do all the things Tayo said, he couldn't possibly know for certain because we weren't in contact with him, and neither could we be. It sounded harsh but I couldn't let his obsession continue to build. It was starting to affect his life. Tayo listened to what I said without comment.

Two days later I found Tayo sitting in his bedroom writing. He showed me the sheets of A4 paper, not at all abashed. They were letters to his father, about half a dozen of them, that clearly would never be posted, but they detailed the horror of living with his mother and asked why his father hadn't come to get him yet. There was no mention of us or the improvement in his life since coming into care, just lines and lines of furiously scribbled prose, which would have been cathartic if it had given Tayo release, but it didn't.

When Sandra called to ask how the holiday had gone, I told her we'd had a good time but mentioned Tayo's growing obsession with his father. She was obviously concerned and said she'd speak to Tayo, and arranged to visit the following day at two-thirty as we were still on the Easter break and there was no school. When she arrived I made her a coffee then left the two of them alone in the lounge for the best part of an hour.

'I see what you mean,' Sandra said when they'd finished and Tayo had disappeared down the garden to the swings. 'He became quite angry when I said there was no way we could contact his father, let alone arrange for Tayo to live with him. For the first time I could see his mother's anger in him.' She paused. 'I'm wondering about art therapy, do you think it might help? Give him some direction for his anger and emotions.'

'I don't know. But it's worth a try. When is it?'

'I'll find out and get back to you. In the meantime, will you explain to Tayo about what is involved in the therapy? I won't say anything to him now. I think he's had enough of me talking for one day.'

That evening when I told Tayo what Sandra had suggested, and explained that I'd looked after a boy before who'd gone to art therapy and had thoroughly enjoyed the painting and clay making, Tayo told me to 'stick it'.

'I beg your pardon?' I said sternly.

Tayo looked at me, eyes wide and angry. 'I don't want art therapy. I like football like my dad.'

'This is as well as football, not instead of. And you don't know if your dad likes football. For all you know, he might be into art.'

'He plays football!' he returned, stopping just short of shouting. 'Every weekend! And he scores all the goals!'

I didn't know what else to say. I couldn't emphatically deny it was true any more than Tayo could claim that it was. So I clung to the belief that given time, Tayo would adjust to being in care and his fantasy would slowly subside.

Chapter Twenty

Anger

School returned for the summer term and I returned Adrian to university. He had his end-of-year exams looming which he would have to pass to enable him go on to the second year. Paula had her GCSEs starting in three weeks, Lucy had her final B.Tech exams in a month, and Tayo would have his SATs. It was going to be an important term for everyone and I was pleased we had managed the Easter break, which had recharged everyone's batteries and set them up for the hard work that lay ahead.

At the end of the third week of term, Tayo's teacher asked to see me. Here we go again I thought. What's he done this time?

But there hadn't been an incident. Rather, Mrs Gillings was worried Tayo was falling behind with his work again, and some homework hadn't been completed. I spoke to Tayo that evening and restated the importance of doing well at school so he could go to university if he wanted, like Adrian.

Tayo shrugged despondently. 'Not fussed,' he said. 'My dad didn't go to university and he makes heaps of money.'

'That's as may be, Tayo but you're going to do your home-work before the television goes on,' I said firmly. Enough was enough – he wasn't going to use his father as an excuse to start failing.

He refused point blank to do the outstanding homework so I stopped his television, but he wasn't 'fussed' about that either. In fact, when I came to think of it, Tayo wasn't fussed about a lot of things that he used to enjoy, and I wondered if he was starting to become depressed. I tried talking to him again, reassuring him, and using my usual philosophy of trying to put things into perspective by balancing the negatives of life with the positives, but he was having none of it. 'Not fussed' and 'not bothered' was his new philosophy and he was sticking to it.

Tayo's despondency also developed an insolent air and I was increasingly finding that when I suggested anything – or insisted on it in the case of homework – he shrugged in a what-are-you-going-to-do-about-it? manner. And there was very little I could do, except for continuing to talk to him and encourage him.

During these weeks, Minty turned up for contact, but was usually late and often incoherent, which I was sure did noth-ing for Tayo's disposition. He switched on the television as soon as he arrived and ignored her when she came in. Accord-ing to Aisha, if he did speak to his mother he was terse or often quite rude.

Meanwhile, phone contact continued spasmodically with Minty answering about every second or third call and occa-sionally managing to ask Tayo how he was, before lapsing into a wail about her own ills, and who had done the dirty on her now. Once when she answered she was so drunk she couldn't put two words together.

'You fucking waster!' Tayo shouted towards the phone, which was on speaker.

I picked up the handset. 'Minty, I'm terminating this phone call. It's not in either of your interests to continue.' I replaced the handset and turned to Tayo. 'Don't you ever use that word again. Do you understand?'

'Why not? She uses it,' he said, referring to his mother.

'And you want to be like her?' I asked, more from annoyance that reason.

'No! I want to be like my fucking father, but none of you bastards will find him!' He stormed out of the lounge and upstairs where he slammed his bedroom door. I gave him five minutes to cool off then went up, knocked on his door and went in. He was lying face down on his bed crying.

'Tayo, love,' I began.

'Go away!' he yelled. 'I don't want you here. You're not my family. Get out. I want my dad.'

I tried again half an hour later but he still didn't want anything to do with me. By bedtime he had calmed down sufficiently to apologize but still didn't want to talk. It saddened me greatly that he couldn't share his feelings as he had done before; he seemed to be pulling away and cocooning himself. He had pinned all his hopes on his father and I'd known from the start he had set himself up for disappointment. Now it was happening. How I wished I could have given him what he so desperately wanted but in reality, all I could do was carry on as we were and keep him safe and well cared for.

* * *

School had noticed a change in him as well. Apart from the standard of his work, which was still dropping, Tayo was becoming increasingly confrontational, his anger brimming over into the playground and classroom. Over one week in April there were three events that were serious enough to be logged on incident report forms. I was called in again, this time to the Head. Tayo was already in her office, looking far from shame-faced. The Head made it clear that she had been very lenient because of Tayo's circumstances but one more incident and he would be formally excluded for the following day. I said I would talk to him again and thanked her for her understanding. I waited until we were in the car before I said anything.

'Tayo, do you realize how serious this is? Exclusion will go on your school report and then follow you to secondary school.'

'No, it won't,' he put in quickly. 'I won't be in this country.'

'You will be, and it's irresponsible not to think about your future.'

'Shut up! I'm not talking to you anymore.' And he didn't for the rest of the day.

I was concerned and astonished by his stubbornness and tenacity. He had a dream of his father taking him to live in Nigeria and he was sticking to it. What worried me was that he was slowly destroying his real life chances for the sake of a dream, and causing himself terrible unhappiness in the process.

* * *

The Guardian Ad Litum finally managed to put in an appearance in the last week of April and I knew why she'd managed to fit it in during this particular week. Tayo's second review was scheduled for May 4th and she could hardly turn up for that not having seen him when he'd been in care for five months. But even when she came it was a perfunctory visit only, and she made little attempt to relate to Tayo. Once she'd satisfied the criteria for actually seeing the child in the foster home, she told him to go and play while she talked to me.

I was disappointed. Her attitude was dismissive of Tayo and all that he was going through. Instead of chatting to me, she should have been talking to him about how things were and trying to get an understanding of his wishes and views. But her manner was generally dismissive and once she had gleaned enough of what was going on from me to satisfy her report, she left. Alison Hemming-Sanders was undoubtedly a Guardian Ad Litum because it was damn sight easier than being at the sharp end of social work.

Tayo's mood didn't improve even with outings at the weekends to places that he had previously asked to go, like Alton Towers. Nothing I could offer seemed to soften his attitude or raise his spirits. He was developing a hard shell around him, encasing himself in an unhealthy mixture of anger and self-pity. I asked him if he would like to talk to someone outside the family about how he was feeling, a specially trained counsellor used to working with young people in care.

His emotionless and cynical response was: 'And he's going to find my father, is he?'

'No, Tayo,' I said. 'He can't, no more than anyone else can. But he might help you to come to terms with what's going on. We all need someone to talk to.'

'I don't,' he said emphatically. And he proved it by continuing to be stone-faced and almost aloof in his dealings with me and the rest of the family.

I missed the exuberant young boy who had gone tobogganing with such excitement, and who had got such great pleasure from owning a few bits and pieces from a car-boot sale. It had all started so well, and now it was slipping away and there was nothing I could do about it.

Tayo's second review was a sharp contrast to the first one. It was the same chair, Maureen Green, with Sandra, myself and the Guardian present. The school had been invited but couldn't make it so his teacher had sent in a report. Minty had been left a invitation at Headline Family Centre but didn't come or send a message. Tayo had completed the booklet that had been sent to him in the post but didn't want to attend either. He told me to tell 'them' that he didn't see any point in coming as no one was listening to what he wanted.

We were a sad little group this time as we sat in the same room at the Social Services offices and remembered how bright Tayo's first review had been compared to the picture that was emerging now. Maureen read out the school's report first and, although Mrs Gillings had tried to make it as positive as possible, it was obvious that not only had Tayo's progress stopped but he was sliding backwards. She commented on Tayo's sullen attitude, some incidents of bullying, his general lack of cooperation, and that he seemed to have lost interest in most things. On the plus side, he did still attend the two after-school clubs, and football was the one activity where he maintained a positive attitude and could lose himself in the game.

I followed with my report, and agreed with what Sonya Gillings had said, confirming Tayo still went to Saturday football club, but whereas he used to bubble over with excitement when he left the pitch, sharing it all with me and the family, he now said nothing. Any enquiry of mine about anything was met with a shrug and occasionally, 'I guess.' It was as though he was trying to freeze me out. But he was still eating and sleeping well which was something, as truly depressed children do neither.

'But when I think of the boy who arrived,' I said, 'who was so confident and full of life, and relieved to be in care, I realize how much he must now be hurting. Looking back, I suppose he was holding it together too well, considering the previous five years. He was bound to have a reaction to what had happened to him. If he was snatched by his mother, he probably never had time to come to terms with how he felt about that.'

Maureen agreed, and noted what I said. 'I hope he'll work through it,' she said. 'He's an intelligent lad and must realize that going to his father isn't a viable option when he can't be traced.'

The Guardian Ad Litum went next, and she more or less repeated what I had told her on her visit, adding that she'd seen Tayo at his foster home and was in regular phone contact with us. I didn't challenge her on this; it wasn't my place. And quite possibly she thought that two brief phone calls in five months was 'regular'. She said she hadn't been able to see Minty yet but had left a message on her mobile asking her to return the call.

'The only way I can see Minty is at the Headline Family Centre,' Sandra advised. 'She still attends contact, although she is often very late.'

Alison Hemming-Sanders made a note. 'I'll try that,' she said, though I wondered just how hard she would try. A Guardian Ad Litum is supposed to see all parties involved in the case a number of times before filing her report into court. In large families the Guardian could see a dozen or more individuals, in fact anyone who had a vested interest in the child including grandparents and aunts and uncles. Given that there was only Tayo and his mother involved in this case, it shouldn't have been too arduous.

Sandra's report served to underline the picture of Tayo that had already emerged. She mentioned that art therapy and counselling had been offered, and his response to them. Meanwhile, Minty had been unable to be assessed because she hadn't turned up for any of the appointments with either Sandra or the psychiatrist, although with four months to go before the reports had to be filed, there was still time, and more appointments had been sent to Minty.

'What are the long-term plans for Tayo?' Maureen asked Sandra.

'As it's unlikely that Tayo will be returning to his mother, it will be a long-term foster placement. We will be holding a Family Finders meeting next month to look at Tayo's needs. I've already had one discussion with my manager and we both feel that in view of Tayo's desperate need for a father figure, he should be placed with a two-parent family.' Sandra looked at me and smiled almost apologetically.

I nodded. I understood and agreed. Although we would obviously miss Tayo, I knew we would keep in touch, and I hoped that in time he would bond with a new father who would go some way to making up for the one Tayo didn't have.

'And what is the time scale on this?' Maureen asked as she wrote.

'The final court hearing is on October 20th,' Sandra said. 'We'll start looking for a family in November.'

'So you'll have Tayo for next Christmas.' Maureen looked at me.

'Excellent,' I said, pleased we'd have this time together, possibly longer, for it took many months to find a suitable family and then complete the long process of introduction.

'I wouldn't say anything about the long-term plans to Tayo yet,' Maureen added. 'Let's hope that nearer the time he'll come to be more positive and accept being in care.'

Maureen then read out Tayo's booklet, what there was of it. The questions asking what he thought about his social worker, carer, where he was living and his school were all answered with: 'OK'. His wishes for the future were predictably: 'I WANT TO LIVE WITH MY DAD!!!!!!'

Maureen smiled sadly as she closed the booklet and made a note. She drew the meeting to a close by setting the date for the next review. This one would be in six months' time and she suggested November 5th.

'Could we make it the fourth?' I asked. 'The fifth is bonfire night and I always have a little party in the evening for family and friends. I'd appreciate having the day clear to prepare.'

'Of course,' Maureen said. 'That sounds nice. Ten-thirty on the fourth then.' And we wrote it in our diaries. As usual, Maureen then thanked me for all I was doing, only this time I didn't feel that I deserved it as I had done at the last review.

When I collected Tayo from school that afternoon, he was completely silent until we were almost at Headline, when he asked, 'What happened at my review?'

'Not an awful lot,' I said. 'Sandra and Alison were there and a lady called Maureen, chairing. We talked about how you were doing and Maureen read out what you had written. Why don't you come next time, then you'll see?'

'And are they going to let me live with my dad?' he asked.

I sighed inwardly. I didn't know how many times we were going to have to keep going over this. 'It's not their decision, Tayo, it's the judge's. And while everyone wants what's best for you, it won't be possible for you to live with your father for all the reasons we've talked about. I think deep down you know that. When you're an adult you can try and find him if you still want to but for the time being you need looking after in a family.'

I glanced in the rear-view mirror and saw his face set in the now familiar look of obstinate anger.

'Fuck off the lot of you,' he suddenly yelled, and kicked the back of the seat so hard I braked as a reflex action.

'Tayo! Don't you dare do that!' I said. 'You'll cause an accident. And don't swear.'

'I will if I want. You can't stop me.'

'No but I can stop your television.'

'How?'

I glanced again in the mirror and he met my gaze, cold and defiant. He was crossing the boundary, challenging my authority, and he knew that the bottom line was I could do very little about it.

'Tayo, don't,' I said evenly. 'I don't want a confrontation with you but you won't speak to me like that, do you understand?'

His eyes blazed and I knew his anger was now spilling over. He had turned a corner but it was not a positive one. Something in him had been released, and I knew it would get worse before it got better. He was still angry as I parked outside the contact centre; although he was quiet his fists were clenched and his whole body was stiff as if ready for a fight. He went ahead and pressed the security buzzer, then marched up to the door. Once inside he continued through reception and stormed straight into Yellow Room. I caught up with him. Aisha was inside sitting at the table but there was no sign of Minty.

'Where is she?' he demanded of Aisha. 'Where's my fucking mother?' Aisha looked shocked.

'Tayo!' I said firmly. 'Sit down and calm down.'

He marched over to the toy boxes and began kicking them over, spilling their contents everywhere.

'Tayo!' I said again louder.

'Fuck off! Get out!' he yelled, his face bulging with anger.

Aisha stood up and pressed the panic button, then came and stood by me at the door. Tayo grabbed the television, pulling it off the table, and threw it to the floor. He was looking round for the next thing he could throw or kick when James appeared.

'Tayo!' he yelled at the top of his voice. 'Stop that now!' He was usually so quietly spoken that even I jumped. Tayo froze.

'Sit down now!' James commanded, going over to him and pointing to the sofa.

Immediately Tayo did as he was told. Like a lamb, he walked to the sofa and sat down, then looked up at James.

'That's better,' James said, lowering his voice and sitting beside him. Aisha and I remained where we were. He waited a moment and then said, 'Tayo, when you've calmed down you can clear up this mess, and then we'll have a chat. Your mum phoned to say she wouldn't be here for another half an hour. Is it all right if Cathy goes?'

Tayo nodded. James looked at me. 'Aisha will bring Tayo home as usual,' he said.

'Thanks, James,' I said. 'See you later, Tayo.' He didn't answer. I left, thinking to myself that if I'd ever seen a good example of a young lad responding positively to an authoritative male role model, that was it.

When Aisha returned Tayo at six she said he was much better, although Minty had arrived an hour late so they'd only seen each other for half an hour. Tayo did seem calmer as he came in, and at dinner managed a stab at some conversation. I didn't try to talk to him about what had happened, James had obviously done a good job and I left it at that.

Once Tayo had finished his homework there wasn't time for television so it didn't become an issue. But as I said goodnight, I felt the atmosphere. Tayo was strengthening his defences and forcing me out even further.

'Do you want a kiss?' I asked, as I tucked him in.

He shrugged. 'Not fussed.'

'Well, but I'd like to give you one anyway.' I leaned forward and gave him my usual kiss on his forehead. 'Night night,' I said. 'Sleep tight.'

But there was no return of 'And don't let the bed bugs bite', so I came out and closed the door.

Chapter Twenty-One

The Phone Call

May gave way to June and the weather turned gloriously warm. The cloudless skies shone blue and the garden burst into life. All the exams came to an end and everyone awaited their results. The only thing Tayo was waiting for was his father, and he struggled on a daily basis to keep his anger under control. He still refused art therapy or counselling but he knew it was available if ever he felt it might be useful. He also knew I was always on hand to listen if he wanted to talk, but he didn't.

I now felt that Tayo's life could go one of two ways – he could gradually come to terms with what had happened and try to look positively on the future, or he could continue with the seething anger and resentment which undoubtedly would send him on a downward spiral towards teenage delinquency.

I was desperate to help him overcome his despair. I'd seen children before whose life chances had effectively been ruined because the damage done to them was so extensive that they would never recover. For a child like Jodie Brown (whose story I told in *Damaged*), who'd suffered such extreme sexual abuse at such a young age that she was virtually stunted in her development, it meant a closed-in life of dependency and lack of choice. For others who had been left too long in terrible situations of confusion and neglect, it meant it was too late to reach them. That way of life, and the anger deep inside, was so ingrained that the path to a life of missed chances and possibly crime and drugs was almost inevitable.

But it didn't need to be like that for Tayo. His character and intelligence meant that he'd been given a chance to get through this and, on the other side, perhaps find a rewarding career and a satisfying life. I knew he was standing at a fork in the road and I yearned for him to pick the right path. It broke my heart to think of him slipping away and ending up at the bottom of the pile.

Adrian returned home from university with all his belongings for the long summer break. I had to take Tayo when I collected Adrian as I didn't feel comfortable leaving him in the care of Lucy and Paula, and it was quite a squash getting everything in. On the return journey Tayo had to sit on Adrian's duvet and pillows, with his head nearly touching the ceiling. He did find this amusing, and actually laughed when we went over a bump and his hair brushed the roof of the car.

Now that he was back, Adrian began spending time with Tayo, with varying degrees of success. Sometimes Tayo was responsive and open to Adrian's input and suggestions, but at other times he gave Adrian the same cold-shoulder treatment that he gave the girls and me.

I had come to realize with sadness that Tayo had a very low opinion of women in general, probably because of the example of his mother. It didn't take much for him to criticize the girls or me, or raise his eyes in disdain. Most of the time we just ignored it, but sometimes Paula rose to the bait before realizing that the best thing to do was simply walk away.

With the weather so good, I encouraged Tayo outside as much as possible. I tried to think of things that would keep him busy and occupied. Tayo liked his sport and physical activity seemed to give him a diversion so I asked him if he would like to go on a local play scheme in the summer holidays, where there were lots of fun activities. If so, I would have to apply soon to secure him a place. He said he wasn't fussed, but Sandra and I thought it would be a good idea, so I sent off the application form. In the meantime, I kept Tayo very busy at the weekends in the belief that this would give him less time for gloomy speculation but I knew we were in for a long haul before I saw any improvement.

June 23rd was a Thursday and also my brother's birthday. Tayo was off school for two days because of staff training, and the weather was set to be even hotter than the day before and was predicted to reach a new record; but then, we always seemed to be setting new temperature records now.

I had decided to take Tayo swimming rather than having him mooching around all day, and while he had his breakfast I phoned my brother at his office to wish him a happy birthday. I replaced the receiver and started upstairs to find the towels for swimming when the phone rang again. I went back and answered it in the hall.

'Hello?'

'Cathy.'

'Hello, Sandra.'

'Is everything all right?'

'Not too bad,' I said. I thought Sandra's voice sounded uneven, emotional almost. 'Are you all right?'

'Yes, just shocked. You're not going to believe what's happened.' She paused to catch her breath. 'I've just had a phone call from a Mr Ondura in Nigeria. He's Tayo's father.'

'What?' I cried in disbelief.

'Yes, I know I can't believe it either. We've been talking for nearly an hour. Tayo's off school, isn't he? He can't hear me, can he?'

'No, he's having breakfast.'

'Good, because I need to think carefully about what we're going to say.'

I was listening hard now, my heart was thumping loudly and my hands shaking. Sandra couldn't get her words out quickly enough.

'I'm not sure where to begin,' she said. 'Mr Ondura phoned me at eight-thirty this morning just as I got to my desk. We're going to speak again later, and he's faxing over Tayo's birth certificate. According to Mr Ondura, Tayo lived with him and his paternal grandmother from when he was a baby. He's on Tayo's birth certificate as his father, although he was never married to Minty. He said Minty had problems right from the start and eventually was persuaded to give Tayo over to the care of him and his mother. Minty had access though, when she wanted, which was variable. Mr Ondura said he paid to have Tayo go to one of the best schools in Nigeria – honestly, Cathy, he's very well spoken, with almost a public-school accent. Apparently Minty wasn't supposed to see Tayo without either him or his mother being present, but one day she went to the school and basically snatched Tayo from the playground. He had the police after her immediately, of course, but she simply disappeared without trace, taking the boy with her. He says that he's been trying to find Tayo for the last five years, but he's been looking mainly in Africa and the Far East where Minty has relatives. He's spent a fortune on private detectives, but any sightings of them led to nothing.'

'Didn't he look here?' I breathed, unable to bear the suspense of Sandra's story.'

'Oh yes, he contacted the authorities here a number of times, and gave both the names Ondura, which is Tayo's correct surname, and Mezer, which is Minty's, but of course, with Minty and Tayo not registered for anything, they were invisible. They weren't on any database in either name.'

I still couldn't really believe what I was hearing. 'But why didn't the Home Office have any record of them entering the country?'

'Mr Ondura thinks they must have used forged passports in completely different names. Apparently Minty associated with a pretty undesirable crowd out there and could have laid her hands on them easily.'

'But I can't understand why Tayo has never mentioned his real surname to us. He must have realized it might have helped trace his father. I remember asking him if his father's surname was Mezer and he said he didn't know.'

'I don't know, we'll ask him at some point. I'm still getting over the shock of speaking to his father.'

'Yes,' I agreed. 'It's absolutely incredible! It's still sinking in. There's no mistake, is there?'

'I don't see how there could be. From what Mr Ondura said, Tayo's recollections of his early years in Nigeria are spot on. Mr Ondura does live in a big house by the sea, and he used to travel a lot with his work, and still does. While he was away his mother, Tayo's gran, looked after Tayo with the help of a nanny when he was a baby. I didn't ask Mr Ondura if he was tall and muscular,' she said with a laugh, 'but when I told him Tayo loved his sport, he said he must have got it from him. He plays golf and goes to the gym regularly. He used to be very good at football and nearly turned professional when he was younger.'

'But that's exactly as Tayo said! And all the time I thought how sad it was that he needed to invent this amazing father …' I sat down on the stairs, completely overcome. 'I can't believe I'm hearing this.'

'What?' Tayo said, suddenly appearing in the hall having finished his breakfast.

'Just a minute,' I said to Sandra, and leaving the mouthpiece uncovered, I said to Tayo, 'I'll be with you in a minute. Go upstairs and do your teeth, and then find your swimming trunks.'

I waited until he'd passed me and was safely out of earshot. 'OK, Sandra, he's gone.'

'Mr Ondura wanted to know all about Tayo obviously. I kept it positive though, there'll be plenty of time for him to learn about the horrors of what happened when he talks to him, and I got the impression that he's feeling guilty enough already. I told him what a big handsome lad Tayo was, how intelligent and well mannered he was. Mr Ondura said he was quite strict with Tayo, although he loved him deeply – he always insisted on respect and good manners, as did the school he sent him to. He said he placed a lot on a good education and the school encouraged self-reliance and traditional values. I said it was probably that grounding that saw Tayo through the last five years.'

'Yes, it must have been,' I said. 'What's the saying? Give me a child until he's seven and I'll give you the man.'

'Exactly. Only in Tayo's case, it was five years. Just shows how important those early years are.'

I imagined poor little Tayo, only five years old, snatched from a safe and happy life where he was looked after and loved, into a nightmarish whirlwind of chaos, hunger and danger. Could it all be over now? 'Does he want Tayo back?' I asked.

'Oh yes – but it's not going to be that easy, which is why we need to be careful what we say to Tayo. This is the first time I've dealt with a case like this and I've got to do some research into the legal position. But from what I know so far, Mr Ondura is going to have to apply to the courts here to become Tayo's legal guardian. Because he wasn't married to Tayo's mother, he has no automatic right to Tayo under English law. Tayo is a Nigerian citizen and he did have a Nigerian passport but obviously that wasn't used to enter the country otherwise the Embassy would have had a record. Now that Tayo is in care, he's under our legal jurisdiction – that means that if Mr Ondura wants Tayo to live with him and his mother in Nigeria, they'll have to be assessed there by our authorities. As you can imagine, none of this will happen quickly. The first thing

Mr Ondura has to do is to become party to the proceedings here and I've told him to instruct his lawyer, which he said he will do today.'

'Oh, Sandra,' I said, a lump rising in my throat. 'This is truly unbelievable! It's like a dream come true! But what shall I tell Tayo?'

I longed to be able to run up and share all the excitement and emotion that was welling up in me, but, for Tayo's sake, we had to think carefully about what was best for him.

'I think you can tell him that his father has been found – or rather he found us – and that I've spoken to him and he's going to phone this evening, that's all. I've suggested seven if that's all right with you. Mr Ondura wants to visit as soon as he can but I've made it clear to him there's no question of him taking Tayo back until the legal position is clarified at the final court hearing. I've also said that when he sees Tayo it will be super-vised contact to begin with, and he understood that. I also told him to bring the original of Tayo's birth certificate with him, which we will need for court.'

'How long do you think it's all going to take?' I said. 'Tayo's bound to ask.'

'I don't know yet. But his father and gran have got to be assessed and the judge has to be satisfied, so it's going to take a while. At least six months, I'd say. We'll have to get the final court hearing postponed.'

'Sandra,' I said, 'how did Tayo's father find him, or rather find you? And why now and not before?'

'It was through the authorities here. The private detective that's been working for Mr Ondura on and off for the last five years was doing another sweep of all possible countries and of course the name Mezer came up because it's now on our systems. They discovered a month ago that Tayo was in this country but they've only just managed to track him down to this authority, and me.'

'Good grief, that must have taken some doing!' I thought of the labyrinthine nature of the Social Services, with its millions of names and thousands of cases. 'Well, he must be serious about having Tayo back.'

'Yes, that's my feeling. Tell Tayo that his father has been looking for him for five years.' Sandra's voice shook again. 'Cathy, Tayo was so sure of it. That little boy had unshakeable faith in his father. I think we owe him an apology.'

'I know.' My eyes moistened. 'It's like a fairy tale. Tayo's knight in shining armour is really coming to rescue him after all.' Then I stopped short as a terrible thought struck me. 'Sandra, nothing can go wrong, can it? Tayo can't lose it all again, can he?'

'I don't think so. Mr Ondura obviously loves Tayo. He was nearly in tears on the phone when he finally spoke to me. He's obviously sincere and committed about looking after Tayo, otherwise he wouldn't have gone to all the trouble to find him, and as long as he can satisfy the court that he can give Tayo a good home, and assuming Tayo wants to go, which I think we can take as read, it should happen. It's more a matter of when. Now, I've got to see our legal department and put them in touch with Mr Ondura's lawyer. Will you tell Tayo?'

'Of course. I've never had anything nicer to tell someone.'

'His dad will call at seven our time.'

'Sandra,' I said, laughing out loud, 'I still can't believe this. I think I'm as excited as Tayo's going to be.'

'My manager was sitting next to me when the phone call came through and she was in tears as well. Now, you go and tell him and I'll speak to you later. Also I'll try and visit tomorrow when I know more and after they've spoken. Good luck!'

'Thanks. But I think this is one time I won't be needing it.'

Chapter Twenty-Two

My Daddy

I walked slowly up the stairs with carefully measured steps that belied my racing heart. How many times had I trodden this path up to the child I was fostering to impart some piece of news – good news, bad news, indifferent messages about changes in arrangements or appointments? Hundreds, possibly thousands of times. Yet I couldn't ever remember being the harbinger of a piece of news that was so welcomed, deserved, and life-changing.

I turned right at the top of the stairs and went along the landing to Tayo's door. I knocked and entered. Tayo was standing with his back to me, gazing out of the window.

'Tayo.'

He turned and looked at me, big eyes dull and unenthusiastic. 'I don't want to go swimming,' he said.

'Then you needn't.' I felt the smile that I could no longer contain spread across my face. 'Tayo, love, that was Sandra on the phone. She's been speaking to your father in Nigeria.'

He looked at me, and no words, photograph, painting, or music could ever capture the transition that Tayo went through. His expression changed in seconds from sullen despondency to absolute ecstasy, as his eyes opened wider than I had ever seen them before and his face, his whole body, lifted as though a ton weight had been taken from his shoulders.

'My dad?' he said, not daring to believe. 'My dad? He's come?'

'He's not here, love, he phoned Sandra from Nigeria, he's going to phone you this evening.'

'My dad,' he said again, still disbelieving. 'My dad has really found me?'

'He has, darling, he has. You were right all along. Your tall, big, strong dad who plays football and does everything you said, has been looking for you for five years. And now he's found you.'

'My dad,' he said again wonderingly. Then he yelled at the top of his voice. 'My dad! My daddy is coming to get me, I knew it!'

Tears streamed down his face as he shouted. I felt my own tears fall. He rushed into my arms, flinging himself at me with such force that I nearly lost my balance. 'My dad! My daddy!' His arms tightened round my waist and he buried his head into my chest as though he would never let go. I held him for all I was worth, my chin resting again his soft shining hair.

'Tayo, love,' I said softly. 'He's really done it. He's found you, just like you said he would.'

Adrian's bedroom door opened and a moment later he poked his head into the room. 'Everything all right, Mum?' he asked, still half asleep.

'They're found my dad!' Tayo cried, lifting his head up to look at Adrian. 'They've really found my dad.'

Adrian looked at me astonished and I nodded. 'It's right,' I confirmed. 'Or rather Tayo's dad has found him. Long story, but he's spent five years looking for him. He spoke to Sandra from Nigeria this morning and he's going to phone here this evening.'

'Cool,' Adrian said. 'Well done that man.'

Tayo began to calm down as the initial euphoria subsided and he realized how many other questions there were to ask. 'Is he coming here?' he cried. 'Is he going to take me back? Has he got a passport? Has he got mine? Is my gran all right?'

Adrian retreated back to his bed, while I took a couple of tissues from the box, passed one to Tayo, and we both wiped our eyes. I took his hand. 'Come on, let's go downstairs and I'll tell you what I know.'

Seated beside him on the sofa with Tayo's hand in mine, I told Tayo what Sandra had told me, of his father's search, which had led to his eventually finding him in this country. 'He's going to visit you, love but it will all take time.'

'Will I go back to live with him?'

'That's what your dad would like but there's a lot of legal things that have to happen and it will be the judge's decision.'

'I'll go and see the judge and tell him I want to live with my dad.'

I smiled and gave his hand a little squeeze. 'Certainly the judge will want to know that, but Alison, your Guardian, and Sandra will take care of it and tell him. All you're going to have to do is be patient; Sandra thinks it will take about six months, but she can't be sure.'

I could see Tayo calculating in his head. 'So I'll b[...]
for Christmas?'

'It's possible,' I said. 'But we won't know anything
nite until the judge looks at all the reports and make [...]
sion. And one of those reports will be from a social work[...]
will visit your dad and gran in Nigeria.'

'Why?'

'So the judge knows that it is a good place and they are g[...]
people.'

'They are!' he cried indignantly.

'I know, love, but the judge must have the report.' I didn'[...]
want to puncture his dreams but he had to have an understanding of the complexity of the case, and realize that he
wasn't going to be sailing off into the sunset with his father in
a week. 'So let's take it a stage at a time, OK?'

He nodded. 'Yes, I understand.' And he nodded again, shaking his head up and down as though his teeth would chatter.

I laughed. 'And I think it would be a good idea to go swimming, otherwise you'll be sitting here all day on edge, waiting
for the phone call.'

'Yes, sure,' he said, bright again and full of enthusiasm. 'My
dad loves swimming.'

I laughed. The old Tayo was back, and it was wonderful to
see him. 'You're right, he does, and golf, and going to the gym.
And he is tall and muscular and you're going to be just like
him.'

'And he's black,' Tayo added. 'And I'm proud I'm his son.'

* * *

We went swimming, although I could see Tayo's thoughts were far from the chlorinated and artificially heated water of the municipal baths. His dream-like gaze suggested he was in the naturally warm water of the South Atlantic as it lapped the white sands of the Gulf of Guinea and Nigeria, while his father and gran watched him adoringly from the beach.

Tayo was quieter in the car coming home, exhausted from the swimming and the emotions of the morning. He spoke intermittently, usually beginning with 'I suppose …' before suggesting what his father or his life in Nigeria might be like.

All I said was, 'It's quite possible; you can ask him when he phones.' I still shook my head in wonderment at the thought that Tayo's father was going to be calling us that very evening. It was truly incredible.

As I drew up outside the house, Tayo said, 'I suppose my dad could have a wife now, with more kids?'

'He might, but Sandra didn't say anything about that. I'm sure he would have mentioned it to her and she would have told us. He still lives in the same house as when you were little, I think.'

'With my gran. And the servants,' Tayo put in. 'I remember servants.'

Lucky them, I thought, one wouldn't go amiss here.

'I don't mind if there are other kids,' Tayo added, 'as long as he has time for me.'

I turned and looked at him. 'Tayo, your father will have all the time in the world for you, love. I've never heard of a man spending five years searching the world for his lost son. Never ever.'

He beamed. 'I guess I'm important.'

'You are, love. That's for sure.'

I tried to keep Tayo absorbed in activities as best I could for the rest of the afternoon, but I was fighting a losing battle. He just wanted to think and talk about his father and what life would be like with him. When Paula and Lucy returned home after school and college, Tayo flew down the hall as soon as he heard their keys in the lock.

'They've found my dad!' he cried, before they'd even got in.

To say they joined in his excitement was an understatement. The whole house was in uproar as the cry of 'They've found my dad!' reverberated round the walls along with screams and cheers of delight. The neighbours must have wondered what on earth was going on next door.

By the time I served dinner, I was on a heightened state of alert, eating with one eye on the clock. Tayo had asked what time his dad was phoning but I'd said that I wasn't sure, then added the warning that sometimes it was difficult to get through on long-distance calls and he wasn't to be disappointed if his dad couldn't get a connection tonight, because he would doubtless try again in the morning. I didn't want to let him pin his hopes on a particular time, and I was even beginning to wonder if I should have promised that it would be tonight.

We finished dinner but I hovered near the phone, unable to load the dishwasher or do anything I was supposed to. Tayo had the television on in the lounge but I doubted he was actually watching it. The clock ticked up to seven and then five past. At ten past the phone rang and I flew into the lounge to answer it. Tayo pressed the remote to switch off the television.

'Hello?' Silence, and then crackles on the line. My heart thudded and my mouth went dry. 'Hello?' I tried again, and the line cleared.

'Is that Mrs Glass?' a highly cultured male voice asked.

'It is. Speaking.' There was a second's time delay before he replied.

'Hello, Mrs Glass, I am Mr Ondura, Tayo's father.'

Tears leapt to my eyes again and I tripped over the words I was trying to get out. 'Oh … hello! Oh, hello. I'm so pleased you've called. So pleased. Really. Tayo is sitting next to me. I'll put him on now.'

I passed the phone to Tayo and watched his expression. If I'd ever had doubts about the joys of fostering, they were dispelled in that instant. His face shone and his eyes glistened as he spoke the words neither of us had ever thought he'd say.

'Hello, Dad, my daddy,' he said evenly. 'Thank you for phoning me.'

Adrian, Lucy and Paula appeared at the lounge door. There wasn't a dry eye in the house as we watched Tayo. We couldn't hear what his father said but could guess from the replies. Tayo sat proud and upright with the phone to his ear and answered his father's questions, then relaxed a little and made conversation.

Strictly speaking, I should have supervised the phone call but after five minutes, as there were no issues with his speaking with his father, I left the lounge door open and came out to give them some privacy. Adrian, Paula and Lucy left too. For the next hour, as Tayo spoke on the phone, I wandered in and out of the lounge occasionally, just to make sure Tayo was all right and coping with all the emotion.

Tayo and his father clearly had a lot of catching up to do and from what I could hear, Mr Ondura was playing it just right. Their talk had started off light as he asked Tayo about his school, hobbies, the food he liked, and his life with us. Tayo then listened as his father told him of his life at home and the search that had led to him finding him. I heard Tayo ask if he was married with 'kids' and from his reply I guessed the answer was no.

'So there's just me then?' Tayo said. And I was pleased because Tayo needed spoiling, he deserved it, and I felt sure his father would more than make up the lost five years.

An hour passed and I dreaded to think how much the call was costing Mr Ondura, but from what I'd heard so far from Sandra and Tayo, his father sounded well off by any standard, so I was sure he could afford it.

Tayo's voice dropped and became more subdued as he talked about some of the things that had happened to him since he'd disappeared from school in Nigeria on that fateful afternoon. His father must have asked him if he knew where his mother was because Tayo said, 'I don't know. She hasn't got an address. No one knows.' I also noticed how respectful Tayo had become in his tone and language as he spoke to his father; at one point he even called him sir.

After almost an hour and a half on the phone, Tayo called me. 'Cathy, Dad would like to talk you if it's convenient.' It was the old Tayo, polite and formal, even though I knew he was repeating his father's words.

I went into the lounge and took the receiver while Tayo hovered. 'Good evening, Mr Ondura,' I said, with a bit more composure than the last time I'd spoken to him.

'Good evening, Mrs Glass. It is a real pleasure to make your acquaintance. Let me begin by thanking you from the bottom of my heart for looking after my son. It is an enormous relief to know he is safe and well at last. You can't begin to imagine what I have gone through in the years since he was taken. I was coming to the conclusion that he must be dead, then he was found, thanks to your Social Services.'

It was the first time I'd ever heard a parent praising the Social Services for taking their child into care, but of course Mr Ondura was seeing it from an entirely different viewpoint. Not only had the care system been Tayo's salvation, it had also made Tayo 'visible', allowing his father to find him.

'I understand from Miss Braxley, Tayo's social worker,' he continued, 'that my son can be quite strong willed. He always was but I have made it clear to Tayo that while you are looking after him he will do as you say.' I glanced at Tayo who was looking slightly apprehensive, and I smiled.

'He's a good boy,' I said. 'And to be honest, I'm amazed at how well he's coped, considering everything.'

'That makes me very proud, thank you, Mrs Glass.' I heard his voice break with emotion before he quickly recovered. 'I have spoken to Miss Braxley a number of times today,' he continued. 'There is much to address in respect of the legal situation. I have said I want my son home to live with me where he belongs as soon as possible. I will not stop until I have achieved that goal. I know my son wants to return.'

'He does. Very much,' I confirmed. 'But I have explained to Tayo that it will take some months, possibly six or more before everything is complete.'

'That is what Miss Braxley said, but I have told her we must do everything to try and speed things up. Tayo has had uncertainty for long enough. Miss Braxley was talking about postponing the final court hearing in October but I have asked her to leave it as it is for now – perhaps we can still make that date. I am in business and have little understanding of child care proceedings but I am learning fast, and I believe that if everyone pulls their fingers out, it is possible.'

It was strange hearing that English colloquialism from a well educated, perfectly enunciated, slightly accented voice, but I wondered if he was being over optimistic. Even if everyone connected with Tayo's case did, as he said, pull their fingers out there was still a lot to do, not least of which was the Social Services visit to Nigeria to assess Mr Ondura and his mother.

'To this end,' he continued, 'my lawyer is already speaking with the Social Services legal department, and I shall see them next week when I visit.'

'You're coming next week?' I looked at Tayo who was nodding furiously.

'Yes, I am booked on a flight for this Sunday. I have told Tayo. I shall arrive in the evening at nine o'clock and I have asked Miss Braxley to arrange for me to see my son on Monday. On this one occasion I should like Tayo to be taken out of school for the day. I assure you I shall not be making a habit of it but I think in this instance I can be forgiven.'

'Undoubtedly,' I said. 'Tayo wouldn't be able to concentrate anyway, knowing you are in the country.'

'Precisely. I can see we are of the same mind. There is a Hilton hotel about twenty minutes from your town, I believe. I have reserved a room there and will use the taxis to get around.'

Struth, I thought, impressed. He really hasn't wasted any time! But then, he's been waiting for five years for this. He probably knew exactly what he'd do when Tayo was found.

Mr Ondura said, 'Now, if I could say goodnight to my son I won't keep you any longer. It is getting late and I think it must be past his bed time.'

'Of course.'

'And, Mrs Glass, let me finish as I started by thanking you. I am looking forward to meeting you, you are doing an incredible job and my mother sends her warmest wishes too. She will speak to Tayo on the phone when I am there. It has all been a bit much for her and she is resting at present.'

'I understand, thank you, Mr Ondura. I'll pass you to Tayo now.'

Tayo sat on the sofa again and I handed him the phone. 'Goodnight, Dad,' he said, then there was a pause and his face opened to a huge smile as he added, 'and don't let the bed bugs bite.' The phrase that had begun all those years ago with his gran tucking him into bed had gone full circle and found its way home again.

He replaced the receiver and snuggled into my side. I put my arm round him and he buried his head in my shoulder and sobbed again. 'I'm sorry, Cathy,' he said. 'I'm sorry for being so horrible to you and your family.'

'It's OK,' I said, reaching for a tissue. 'You've been through a lot. We understand, and I know you'll be fine now.'

'Yes, I will,' he said, raising his head to blow his nose. 'Fine, really really fine.'

'Tayo, I think the best thing now is bed. You must be exhausted and I know I am.'

I eased him from the sofa and led him upstairs. I waited on the landing while he quickly washed and changed and then got into bed. A warm summer breeze wafted through the open window and a nearly full moon shone between the parted curtains.

'It's funny to think my dad is seeing the same moon,' he said. 'All those miles away. I used to think about that a lot.'

'Did you, love?' I sat on the bed and stroked his hair.

'All the time I've been away from him I thought he was out there somewhere looking up at that moon and thinking of me.'

'Well, you were right weren't you?' He smiled and yawned. 'Now, off to sleep. You haven't got school again tomorrow so you can have a lie in. Sandra is coming at some point, and you're seeing your mother in the evening.'

He suddenly looked concerned. 'What do you think she'll say about my dad?'

'I don't know, why? Are you worried?'

'Sort of. I think she'll be angry.'

'Possibly, but not with you. And Sandra will know how to handle it. Don't you worry, just be happy, OK.'

'Will you say sorry to Adrian, Lucy and Paula for me? Sorry I was so horrible.'

'I will.' I stood up and kissed his forehead, his eyes were already closing. 'Night night, sleep tight.'

'And don't let the bed bugs bite,' he said sleepily, then added, 'my gran will say that to me again soon.'

Chapter Twenty-Three

Arrangements

Far from having a lie in the next morning, Tayo was up before the girls left for school and college.

'Sorry for being such a pig,' he said as they collected their bags from the hall and prepared to leave.

'You're forgiven,' they said in turn and gave him a hug.

'You guys coming to visit me in Nigeria?' he asked.

'Yeah!' Lucy and Paula readily agreed.

'We'll see,' I said, not wishing to dampen anyone's enthusiasm but being realistic. 'It's a nice thought though.' And it was.

I kept Tayo occupied with little jobs in the garden for the rest of the morning. He liked helping and doing what he called 'man's work'. He pruned a couple of bushes for me, sawed up a small log and then swept the patio. None of the jobs was urgent but it gave him something to do. We had a sandwich lunch with Adrian, who'd come down to find a letter from Tesco confirming they would be employing him again for the summer. He was pleased, as student jobs seemed to be increasingly difficult to secure; many of his friends hadn't been able to find anything this year.

Sandra arrived shortly after one, and Tayo came in from the garden as soon as he heard her voice through the open French windows. She didn't have to ask him how the phone call from his father had gone, because he began telling her without pausing for breath. She listened patiently, her face mirroring Tayo's in delight and enthusiasm. He finally ran out of breath with, 'That's right, isn't it? He *is* coming on Sunday?'

Sandra said, 'Yes, and you will see him at twelve-thirty on Monday. At Headline.'

'Oh,' Tayo moaned. 'Can't he take me out? He wants to play football with me, and go to the cinema, and the castle.' The castle was a ruin about half an hour's drive from the town and I'd taken Tayo to see it the month before, but clearly it would be a whole new experience to have his father there.

'Your dad will be able to take you out later in the week,' Sandra said. 'But Monday's contact will be at Headline, and I shall be there as well. He'll come to my office first, because we have lots of thing to discuss, and papers and forms to exchange and complete, then I'll bring him to Headline and you'll see him for two hours. If it all goes well, which I'm sure it will, he can take you out during the week. You don't mind missing some school, do you?'

Does a duck mind water? Tayo shook his head vigorously.

'As you know,' Sandra continued, smiling, 'he's staying for the week and I've left a message with the secretary at your school to say you won't be in Monday, Wednesday or Thursday, because you're seeing your father. You will also see your dad for the whole of next Saturday and Sunday.'

'Why not Tuesday and Friday?' Tayo asked, frowning.

I knew the answer.

Sandra said, 'Because that's when you see your mother and my manager has agreed with me that it would be too much for you to see your father all day and your mum in the evening.'

Tayo opened his mouth to protest but he didn't say anything. I could see him thinking it through and while he would have liked to see his father every day, he knew he wouldn't be allowed to abandon his mother for the week. Despite all her failings, she was his mother and until the court decided otherwise, Minty was entitled to see her son as set down in the Care Order.

'He can phone you on the Tuesday and Friday,' Sandra added.

'Will he be allowed to come here to collect me?' Tayo asked. 'I want to show him my bedroom and all my things.'

'As long as Cathy agrees,' Sandra said, looking at me.

'Yes. There aren't any concerns, are there?'

'No. We've run a police check and it's clear.'

'Police check?' Tayo picked this up immediately, ever astute.

'It's a formality,' Sandra said. 'We do it with everyone who comes into contact with children. Now, Tayo, you must be patient. I'm sure you've thought about this already, but when your dad returns to Nigeria, it's going to be a bit sad for you. You won't be seeing him again until the court case, although you'll speak on the phone of course.'

'October!' Tayo cried. 'That's only three months to go!' It was nearer four but I didn't correct him. 'And then I'll go home with him?'

'I hope so. We'll do our very best, I promise,' Sandra said. She gave Tayo a hug and stood ready to leave. 'I'm sorry I must go, I've so much to do and I want to see Minty before contact tonight at Headline. I've left a message on her phone asking her to get there half an hour early. See you later Tayo.'

I walked with her down the hall with Tayo hopping and skipping beside us. Before I opened the door Sandra paused and looked again at Tayo. 'There is one thing I wanted to ask you. You know your surname, Mezer? When did you start using it?'

Tayo stopped bouncing up and down and was suddenly still and on guard, his old protective instinct kicking in. 'Why?' he said.

'I'm curious. Because your real surname is Ondura, that's what's on your birth certificate. It's not a problem, I just wondered why you didn't tell me or Cathy.'

His face clouded. 'My mum said it wasn't Ondura. I asked her when we came to this country because at my school in Nigeria I was always Ondura. Mum said I'd made it up and got very angry. I believed her because there were lots of other things I thought I'd remembered about my life before but she said it was all lies and I wasn't to say it again.' He paused, and looked carefully at Sandra. 'If I'd told you, it would have helped find my dad sooner, wouldn't it?'

'No,' Sandra lied. 'I doubt it.'

Though in truth, we would never know.

'Who the fuck does he think he is! Wait till I get my hands on him! I'll fucking kill him!'

Minty's voice could be heard raging through the centre. That answered any questions we'd had about how she would take the news that Tayo's father had been found.

Tayo stood close to me, subdued. Who did his mother want to kill this time? His father or Tayo himself? We stayed where we were in reception, and I kept the door open behind me in case we had to make a quick escape.

Aisha appeared from the corridor. 'Wait there a moment,' she said unnecessarily. 'I'll tell them you're here. James and Sandra are trying to calm Minty down.'

She went back down the corridor and I looked at Tayo who had visibly paled.

'Don't worry,' I reassured him. 'We won't stay if Mum doesn't calm down.'

'I don't want to stay,' he said. 'She's been drinking, I can hear it in her voice.'

I didn't doubt what Tayo said, as he'd lived with her long enough to know the signs, even if Sandra and James didn't. We waited, the shouting stopped, five minutes passed and then Aisha reappeared.

'We're not going ahead with contact tonight,' she said. 'Your mother is all right now, Tayo, but Sandra thinks it's best to leave it until Tuesday. You can phone her as usual tomorrow.'

'She's drunk,' Tayo said.

Aisha looked at me and didn't know what to say.

'You can tell him,' I said. 'Tayo thought he heard something in her voice.'

'It's possible,' Aisha said. 'She's had some water now and we're going to pay for a taxi to take her home.'

Tayo shrugged dismissively and turned ready to leave. 'See you next Tuesday,' I said to Aisha. Tayo and I left. He said nothing until we were in the car again returning home.

'What do you think will happen to her when I go for good?' he asked, concerned.

I caught his gaze in the rear-view mirror. 'I know you love your mum, but please try not to worry. Your mother is an adult and adults can take care of themselves. It's not a child's responsibility.'

My reassurance sounded hollow to my ears, as I'm sure it did to Tayo's. The clear evidence was that Minty wasn't functioning as a responsible adult and she had needed Tayo to take care of her when he was with her.

But he had to grasp his own chance of happiness – Minty had had her own chances, whatever they had been. Tayo was the important one now.

Saturday morning football provided a good two-hour diversion for Tayo, and afterwards he was more than happy to share his triumphs with me. When we phoned Minty's mobile that evening she didn't answer, so Tayo left a message.

'Hello, Mum. I hope you're feeling better. You know I worry about you. When I see you on Tuesday, please be OK. I love my dad and I want to live with him, but I love you too. Bye.'

I could have wept.

We went to my parents' house for Sunday dinner. They'd built up quite a relationship with Tayo and were fond of him and were delighted to hear his news. That visit took care of most of the day, so that by the time we arrived home, stuffed full of homemade puddings and cake, it was bath and bed time for

Tayo. It had been another lovely summer's day and the sky was still light at nearly nine when I tucked Tayo into bed. He wanted his curtains left open so he could see the moon.

'He's here,' Tayo said dreamily. 'My dad has landed in this country. I'll see him soon, Cathy. Only till tomorrow to wait.'

A few more hours, and Tayo's long wait to see his father would be over.

Chapter Twenty-Four

The Lost Son

I'm not sure who was more nervous on Monday morning as Tayo and I changed into our smart clothes ready to meet his father.

Tayo wanted to leave at eleven o'clock, and it had taken some doing to persuade him that the twenty-minute journey to the Headline Family Centre was not going to take an hour and a half, even if the traffic was heavy.

'But supposing there's been an accident,' he persisted. 'The high street might be blocked then we'd have to go the long way round on the by-pass.'

'Yes, and there might be a hurricane and earthquake, but thirty minutes is plenty of time to get there.'

And it was.

We drew up outside the family centre at twelve-twenty. My stomach was churning and my heart fluttered as we walked up the path. Of all the reunions of all the children I'd looked after in all the years I'd been fostering, no meeting had ever caused either me or the child so much nervous anticipation and excitement.

At the door Tayo straightened his trousers and brushed his hands over his hair.

'You look fine,' I said. 'I'm proud of you and I know your dad will be too.'

I heard him take a deep breath and I could almost hear his heart thudding as mine was doing. We went in and James met us in reception with a broad smile. He put his hand on Tayo's shoulder. 'You dad's here with Sandra,' he said. 'In Blue Room.'

We followed him down the short corridor. I could feel Tayo's nervousness; his breath was coming fast and shallow, and he kept licking his bottom lip. Before we turned the corner into Blue Room Tayo grabbed my arm. I put my hand on top of his and gave it a reassuring squeeze. We went in.

Sandra was standing in the middle of the room and next to her stood Tayo's father. He was well over six feet tall, in his mid-thirties, broad shouldered, handsome, and incredibly smart in a light grey suit and open neck white shirt. He looked at his son and his eyes filled with tears as he held out his arms to him. There was a second's hesitation before Tayo let go of my arm and rushed into his father's waiting embrace. He was so tall and broad that he seemed to engulf Tayo completely. Hugging him close, he cried openly. 'My son. Dear God, thank you. My son,' was all he could say.

Tayo began to cry. I was weeping and the tears were pouring down Sandra's face. Behind me, James left discreetly.

'My son,' Tayo's father repeated, his cheek pressing against the top of Tayo's head. 'My son, my lost son. I never thought I'd see you again.' Tayo sobbed louder. I reached into my pocket for tissues and passed one to Sandra, who sniffed and smiled gratefully.

After a few moments Mr Ondura looked up, his eyes and cheeks wet. Tayo still had his arms tightly around his father's waist with his head buried into his chest. Slowly straightening, Mr Ondura gently eased Tayo from him. With one arm around his son's shoulders, he took the few steps across the room to me, and struggling to compose himself, he offered his hand for shaking.

'I can't ever thank you enough,' he said, his voice breaking again.

I looked into the dark eyes that were an older version of Tayo's and smiled. 'You're welcome,' I said. 'I'm so pleased to meet you at last. Tayo's a lovely boy. We'll have time to talk later but for now I'll leave you two to get to know each other.'

I would have loved to have stayed and watched them get to know each other but this was their time, an intimate, emotional occasion for themselves alone. I had been privileged to see their first reunion and that would have to be enough for me.

'I'll see you later,' I said to Tayo, then to Sandra, 'Shall I collect Tayo at two-thirty?'

'Yes, please.'

Mr Ondura thanked me again, and as I left he was walking towards the sofa with an arm round Tayo's shoulder, father and son together.

Chapter Twenty-Five

My Son's Child

When I returned to collect Tayo from the centre I was early and I lingered in reception, taking time to compose myself again. The lump had returned to my throat and I could feel my eyes start to moisten at the very thought of Tayo with his father. Come on Cathy, I said, get a grip. Fostering was full of emotional highs and lows, with the meetings and partings in the break-up of a family, but this was in a category all of its own. If I was finding the emotion difficult to cope with how much more was Tayo? I was going to have to be very strong for him, particularly over the coming months when his father had returned to Nigeria.

While I waited for Tayo, I occupied myself with looking at the drawings and paintings that the children attending the centre had done over the last year. They were pinned on three large corkboards that I passed all the time on my way in and out of reception but had never looked at. One was of a large plane flying high in the air with a bright blue sky and shining yellow sun. It looked familiar. I peered closer at the signature in the right-hand corner and sure enough it was Tayo's. Beside his name was the date — 22nd February, the month after he'd come to stay with us, when his father was just a memory, and any hope of him seeing him again was as distant as the land below the plane.

I heard a door open along the corridor and I looked up. Sandra came out first, followed by Tayo and his father, both smiling openly and looking so very proud of each other. As they approached me, walking side by side, I could see that Tayo was the spitting image of his father, in stature, features and the way they walked. Tayo was just that much smaller.

'All right?' I asked unnecessarily as they approached.

Tayo nodded while his father shook my hand again. 'We must speak more another time. Tayo has told me so much and I need time to recover.'

I nodded. Although Mr Ondura was still smiling there was sadness behind his eyes, and I guessed Tayo had been telling him of his life with his mother and some of the horror he had endured. Tayo, for his part, looked the best I'd ever seen him. Standing tall and proud, he was beaming from ear to ear.

'My dad's brought me presents,' he said. 'He'll bring them to the house on Wednesday.'

'That's nice,' I said. 'I hope you thanked him.'

'Thanks, Dad,' he said.

His father smiled and ruffled his hair. 'I'm pleased to see you haven't forgotten your manners, Tayo.' He winked at me.

Mr Ondura was so charming, well educated and polite, as well as utterly devoted to Tayo, that it was hard to understand how he had met and had a relationship with Minty who, bless her, was hardly his match, and I doubted she ever had been. He saw Tayo into the car and then he and Sandra waved until we were out of sight.

'Sandra's taking Dad back to the hotel,' Tayo said. 'And he's going to phone me at seven to say goodnight, and so is my gran.'

'Good. I'll make sure the line's free.'

'Cathy?'

'Yes, love?'

'Dad says he has a partner and he showed me her photo. She doesn't live with him but she's really nice and he said she's looking forward to meeting me. I asked him if my gran liked her, and Dad said yes.'

I glanced at him in the rear-view mirror to see how he'd taken this news. 'So that's good? Yes?'

He nodded. 'Gran never liked my mum. I didn't know why. But I guess she was right and knew things I didn't.'

'Possibly. But we won't be too hard on your mum, Tayo. She's made mistakes but I'm sure they weren't intended.' It was easier to be kinder to Minty now that Tayo had his father back, and it wouldn't do Tayo any good to have his mother demonised now when, in a few months' time, he would possibly be saying goodbye to her forever.

When Lucy and Paula returned home from school and college, Tayo was in the garden on the swings, so they went straight to find him and ask how it had gone.

They were still talking about it over dinner.

'So we're really going to meet this phantom father on Wednesday?' Lucy teased Tayo across the table.

He rose to the bait. 'He's not a phantom!' he retorted, 'He's real. And anyway he's the wrong colour for a ghost.'

We laughed, and I thought how far Tayo had come. In the time he had been with us, his racial identity was now so secure that he could even risk a joke.

That evening his father phoned from the hotel at exactly seven o'clock and after we'd exchanged 'good evenings', I put Tayo on. They chatted easily, mainly about Tayo's school the following day and how he must work because it was important for his future. Tayo asked his father if he had gone to university and his father said that he had. This was the only detail about his father that Tayo appeared to have got wrong, possibly because he'd made it up in order to get out of schoolwork. They were on the phone for about twenty minutes when Tayo said goodbye and immediately replaced the receiver.

'Dad said Gran's phoning at seven-thirty from Nigeria,' Tayo said, then sat beside me and waited, looking over my shoulder as I flicked through the newspaper. Sure enough at seven-thirty the phone rang and I let Tayo answer it.

'Hello?' he said tentatively, then, 'Hello, Gran!' A grin spread from ear to ear and I suspected the same was true of his gran all those miles away, who was finally speaking to her lost grandson.

The phone call was very much the same as he had had with his father on that first night, as he spoke about school and his life here with us. Then his gran must have started reminiscing about the time when Tayo was with her, for he was listening hard and every so often burst out, 'Yes! I remember that!'

She was on the phone for nearly an hour and I sat beside Tayo with the newspaper still open but not reading a word.

Then Tayo said, 'OK, Gran, I will. Goodnight. I love you too.'
He passed the phone to me. 'Gran says it's my bed time.' And
planting a kiss on my cheek, he jogged off up stairs.

Sensible woman, I thought, we'll get along just fine. 'Hello,'
I said. 'It's lovely to speak to you at last. I've heard so much
about you from Tayo.'

'And you, Cathy,' she said. 'I must add my own heartfelt
thanks to my son's. Thank you for looking after my grandson. You can't imagine what we've been through since he was
taken.' Her voice broke with emotion. It was a beautiful
singsong voice that was full of warmth and had more of an
accent than her son's. She began telling me about the day Tayo
disappeared from the school playground and the immediate
search that ensued when they found he was gone. 'I don't
know why Minty took him,' she said. 'He had a good life with
us, and she could see him whenever she wanted. She never was
a mother to him, she was always coming and going. We never
knew where she was or even which country she was in. She'd
been gone for five months when she took him. We didn't even
know she was back in the country. It was Tayo's school friends
that gave the police a description of the woman who'd taken
him.'

'Did he leave with her voluntarily?' I asked.

'Yes but he was tricked. His friends said that she'd told him
I was very ill and that I had asked her to fetch him and bring
him home. Tayo didn't know to check, he trusted her, he was
only five years old. We were beside ourselves with worry as
you can imagine, and it didn't get better over the years. Ajani,
my son, has spent a fortune trying to find Tayo, but any sight-
ing of Minty and Tayo proved false and led to nothing. I think

she was protected by the type of people she mixed with. They were bad people, not our sort of people.'

I was pleased that Tayo wasn't around to hear this, even if it was more than likely true.

'What about Minty's family?' I asked. 'Did they ever have any involvement with Tayo?'

'She hasn't got one as far as we know. But, Cathy, we don't really know Minty very well at all. I will tell you something that Tayo must not know. It's not for his ears. Minty was a lap dancer in a club in Lagos. Men give these women money to dance and take off their clothes, and then there are other favours later for more money. I didn't like Ajani going there but he's a man and his own person. Minty was very attractive, I'll give her that. According to Ajani, he slept with her twice and then she announced she was pregnant.' She paused and I heard her sigh. 'Cathy, my son is a good boy and he felt he had responsibility for the unborn child. I had my doubts that he was the father. What woman sleeps with a man as part of her work and doesn't use contraception? I told Ajani I thought he should do a DNA test when the child was born and he was very angry with me. It was the only time we have ever really argued. Since his father died he has looked after me well and taken all the responsibility. I apologized to him and when the baby was born there was no need for a DNA test because it was obvious he was my son's child, they are so alike.'

'They still are,' I agreed. 'The family likeness is remarkable, I noticed it straightaway.'

'Yes, Ajani said so too. Anyway, he forgave me and I forgave Minty. A new baby mellows all hostility and Tayo was my first, and remains my only grandchild.'

I was gripped by the story, imagining a young and beautiful Minty, holding baby Tayo. That must surely have been a moment when she could have grasped a chance of happiness.

'We opened our house to Minty,' she continued. 'And for the first three months of Tayo's life she stayed with us. But even then it wasn't every night. My son was away a lot on business and when he was not at home Minty used to stay out all night. Ajani had stopped her working at the club as soon as she said she was pregnant. He gave her a generous allowance to live on, there was no need for her to stay out at night.'

'Where was she?' I asked.

'I never knew for sure, but I could guess. She liked the attention of men, but I could never say that to my son. By the time Tayo was nine months old Minty had taken to spending more days and nights away than she was at our house. And when she was with us she barely looked at the child. I bathed and fed Tayo from the start. Sometimes she'd arrive in the middle of the night drunk and I'd have to put her to bed as well. Even my son was losing patience with her. By the time Tayo was two, Minty had taken to visiting for a few hours every so many weeks. She'd have a bath and good meal and either my son or I would give her money and she'd disappear again. I looked at her passport once; it was sticking out of her bag. She'd been visiting neighbouring countries and also Malaysia. She's part Malaysian, that's all I know of her family. I did wonder if she was smuggling drugs, but I didn't ever say anything to my son of this. Their relationship had finished by that time, although you could hardly call it a relationship in the first place. If she hadn't got pregnant I doubt Ajani would have seen her outside the club. He has a lovely lady now and it is my hope that one day they will marry.'

'Yes, so I understand. He showed Tayo a photograph.'

'Good. She is a kind, sweet person, a nurse at our local hospital. I know she will be very good to Tayo.' She paused. 'Cathy, what worries me most is what living that sort of life for five years has done to Tayo. My son told me what Sandra and Tayo have said about his life, that he didn't go to school, and for a year he worked in a factory. I didn't think that happened in England.'

'No,' I said sadly. 'Neither did I. Tayo has coped remarkably well under the circumstances. Like all children, he appreciates routine and firm and consistent boundaries. He's had his moments but he's a good boy and has been very resilient, thanks to the good start you gave him. But you may have to be firm with him when he first arrives. He went through a bit of a testing time here, but a lot of that was to do with not finding his father. From the day he first came to me Tayo had his heart set on returning to you.'

'Thank you Cathy, I'm so pleased. That is what I wanted to hear. I will say goodnight now.'

I smiled. 'We have a little nighttime saying here and Tayo remembers you saying it when you used to tuck him into bed.'

Tayo's gran said at once, 'Night, night, sleep tight. Don't let the bed bugs bite.'

'That's right.'

'Does he really remember that?'

'He does. We've said it every night since he first arrived.' She was quiet again, and I knew she was struggling with all the emotion. 'Goodnight,' I said. 'We'll speak again soon.'

'Yes, and thank you, Cathy. God bless.'

Chapter Twenty-Six

Time with Dad

I warned Sonya Gillings, Tayo's teacher, that he might be a little excitable at school on Tuesday. She understood when I explained why and was delighted that the reunion with Tayo's father had gone so well.

'He has contact with his mother today, though,' I said, 'and it might cause him to feel a bit up in the air emotionally.'

'Understandable,' smiled Mrs Gillings. 'I'll keep a special eye on him.'

As it turned out I needn't have worried about Tayo being unsettled, for when I collected him that afternoon Sonya said he had been fine, if just very excited. When we arrived at Headline for contact, though, Minty wasn't there. James said she had just phoned through to say she couldn't make it as she had an appointment with her solicitor.

As we trudged back to the car, I felt disappointed in her and very dubious about her excuse. She'd used it a few months previously, and nothing had ever come of it.

Tayo clearly thought the same. 'Solicitor! My arse!' he muttered as we headed for home.

'Tayo,' I admonished. 'Please don't use that word.'

'Well, she didn't see a solicitor,' he said. 'It's an excuse. She's worried my father might have turned up, then she'd be in for it.'

That sounded the most likely scenario to me, even if I didn't say it, for Minty would have a lot of explaining to do when or if she met Tayo's father again.

Mr Ondura phoned at seven and wanted to speak to me first. He told me that he'd had a meeting with the Guardian Ad Litum that afternoon and he'd felt it had gone well, although she hadn't said much. I told him at this stage he was unlikely to get much feedback from the Guardian as she was still compiling her report. Mr Ondura said he had also used the day to see a solicitor here, one appointed by his solicitor in Nigeria. 'I'm due to see him again on Friday,' he said. 'Then the rest will be taken care of after my return.'

I told him that Minty hadn't attended contact, to which Mr Ondura simply said, 'I see.' I thought it said a lot about him that he had made no attempt to condemn or criticize Minty in any way and hadn't done so to Tayo.

I passed the phone over to Tayo and left them discussing all the things they would do and places they would visit over the next two days. His father would come to the house at nine the next morning to collect him.

Tayo went to sleep early, saying that it would make the morning come that much quicker, and he was up early, very early

indeed. By seven-thirty, he was washed and dressed and waiting for his father.

After breakfast I persuaded him to read a book for a while,
to save the strain on his nerves and those of the rest of the
household as the girls prepared for school and college, and
Adrian left for work.

Tayo wasn't the only one who was early; Mr Ondura was on
the doorstep at eight forty-five. Tayo wanted to show his father
his bedroom so we invited him in. Although he had a cab waiting outside, he spent a good half an hour looking at Tayo's
(very neat) shelf displays, the clothes hanging and folded in
his wardrobe, and his half-completed homework lying open
on his desk. I saw them off at the door and told them to have a
lovely day, which was completely redundant for the day was
guaranteed. But it was strange not having Tayo around, and
we all missed him at dinner time. It made me realize just how
much of a family member he had so easily become, and I knew
the girls and Adrian felt the same. When the doorbell rang at
just gone eight, I leapt to answer it and Tayo and his father
came into the hall.

'I won't stay,' Mr Ondura said. 'I know you're busy and we're
both exhausted.' They looked it.

'Can Dad just meet our family?' Tayo said.

'Of course.' I was touched that Tayo had said 'our family',
and I felt that he was including his father in it, so that we'd all
become part of the same extended family.

I called Adrian, Lucy and Paula down and introduced them.
They all shook hands with Mr Ondura and he asked them how
they were and they replied a little formally that they were fine.
After some polite chat, Mr Ondura bid us all a good evening

and, confirming he would be collecting Tayo again as arranged at nine the following morning, returned to the cab waiting again outside.

'Did you have a taxi with you all day?' I asked Tayo.

'Yes, Dad's got the same one booked for tomorrow and the weekend.'

Struth, I thought, he really wasn't short of money. I couldn't remember the last time I'd used a cab but I knew they didn't come cheap.

When I went up to say goodnight to Tayo he was already fast asleep.

'Night night,' I whispered, as I closed the curtains, then added, 'Sleep tight and don't let the bed bugs bite.'

Well, I couldn't let the ritual lapse even if he was asleep.

The following morning Tayo was so exhausted from the day before, he slept until eight and I had to wake him. Over breakfast he told me about the day before: their visit to the castle and accompanying museum, their walk in the botanical gardens, the cinema, and dinner at a very expensive restaurant.

'The only thing is,' Tayo said, 'Dad forgot my presents.'

'Don't worry,' I said. 'He's got rather a lot on his mind. I'm sure he'll remember them soon.'

Tayo told me the plans for the day ahead, which included Tayo seeing the hotel where his father was staying. He asked if he could take his swimming trunks as there was a pool there. 'I don't need a towel,' he said rather haughtily, 'the hotel provides them.'

His father arrived at nine and I watched them get into the cab and waved them off. Sandra phoned during the morning to ask how it was going and to tell me that her manager had identified a social worker who could visit Mr Ondura and his mother in Nigeria, possibly at the end of July, although the date hadn't yet been finalized. The social worker was Nigerian herself and would stay in a hotel near to Mr Ondura's house and make a number of visits over a two-week period, and then file her report in August.

'So we could still make the October hearing?' I asked.

'It's looking good,' Sandra confirmed. 'But I'm concerned that Minty didn't turn up for contact on Tuesday. She also phoned the duty social worker at midnight, very distressed and threatening suicide. I've called her lots of times but her mobile's always switched off. It still is now. I just hope she's all right and calm enough to make Friday's contact.'

I hoped so too. Minty's threat of suicide coupled with her absence were a real worry; given her fragile mental state, exacerbated by drink and possibly drug abuse, and now with the added trauma of Tayo's father's arrival, she could easily have been tipped over the edge.

I obviously said nothing about this to Tayo when he returned in the evening after another fun-packed day and clutching a bag of presents. Mr Ondura didn't come in this time but said that he would see Tayo at nine on Saturday morning, when they were planning on going into London.

'By cab?' I asked, unable to hide my astonishment. 'All the way into London?'

'Yes, why? Is there a problem?' Mr Ondura asked.

'Er, no, I was just thinking of the cost.'

He gave a little laugh. 'Don't worry, the cab won't be on meter. I've done a deal with the driver – two hundred pounds for the day.'

I supposed that wasn't too bad, considering the journey, but it still caused me a hiccup when set alongside the £23 rail fare they could have paid.

Minty didn't arrive at contact on Friday, or leave any message. Telephone contact hadn't taken place during the week because Tayo had been out with his father until late in the evening, so I didn't know if Minty would have answered or not.

Tayo was too full of the weekend ahead to be angry with her for not showing but I knew that if she failed to attend contact on Tuesday without a word, there would be serious concerns for her safety. Not only that, but there was a good chance that future contact would be suspended. It would be deemed unfair for Tayo to keep turning up, only to be disappointed.

While Tayo was out with his father on Saturday, Paula spent a couple of hours downloading music from the Internet on to Tayo's MP3 player for him. It was one of the presents his father had given him, together with a hand-held gameboy with games, a book on Nigeria and T-shirts with the names of countries Mr Ondura had visited emblazoned across the front. There were a dozen or more T-shirts in various sizes and I guessed Mr Ondura had been collecting them for some time in the hope that one day he would be able to give them to his son.

* * *

It was nearly ten by the time they returned but Mr Ondura had phoned from his mobile at eight so that I wouldn't be worried. He saw Tayo into the hall, saying that he was going back to his hotel to confirm a few details before his flight back early on Monday morning. At the mention of his father leaving, Tayo's face dropped. He'd already calculated that tomorrow was their last day together for sixteen weeks. Fortunately he was so tired from seeing the sights of London that he didn't have time to dwell on his father going, and was in bed and asleep in no time.

The next morning Mr Ondura collected Tayo at nine and took him away for a relaxing day together.

'I'll bring him back by eight,' he confirmed, 'as I know that he has school tomorrow.'

I dreaded to think what state Tayo would be in when he returned from his last day with his father. It was going to be very hard for him, especially with six weeks of summer holiday approaching and no school to distract him. I was relieved that I had booked a place on the play scheme, which would help to occupy him and keep his mind off the wait until the court hearing in October. I wished I could have afforded to take us all away again, but there was no way we could manage it so soon.

When I heard a taxi pull up outside the house at seven forty-five that evening, I steeled myself, expecting Tayo to be more or less in tears at having to say goodbye to his father. As it was, he seemed quite positive.

'Tayo and I have done a lot of talking,' said Mr Ondura, his arm round his son's shoulders. 'We've put things in perspective, haven't we, son?' Tayo grinned and nodded. 'After all, he's already waited five years, so what is a few more weeks? It will pass in no time and he has plenty to keep himself busy until then.'

A man with a philosophy after my own heart, I thought.

Tayo presented me with a large box of chocolates from him and his father. I asked Mr Ondura if he'd like to come in for a while, but he declined politely and I guessed that he thought it wise to keep the parting short.

'Right, son,' he said, opening his arms for a hug. 'Be good.'

Tayo hugged him for all he was worth. After a minute Mr Ondura gently released Tayo's arms. 'I'll phone as soon as I'm home, son.'

Mr Ondura then warmly shook my hand and kissed my cheek. 'Thank you again, and please say goodbye to your family. I hope to meet them again in October.'

'I will,' I said. 'Have a safe trip.'

He gave Tayo a last brief hug and then went out, down the path, and into the taxi. I held Tayo's hand as we waved him off, and then I closed the door.

I looked at Tayo. 'Are you OK?' I asked gently. His bottom lip trembled and he threw himself into my arms and sobbed against my chest. 'It's all right,' I soothed. 'He'll soon be back again.'

Having been so strong for his father, he was now able to release all his pent-up emotion, and he held on to me and cried for some time. I suspected that Mr Ondura wasn't completely dry-eyed either as he sat in the back of his cab.

When he was calmer, Tayo came with me to the sofa and we sat down.

'Look what my dad gave me,' he said, producing an envelope. It was full of photographs. There were some of Tayo as a baby, a toddler, a boy of three, and on his first day at school. There were also head-and-shoulders portrait photos of his father and gran. She was just as I imagined her, with a round open face smiling warmly. I suggested to Tayo that I buy some frames for the photos of his dad and gran so that he could put them on his shelf.

'And I should have one of my mum as well,' he said.

'Good idea. I'll buy one of those disposable cameras so the next time your mum comes to contact you can take some pictures?'

He smiled and gave me a big kiss on the cheek. 'I hope my mum comes to contact on Tuesday. I want to tell her that I love her too, as well as my dad.'

'I know, sweet. I hope so, too.'

Chapter Twenty-Seven

Countdown

Tayo went to school on Monday, full of happiness and eager to tell everyone about his father and their trip to London. Mr Ondura phoned in the evening to say he'd had a good journey and had returned home safely. Tayo also spoke to his gran.

To everyone's disappointment, especially Tayo's, Minty didn't attend contact on Tuesday, but at least she left a message this time. She said that the buses weren't running and to tell Tayo that she would be there on Friday.

I was glad she was safe but concerned that she was still causing Tayo distress. It wasn't fair to keep building up his hopes and then knocking them down. Sandra left another message on Minty's mobile saying that if she didn't attend contact on Friday then Social Services would apply to the court to have contact terminated.

Minty seemed to have a knack for knowing when she had sailed too close to the wind. On Friday she was at contact, albeit half an hour late. I said hello to her and left, glad that Tayo hadn't been let down again. He'd taken the disposable camera I'd bought with him as I'd suggested and had tried to take a picture of his mother, but – as Aisha reported later – Minty had not been at all happy at having her photograph taken and had refused to sit and pose.

We had the film developed the next day, and all the pictures showed Minty turning away or covering her face as Tayo had tried to photograph her. There was only one that was a full face and although she wasn't smiling it was a good likeness so I bought another frame and Minty took pride of place beside Tayo's father and gran on the top shelf.

'Pity it's not true in real life,' Tayo said. 'Mum, Dad and Gran, all together.'

'I know, sweet. But that's true for a lot of children now. At least you have parents and a gran who love you.'

His little collection of photographs gazed down on him while he slept.

The summer holidays began towards the end of July and Tayo started at the play scheme the following Monday. It was nine until four each day and he came home happy but tired from all the activities and outings, and it kept his mind off the waiting. His dad and gran phoned him every Sunday and Monday evening, nights that wouldn't clash with Tayo seeing or phoning his mother.

Tayo began every phone call by telling his dad how many days it was until he returned for the court case in October, as indeed he was now telling me each morning at breakfast. Meanwhile, the slow wheels of the legal and social work processes ground on. At the beginning of August Mr Ondura was able to tell Tayo that the social worker from England had arrived for the two-week assessment; she was visiting them every other evening and also speaking to some of their friends and neighbours, and visiting his offices in Lagos. She had suggested that his dad took some photographs of the house and the area where they lived and send them to Tayo, which he said he would do.

Sandra and I were in regular contact during August. Everything was going along as it should, but Minty had stopped attending contact again, and I simply couldn't understand it. Surely she must realize that she was jeopardizing the slim hopes she had of having Tayo returned to her care? Or perhaps she was concerned that each time she made an appearance there was more chance of the Home Office finding and deporting her. Or possibly she was preparing herself for a separation from Tayo by slowly and deliberately pulling away from him, to make his departure easier for them both. Or maybe she was simply too drunk or drugged to get out of bed. No one knew.

'I suppose it will make everything easier at the final court hearing if Minty isn't there to contest it,' I said to Sandra. 'But her lack of interest is giving Tayo the clear message that she doesn't care about him enough to attend contact or put up a fight to get him back.'

'I know. And my manager is loath to apply to court to stop contact completely as it could be Tayo's last chance to see his mother if he returns to live in Nigeria. And anyway it's doubtful a judge would agree to stop it at this late stage in the proceedings,' Sandra replied. 'I think we'll just have to keep going for now and hope Minty attends.'

So I kept taking Tayo to the Headline Family Centre and an hour later he would return with Aisha, having not seen his mother and angry that she hadn't even bothered to phone to say she wasn't coming.

We were still making the twice-weekly phone calls to Minty, though she rarely answered those either. Tayo sometimes left a message, or I left a voicemail saying Tayo was well.

Perhaps it's just as well, I thought, for Minty must realize that it would be best for Tayo if he returned to a stable life with his dad.

Tayo seemed able to cope, even if he wasn't happy about it, and the summer holidays ticked by, warm and relaxing, with all of us in a more mellow routine. The social worker returned from Nigeria and wrote her report, which Sandra told me was very detailed and very positive: there were no concerns or issues about any aspect of Tayo's care were he to return to his father and gran. Apparently she'd even visited the school where Tayo would eventually go – it was a private school with a reputation second to none.

The GCSE results came out and Paula had done very well so she intended to return to the sixth form in September to do her A levels. Adrian passed his end-of-year exams, and Lucy was awarded her B.Tech diploma. Tayo continued his daily countdown to October 18th when his father would arrive, two days before the final court hearing on the 20th.

It was the first week of September and Tayo had returned to school for the first day of the autumn term looking very smart in his new grey trousers, having grown out of the previous pairs by two inches.

Then Sandra called me. 'Cathy, I've got some bad news. Our legal department has received a letter from a solicitor acting for Minty. It says she has a flat and regular job and is going to fight for custody of Tayo.'

'Oh no,' I said, and my heart sank. 'Is she serious?'

'Well, if that's the case, she'll need to be assessed and that means there's no chance of us making the court hearing next month. The next free court time isn't until the end of February, next year.'

'Damn and blast,' I said, almost in tears of frustration. 'Why is she doing this? She must know that Tayo wants to go home to his father! He'll never forgive her if she stops him.'

Sandra concentrated on the facts of the case for the moment. 'Minty phoned me for the first time this morning and I've told her I'll need her address and details of her employer. She couldn't remember them offhand but said she would bring them to next contact. It looks like she's serious in contesting it.'

'Can she make a good case for getting Tayo back?'

'I'd say it's unlikely. There's her immigration status to consider for one thing, and the behaviour of the previous five years. She's also done herself no favours with the way she hasn't turned up to contact. And Tayo's wishes will be considered, although of course he might change his mind about living with his dad if Minty has really turned herself around.'

'I don't think he's likely to do that,' I said. 'And I'm pretty sceptical that Minty's managed to sort herself out, if it comes to that.'

'I know. I understand your frustration but Minty must be given a fair chance. I think we need to tell Tayo the situation before Minty does tonight at contact. She assures me she will be there. Can you tell him when you pick him up?'

A blanket of depression settled on me. 'Yes. I will.'

I put the phone down, unable to believe that all of Tayo's hopes and desires had been put in jeopardy. If Minty was telling the truth about her new circumstances, then there was no way he would be able to go to Nigeria in October. Was she really sorting herself out? I couldn't believe it, after everything we'd seen so far. While I didn't wish Minty any ill, I couldn't help feeling that everyone would be a lot better off if she'd continued as she was, and let Tayo go.

I couldn't bear to think about his anguish when I told him the news.

There was no point in procrastinating so as soon as I collected Tayo from school and we were in the car heading towards the family centre I explained, as tactfully as I could, what had happened.

Tayo said absolutely nothing, though in the rear-view mirror, I could see his face had set hard and defiant. I asked him if he was OK and he said, 'Yes.' Then he was silent until we were in Headline and had entered Yellow Room, where Minty was already waiting. She was sitting on the sofa and although her hair was very dishevelled, she'd managed to cover up most of her breasts and midriff with a slightly more appropriate top.

As soon as he saw her, Tayo stormed forward, shouting, 'What the fuck do you think you're playing at, you useless cow! I'm going back to my dad and you can't stop me!'

Minty stood up in alarm. Tayo advanced at her with such anger that I thought he was going to hit her. Minty looked scared – she must have had the same thought. He didn't, but his face seethed with anger and hatred as he yelled at her. 'I'm not staying with you! I don't believe you've got a job or a flat! You're just a waster!'

'Tayo!' I said, trying to intervene. I'd never seen him so angry and, I guessed, neither had Minty. She opened and closed her mouth and then collected her wits, and started screaming abuse at him, most of which was unintelligible.

Aisha pushed the panic button and James arrived, just at the point where Minty slapped Tayo hard across the face. James rushed over and stood between them.

'I'm going! Waster!' Tayo yelled. 'Take me home, Cathy! Please!'

'Go, you little runt!' Minty screamed back. 'You're just like your fucking father!' She had worked herself up to a fever pitch and was now completely out of control. James put his hands on her shoulders to stop her attacking Tayo and possibly Aisha and myself, while Tayo came to my side.

'Can we go now please?' he said in a more even voice.

I looked at James who was still restraining Minty by the shoulders. 'Take him,' James said. 'Aisha, you stay, please.' I knew he needed Aisha present as a witness in case Minty made an allegation or complaint about the restraint.

Tayo and I left the room and quickly walked along the corridor with the sound of his mother screaming abuse at James. 'Let go of me, you cunt! Fucking arsehole!'

We continued out through reception and got into the car. I pressed the internal locks, started the car and drove away. I wasn't sure which of us was more shocked, Tayo, who sat pale and withdrawn in the back, or me. I could feel my heart racing and my hands trembled on the wheel. Tayo didn't say anything on the drive home and I was silent too, though my thoughts were racing.

When we got home I tried to talk to Tayo but he didn't want to know, retreating back into the shell I thought he'd put away for good.

I briefly explained to Lucy and Paula what had happened; they'd realized as soon as we walked in that something was wrong. Tayo remained silent and withdrawn over dinner and we had a very sombre meal. When Adrian came in, I heard Tayo telling him that his mother was trying to stop him going home and how angry he'd been and that she'd slapped him. Adrian, bless him, said exactly what I would have said: that although he could understand why Tayo had been upset he shouldn't have spoken to his mother like that, and she certainly shouldn't have hit him.

We spent a miserable weekend trying to forget about what had happened. Tayo went to football but didn't want to do anything else and I couldn't really summon up the enthusiasm to persuade him. He didn't want to phone his mother on Saturday, which was understandable. I made a note in my log about how he had been over the weekend and emailed a copy to Sandra so that she would have it first thing on Monday.

When Tayo's father phoned on Sunday Tayo told him what had happened and when they'd finished, Mr Ondura spoke to me. He knew that Minty was contesting the case because Sandra had emailed him and his solicitor when she'd found out.

'I wouldn't have wished that awful scene with his mother on Tayo in a million years,' he said sadly. 'But perhaps it will have one positive outcome. She has shown her true colours now, and that might help to swing things in my favour.'

I'd been thinking exactly the same thing.

On Monday, Sandra phoned me, having received my email and also the report from Headline about Friday's contact.

'The good news is that we've decided to keep the October court date for now, although it might have to be postponed later.'

'Does Minty's behaviour rule out her being able to contest the case?' I asked hopefully.

'No, I'm afraid not. She's still part of the proceedings and if she wants to be assessed, then the hearing will have to be deferred. Everyone's interests have to be protected, to make sure they get a fair hearing.'

'I know,' I said, 'but it's still frustrating.'

Tayo was once again in a state of limbo and there was nothing I could do about it. He became sullen and withdrawn again, and who could blame him? Just when he thought his life was sorted, it had again been thrown into disarray. A six-month postponement would seem an eternity to him.

Meanwhile, Minty didn't attend the next two contacts although she had been in touch with her solicitor who passed on a message: she wouldn't attend contact because it had a bad effect on Tayo and also she'd moved and it was too far to travel. Sandra said that Minty still hadn't given her solicitor the address of her flat or her employment details, although she insisted she could provide a stable environment for Tayo and would be in court to fight for custody.

This situation continued for the rest of September. Tayo and I arrived at Headline every Tuesday and Friday but now I brought Tayo straight home if Minty wasn't there, as it had been decided that he didn't need to wait on the off chance she would turn up. And she never did.

Tayo didn't want to phone her either, although I asked him every Wednesday and Saturday, then made a note in my log. His dad and gran continued to phone on Mondays and Sundays but even their conversations were subdued.

At the beginning of October, when Minty hadn't attended a single contact session in two months, or produced her address or details of her employment, Sandra and her manager decided definitely to go ahead with the October hearing. Minty would not be assessed. She couldn't be, for no one knew where she lived or how to contact her.

Tayo brightened up a little at this news, and so did the rest of us. Here was a small glimmer of hope, but it was far from over yet. If Minty arrived in court with a good barrister and contested the case, then the judge might be persuaded to adjourn the hearing so she could be assessed. But as time went by, I felt this was becoming less likely.

Then Sandra called with more bad news. 'I've received a letter from Minty's solicitor confirming that she'll be in court with a barrister.'

'How can she afford one?' I asked, and dearly wished that for once Minty could put Tayo first and simply let go.

'It will be covered by legal aid,' Sandra replied.

'Even though she's here as an illegal immigrant?'

'Yes. She still has a right to representation.'

'I see.' I didn't comment further, but when I'd put the phone down, I fumed with frustration. I couldn't believe that Minty was really prepared to try and take away Tayo's chance of happiness. And now she had a barrister there was a chance she could succeed.

Chapter Twenty-Eight

The Verdict

Tayo's spirits lifted as Monday 18th October drew closer, bringing with it the longed-for return of his father. I also felt more positive. Surely one look at Mr Ondura would convince anyone that he was by far the best parent for Tayo to live with. But I knew that there were no guarantees. Until the judge had all the evidence before him and had made his decision, we could not be sure of anything.

'Don't tell Tayo,' Mr Ondura confided to me in his last phone call before he flew to England, 'but when I booked my return ticket to Nigeria for the twenty-fifth of October, I booked one for Tayo too. I just pray he will be able to use it.'

'So do I,' I said fervently. 'So do I.'

The doorbell rang just after six-thirty on October 18th, as I was serving up dinner. Tayo flew down the hall to answer it, and opened the door to his father, jumping into his arms with whoops of pure joy.

I welcomed him in and then left them alone in the front room for a while, before asking Mr Ondura if he would like to join us for dinner. He accepted and told the cab driver to get himself something to eat and he'd phone him when he was ready to leave.

That cab driver must welcome Mr Ondura back as much as we do! I thought.

The five of us sat down to eat and, while it was very pleasant and we all made a big effort to appear at ease, there was a feeling of doom in the air. Forty-eight hours later Tayo's future would be decided, and I could tell that Mr Ondura felt the strain. He looked very tired and drawn. Just before nine o'clock he thanked us all for our hospitality and left. Tayo would not be attending the hearing, so the next time he would see his father would be after the court case and it was a strange farewell for them. Neither could guess what the circumstances would be the next time they were together.

It was a tough time for Tayo, but he behaved admirably. He went to school without complaint on the Tuesday and, despite Minty not having turned up for weeks, we went to Headline afterwards. She didn't show up, so we went home, both trying to remain positive. What Minty was playing at I'd no idea but the uncertainty was agonizing.

The following day, the final court hearing began. It had been allocated three days, at the end of which the judge would make his decision.

Mr Ondura had told me on the phone that he already had a replacement Nigerian passport for Tayo, so that they could leave immediately if that was what the judge decided. There would be plenty of other paperwork if he got legal custody, but that would follow on. Everything was prepared for Tayo's return, but for now we had three days of nail-biting uncertainty while the lawyers battled it out. In court, apart from the judge and court staff, there would be Mr Ondura and his solicitor and barrister; Minty and her solicitor and barrister; Sandra with the Social Services solicitor and barrister; and the Guardian Ad Litum. It was a relatively small case compared to some child-care hearings.

At the end of the first day, Sandra phoned me after she'd left court and said she'd spent four hours in the witness box giving her evidence and being cross-examined by Minty's barrister. Minty had arrived late and the judge had delayed the start of the case at her barrister's request, while making it clear he would not do so the following day. Mr Ondura had tried to talk to Minty when the court had adjourned for lunch but she'd spat at him and walked away.

'Did the judge see it?' I asked.

'No, but her barrister did and he wasn't too impressed.'

Mr Ondura phoned Tayo in the evening but didn't talk about the case. Tayo asked if he had seen his mother and he said, 'Yes.'

'Which is a bloody sight more than me,' Tayo said. In answer to that, he got a good ticking off from both his father and me for swearing.

But of course Tayo had a point – how ridiculous that Minty could attend court to fight for her son but couldn't attend contact to actually see him. The only consolation was that the judge would be aware of these anomalies because details of contact were included in Sandra's and the Guardian's reports.

Tayo went to school as usual on Thursday, trudging off with the burden of the long wait on his shoulders. We could expect no news until Friday afternoon. Then, at lunchtime, Sandra phoned me to say that the judge was going to give his ruling that afternoon.

'Why?' I said, unsure if this was good or bad news. 'How can he deliver his verdict a whole day early?'

'He's heard from all the parties now – except for Minty. She was an hour late this morning,' Sandra explained, 'and she was so drunk she could barely stay upright. The usher had to fetch her a glass of water, and the judge asked her to sit quietly because she kept singing a sea shanty, whereupon she told the judge to fuck off. She was far too drunk to take the stand.'

I could have laughed but I didn't, and neither did Sandra. It was sad really. Minty had gone to all the trouble of going to court and then blown her chances in a way that looked almost wilful. She'd never been able to look after Tayo since he had been a baby but had clung to him almost as a right. Her drink and drug-fuelled lifestyle had doubtless contributed to her inability to parent Tayo or even to look after herself properly. I didn't doubt that in her own way she loved Tayo, and despite everything my heart went out to her.

'Will you call me when you hear anything?' I asked Sandra.

'Of course.'

When I collected Tayo from school at three-fifteen that afternoon, there was still no news. Tayo wasn't expecting to hear anything until the following day so he was no more anxious than usual.

We'd been at home for half an hour when the phone rang. It was Sandra.

'Cathy,' she said breathlessly, 'you can tell Tayo the judge has made his decision and he will be going back with his dad on Monday.'

There was a pause while it sank in. 'Thank God,' I whispered, my eyes immediately brimming. Then I found my voice again. 'Thank God! Hurray!'

I could hear the emotion in Sandra's voice too, utter relief mingled with excitement. 'Tell Tayo his father already has his passport and ticket and Tayo will spend the weekend with him at his hotel before going back.'

'I'd be delighted to,' I said. 'And what about tomorrow?'

'It's up to you, Cathy, but I suggest you take Tayo into school to say goodbye in the morning, then pack. Tayo can either go with his dad tomorrow evening or Saturday morning. I'll leave it up to you and Mr Ondura to decide. I'll come round to say goodbye to Tayo tomorrow about midday if that's OK.'

'Yes, fine,' I said quickly. 'See you tomorrow then. I'm off to tell Tayo. And well done, Sandra.'

'And well done you,' she said.

Chapter Twenty-Nine

Goodbyes

Tayo was in his bedroom watching television when I told him. I simply went in and repeated what Sandra had said: 'The judge has made his decision and you'll be going back with your father on Monday.'

Tayo gasped, then shouted, screamed and yelped for joy, jumping up and down so hard that I thought he might go through the floorboards. Lucy and Paula heard the commotion and came out of their rooms – it said something about the noise that Tayo was making that he could be heard above their music.

We all congratulated Tayo, hugged and kissed him, and hugged and kissed each other. Then I told Tayo of the arrangements for Friday and the weekend.

'It's important we go to school tomorrow to say goodbye,' I said. 'Particularly to Sam. Then when your dad phones later today we'll decide whether you leave here Friday evening or Saturday morning.'

'No offence, Cathy,' Tayo said, 'I love you all but I'd really like to go as soon as possible. It will be the start of my journey home.'

I smiled. 'Of course, love, I understand. As long as it suits your dad.'

Mr Ondura phoned ten minutes later and after speaking to Tayo (more shouts and yelps of joy this end) he asked for me. He said he'd managed to bring the return tickets forward to Saturday's flight so he would like to collect Tayo on Friday, at about five o'clock.

'Of course,' I said. 'That will be fine. We'll see you tomorrow at five.'

That meant some hasty packing and quick goodbyes, but it was definitely what Tayo wanted. When children move from us, we usually give them a small farewell party and a present. There wasn't time to arrange a party but I'd bought Tayo a present in anticipation. I'd wrapped it and we had all signed the farewell card (I'd added Adrian's signature). After dinner we gave it to Tayo. It was a camera and came with the proviso that he sent us lots of photographs of himself in Nigeria. He was tremendously pleased and insisted on taking photos of us, the house, his bedroom and the garden. He said it was a pity he couldn't have a photo of Adrian and I promised I'd take one and send it to him.

Aware we'd be busy the following day, we began Tayo's packing after dinner. Lucy and Paula helped. Tayo had arrived with what he'd stood up in and now his belongings filled three suitcases (which I'd also bought in anticipation), plus a large piece of hand luggage. It was sure to go over the airline's baggage allowance.

It was after ten by the time we'd finished and all that was left out was Tayo's pyjamas, a change of clothes for Saturday, and his washbag. He climbed into bed tired but happy, and I kissed his forehead and said for the last time, 'Night, night, sleep tight.'

'And don't let the bed bugs bite.' He grinned, then added, 'Cathy, the next time I say that will be to my gran in Nigeria.'

'Not your dad tomorrow night?' I asked.

He shook his head. 'No, it's a woman's thing.'

I smiled and left him to sleep.

It was just as well we had done the packing on Thursday evening because Friday flew by. We went into school at nine-thirty and Roberta de la Haye came to take us through to Tayo's classroom. She interrupted the lesson to make the announcement that Tayo was going to live in Nigeria. Tayo and I stood at the front of the class while they all clapped and cheered, and I realized that not only Sam but the whole class, and particularly his teacher Mrs Gillings, had been rooting for Tayo.

Tayo thanked them all and said he would miss them, then added a special 'miss you' to Sam and thanked him for being a good friend. He shouted a final 'Goodbye!' and we left the class-room to the sound of more rapturous applause. I wondered how long it would take Mrs Gillings to settle them down and resume the lesson.

Back at home, I made a sandwich lunch and Sandra arrived.

'All packed?' she asked, joking, and was surprised to find we were.

'I've got three massive cases,' Tayo said proudly. 'And a back pack.'

'I hope Mr Ondura doesn't mind paying the excess,' I said.

'Shouldn't think it's a problem,' Sandra said wryly. 'And it's important Tayo takes everything with him, it's part of his life here.'

She had spoken to Mr Ondura and knew he had changed the flight and was collecting Tayo at five. 'Before you leave, Tayo, I want you to phone your mum to say goodbye.' She glanced at me and I nodded. I knew how important it was. 'I know you're not happy with her at present,' Sandra continued, 'but everything has worked out as you wanted and you can't leave without saying goodbye. If she doesn't answer you can leave a message.'

Tayo agreed.

'Also,' Sandra went on, 'in the court order the judge has said you can phone your mum once a month. Your father has agreed to this, and also if your mother returns to Nigeria and wants to see you, your dad will make the arrangements.'

Tayo opened his mouth to protest.

'It will be supervised contact, Tayo,' Sandra said. 'There's no way your mother can snatch you now, anyway. You're far too big and streetwise.'

Tayo grinned.

Sandra then wished him all the best for the future and said she would be staying in touch with him for the first six months, which was normal when a looked-after child went to live abroad, and was also part of the judge's order.

'Cool,' Tayo said.

'And I know Cathy will want to hear from you, even if it's just to say you're OK.'

'Yes, of course,' Tayo said. 'And she's going to come and visit me, aren't you, Cathy?'

'You never know,' I said. 'I just might.'

Sandra gave Tayo a present of a game for his gameboy and a leaving card. Tayo gave her a big hug. Then she and I walked down the hall together to the front door.

'Tayo couldn't have had a better social worker,' I said, and I meant it. 'You've been excellent.'

She smiled, almost embarrassed. 'Thank you, too, Cathy. Your hard work has been brilliant. Tayo was very lucky to end up with you.'

'I'm glad he did.'

Tayo came down for a final hug on the doorstep and we watched as she got into her car, and waved her off.

'It's sad saying goodbye to everyone,' Tayo said.

'I know, love, but after this evening it will all be all hellos, and won't that be good?'

But I was aware that the most difficult goodbye was looming and I thought now would be a good time to make the call to Minty. She never answered her mobile so the timing of the call didn't really matter. I told Tayo we would phone his mother as Sandra had asked, and we went through to the lounge. Sitting side by side on the sofa, like we had done so many times before, I keyed in the number to Minty's mobile and listened as the voicemail message cut in.

'Minty,' I said. 'It's Cathy. I hope you're well. Tayo would like to say goodbye as he'll be leaving soon.'

I passed the phone to Tayo and he took it slowly to his ear. His voice was flat and emotionless as he said, 'Goodbye, Mum. I wish things could have been different. I love you.'

* * *

With the packing done, Tayo and I spent the rest of the afternoon in the garden, Tayo listening to his MP3 and the music Paula had downloaded for him while I pulled up a few weeds, more to keep busy than anything. I made Tayo a snack at four o'clock because he was having his dinner later with his father at the hotel.

Lucy and Paula returned home from school and college and chatted to Tayo until just before five when I called them into the house. We brought Tayo's cases down and stacked them in the hall. Just as we'd finished, right on cue, the doorbell rang, and Mr Ondura stood on the doorstep with the biggest, most lavish bouquet of flowers I'd ever seen. The gift card attached said, *Thank you for looking after Tayo.*

'They're beautiful, thank you so much!' I said.

'The very least I could do,' Mr Ondura replied, kissing my cheek.

He and Tayo loaded the bags into the waiting taxi while we waited in the hall.

'Well, this is it then,' I said, as they returned to say goodbye. A lump had come into my throat but I didn't want to cry. I wanted Tayo to remember me smiling and waving him off at the door. It was hard, though. He'd been a member of my family now for ten months and with all the ups and downs we had formed a strong bond in that time. Farewells were never easy but somehow knowing how far away he was going and how different his life was going to be made saying goodbye to Tayo all the more difficult.

Mr Ondura nodded and looked far from composed himself. I could see Tayo's bottom lip trembling and I knew Lucy and Paula were about to burst into tears. The girls and

I took it in turns to hug Tayo and then shook hands with Mr Ondura.

He kissed my cheek, thanked me again and said he'd phone as soon as they were home. We watched them get into the taxi and Tayo wound down his window. 'Thanks for everything,' he shouted. 'Love and miss you.'

They pulled slowly away with Tayo's arm waving from the open window. Once they were out of sight we walked slowly into the house and closed the door. There was emptiness, an immediate feeling of something, or rather someone, missing and I knew the girls felt it too. Even when a child leaves in such positive circumstances as Tayo had done, returning to his family to start a new life, we, the foster family, had lost a family member, and it hurt.

The loss would continue until the next child arrived, and we started all over again.

Epilogue

Tayo and his father phoned the evening they arrived home, and have continued to phone every couple of months during the year that has elapsed since Tayo went. He has settled well into his new life and has made friends at school and at the clubs he attends: football, rugby, cricket, archery and swimming. As promised, he sent us lots of photos, of his house (which looks like a mansion), the swimming pool in the garden, him in his bedroom on his computer, his gran, his dad, and his dad's partner, Renee, who Tayo really likes. Mr Ondura is planning to marry Renee next year and Tayo tells me he will be an usher in the church, which is a very important role as he will have to give out hymn sheets and show guest to their seats. Tayo also tells me that he is hoping for a baby brother or sister, though he hasn't told his dad yet.

There were a few teething problems to begin with when Tayo, not used to his father's strict but loving parenting, tried to play off his gran against his dad by asking her for something when his dad had said no. However, Tayo soon came to realize that far from getting him what he wanted, the attempted manipulation only served to strengthen his father's resolve.

Tayo phones his mother once a month but has only managed to speak to her twice. She is still in England and, as far as anyone knows, she is living the life she has always lived here, on her wits, underground, and beyond the reach of the authorities. Sandra told me that the Home Office made no attempt to detain and question her, let alone deport her, although they knew she would be at court for the final hearing. I wonder what her life will become and I can't imagine there will be any improvement unless she can take herself in hand and get off the drink and drugs. But as she wasn't able to do this when she had the chance to win back Tayo, sadly there is now even less reason.

We haven't visited Tayo and his family yet, though that's not to say we won't. Adrian is planning on taking a gap year after he finishes university and before he starts work, and has said he will definitely include Nigeria (and Tayo, of course) in his world travels. I would love to go to see Tayo and Nigeria and so would the girls, but it will depend largely on time and money, and also Peter, who is talking about us all going on holiday together.

For me, I carry on with a busy and rewarding life, looking after my ever-changing family. I've witnessed many stories in the course of my fostering career, but none has ended as happily as that of Tayo, and the father who didn't stop looking for his little boy until he found him. Perhaps it shows that love can truly win out in the end. I hope so.

* * *

Two months after Tayo left us, I attended a training course dealing with child protection and first heard that there are estimated to be as many as one million children living in the UK who are unregistered, and therefore unknown and unprotected by our society. It is a staggering number and many of them will be living in circumstances similar to or far worse than Tayo's. Often they only come to our attention when they make news headlines and sometimes then it's too late.

Tayo was fortunate – enough people raised concerns about him to allow the Social Services to act. So often in our society, we feel that other people and other children are none of our business and we don't like to interfere. Sometimes we assume that Social Services must already know about the situation and are taking care of it. But they can't act if they don't know these children exist.

The Children Act 2004 set up provision for every detail of every child in the UK to be recorded on a central database, with all professionals being able to access it. If it had existed earlier, it might have given a vital lead in finding out where Tayo had been. It is a contentious project, but it could help many children like Tayo. Even if a child is 'hidden' and here illegally, he or she is likely to appear on record at some point. If they went to school for one day, or attended a doctor or a hospital, the details would be recorded. Under the present system, agencies work together but children can and do slip through the net, sometimes with horrendous results.

Tayo was one of the lucky ones, but I can't help wondering – how many other 'hidden' children are out there now?

Author's Note

People often ask why I foster, particularly given the challenging behaviour of some of the children I look after. It is about making a difference. If, in some small way, I can improve a child's life, and help them come to terms with their past experiences and therefore hopefully have a better future, then the rewards are immeasurable.

My first book, *Damaged*, received an incredible reaction from the public. I was moved and very touched by the number of people who emailed and wrote to me, some because they were profoundly affected by Jodie's story and others because they had experienced something similar in their lives. I include here a small number of the many messages I received after publication, and if you would like more information about *Damaged*, *Hidden* or my forthcoming books, then please visit www.cathy-glass.co.uk.

Cathy Glass

Reactions to *Damaged*
by Cathy Glass

'It gave me an insight into a world that was so tragic, it broke my heart. But it is also a world I am familiar with, for my life was the same as Jodie's for two years … The book shows people like us that there is no need to live in shame and fear as Jodie did and so did I.' *Warren, England*

'Many thanks for letting us share in your life. We both read it and we both cried.' *David and Louise, England*

'I was a foster child myself and I was touched by your patience and kindness in your care of Jodie. I couldn't put your book down but it made me cry, I know how Jodie must have felt … You are very special, Cathy, I felt reassured that there are people like you. Thank you for telling us Jodie's story.' *Sue, Scotland*

'My memories of being in foster care are fabulous and will live with me for the rest of my life. You are right in your book, there are so many children out there who need love. You are doing a fantastic job in giving unfortunate children your time and love.' *Wendy, UK*

'I finished reading *Damaged* at midnight last night. It took me just two days to read it. I could not put it down … It took a lot of courage for me to read it as I was abused by a family member when I was eight years old … I am looking forward to Cathy's next book. Cathy is truly an angel from heaven, and one of the people I admire most in the world.' *Debby, hotmail.com*

'As a foster carer of almost ten years I saw in this book some of the things I have seen in the children I have cared for, although nowhere near as extreme. The book reduced me to tears. I hope others reading it are now more aware of the extreme circumstances some of the children we care for have to endure before they are found a place of safety. I also hope that it will raise awareness into fostering. Many thanks for a fantastic book and I look forward to more in the future.' *Jeanette, aol.com*

'I picked up *Damaged* and couldn't put it down … I want to thank Cathy for enlightening us. Without people like her, there would be absolutely no hope for helping children and opening our eyes to what we knew existed but not to the extent I have read … I am so glad that Cathy remained a foster carer.' *Elizabeth, aol.com*

'Your book affected me so much … I would like to know what I can do to help other children like Jodie … I am so angry that this is potentially happening all around us … Thank you for writing this book … you are an inspiration.' *Lisa, Australia*